REFLECTIVE FAITH

AUSTIN FARRER

REFLECTIVE FAITH

Essays in Philosophical Theology

Edited by Charles C. Conti

LONDON SPCK 1972

First published in 1972
by S.P.C.K.
Holy Trinity Church
Marylebone Road
London NW1 4DU

Printed in Great Britain by
The Camelot Press Ltd, London and Southampton

SBN 281 02714 5

Contents

Acknowledgements

Thanks are due to the following for permission to quote from copyright sources:

Allen & Unwin, Ltd: 'A Starting Point for the Philosophical Examination of Theological Belief', by A. M. Farrer, in *Faith and Logic*, edited by B. G. Mitchell.

Baker Book House, Grand Rapids, Michigan: 'Analogy', by A. M. Farrer, in *Twentieth Century Encyclopedia of Religious Knowledge*, edited by Lefferts A. Loetscher.

The Editor of *Downside Review*: an article entitled 'The Extension of St Thomas's Doctrine of Knowledge by Analogy to Modern Philosophical Problems', by A. M. Farrer, which appeared in Vol. 65 (1947).

Routledge & Kegan Paul, Ltd: part of A. M. Farrer's 'Editor's Introduction' to *Theodicy: Essays on the Goodness of God, and the Freedom of Man, and the Origin of Evil*, by G. W. Leibniz.

Stella Aldwinckle, ed. *Socratic Digest*, for use of 'Does God Exist?'

Editor's Preface

Austin Farrer was a philosopher and a theologian—a synthesis valuable as it is currently rare; for his writings combine, to an unusual degree, the qualities of philosophical sensitivity and penetrating faith. He was also a remarkable man.

He came to Oxford as a Scholar of Balliol, and took firsts in Honour Moderations in 1925, in Literae Humaniores in 1927, and in Theology in 1928. He distinguished himself further by receiving the Craven Scholarship in 1925 and the Liddon Studentship in 1927. In 1931 he became Chaplain and Tutor at St Edmund Hall; and was appointed Speaker's Lecturer from 1937 to 1940. From 1935 to 1960 he was Fellow and Chaplain of Trinity; and in 1960 he was appointed Warden of Keble where he remained until his death in 1968.

He wrote what is now a classic in theistic metaphysics, *Finite and Infinite*, in 1943. He delivered the Bampton Lectures for 1948, *The Glass of Vision*; the Edward Cadbury Lectures for 1953–4 on *St Matthew and St Mark*; the Gifford Lectures for 1957 on *The Freedom of the Will*; the Nathaniel Taylor Lectures, 1961, *Love Almighty and Ills Unlimited*; and the Deems Lectures in 1964, incorporated into *Faith and Speculation*. He was a founder member of the Metaphysicals, an informal society of Oxford dons responsible for publishing *Faith and Logic*, to which he was a contributor. He was also an Anglican priest, a Doctor of Divinity, and from 1962, a member of the Church of England's Liturgical Commission. Shortly before his death, he was elected a Fellow of the British Academy.

Despite these accomplishments and impressive credentials, his personal qualities were the most arresting. My impression of him, formed during the last year of his life and as my doctoral supervisor, was of a man who seemed to have reached a pinnacle of consciousness incisive as it was luminous. 'Seemed to'—for the

quality which belonged to the man was as elusive to define as it
was undeniably experienced. His effect on people must bear some
analogy to the transparent impact of the saints. There were human
qualities too. Whether magisterially wiggling his ears, fanning
embers of thought into an incandescent utterance, dashing off
limericks, or releasing the most eloquent of speculations as if to
take flight beyond his study window, he moved in bursts of mental
energy. And the vitality was evident in his penmanship and gait.

Such a quality pervades this collection of lectures, papers and
broadcast talks, spanning his career at Oxford. Written for select
and usually small audiences, they display a warmth and spontaneity
enabling one to draw close to their author; and in so doing, to
appreciate his wit and breadth of scholarship. They also expose the
foundations of Farrer's philosophical theology, and in some cases
provide an abridged version of theses developed elsewhere—a
valuable summary or introduction as the reader's case may be. For
those who wish to delve further, a chronologically arranged bibliography is provided. The study notes are also intended as a guide to
Farrer's other works. They function additionally to integrate the
book into a coherent whole. For the papers included are not only
diverse—a fact which, in my estimation, adds interest—but are of
widely differing dates. Exegetical clues in the notes are relevant
in those instances where Farrer changed his mind or, over the
years, altered his position. They also alert the reader to the fact
that Farrer's writings have a cumulative effect. Some of these
selections, therefore, represent stages within a process of refinement whose full significance cannot be assessed apart from that
corpus indicated in the study notes and bibliography.

The reader will also notice that the selections vary in degree of
formality. It has, nevertheless, been the editor's decision to publish
rather than not, in the belief that Farrer seldom failed to illuminate
a topic in whatever manner he chose to handle it, and that it can be
left to the good sense of the reader to make allowances for style,
substantiality or period flavour. There is another, more important,
reason for publishing.

It is now generally admitted that Farrer deserved a wider
audience than he received during his lifetime. If he was to some
extent neglected, it was due (in part) to his intellectual independence; at odds with the then-current fashions of Form Criticism,

Positivism and neo-Orthodoxy. Then too, he was never an easy writer to understand. A genuine humility led him to assume in others a mind as agile as his own. In his presence the effect was exhilarating; but in a written work, his philosophical leaps could—and often did—leave the reader stranded. This collection mitigates that handicap; for the compact and informal style of these pieces both lends itself to a ready appreciation of Farrer's thought and provides a key to the understanding of his larger works. This fact, coupled with the present revival of interest in philosophical theology, makes it desirable that a representative book of Farrer's should be available to the public.

There are, then, at least three dimensions to these essays. What is immediately obvious is Farrer's rare and individual qualities. By writing with a lucid precision and not allowing the conventions of literary style to interfere, he grants the reader access to his inner meditations—a world rich in the subtleties of logic and language. There is also a high degree of poetic intensity so that, whether he is writing in the compressed almost diagrammatic style of *Finite and Infinite*, his first philosophical essay, or in the discursive mode of *Faith and Speculation*, his last, the flow of words is subject to a rigorous scrutiny, yet one that displays a quicksilver sensitivity. Except that to describe the molten state of his mind as a 'flow' is to overlook those bursts of brilliance native to his pen. These abound on nearly every page, whether in the form of irrepressible quips or glowing insights, and are so characteristic as to provide a clue to the personality of the man himself. Here then, we are confronted *not* with the literary remains of a ghost, but with a tangible reminder of the facility with which he allows us to move in the circumference of his mind.

Such a glimpse of Farrer can only enrich his philosophical legacy; for within the covers of a single book, the evolution of Farrer's thought over the years can be traced. One sees his early origins in scholastic theology and his eventual movement towards what we now call 'the philosophy of action'. Indeed, the latter is prefigured in the former; and it is ironic that descriptive metaphysics, constructed on our actual or active use of language, was being attempted by Farrer years before the strictures of Positivism were (officially) lifted by the work of Hampshire and Strawson. Readers of these essays will notice examples of Farrer developing themes which tend to be associated with philosophers writing within the tradition of linguistic philosophy. I mention this not to detract from the profound influence of these men, or the movement of analytic philosophy, but in protest against the prejudice of those who tended (or may still be tempted) to write off Farrer's philosophy as merely the working out of theological presuppositions.

Finally, there is the theological significance of these selections which, to use traditional language, involves the insistence that faith and reason—man's spiritual and intellective capacities—must be kept in tension. Farrer achieved this balance, not by discarding traditional foundations, but by utilizing them. Indeed, his God was the God of Abraham, Isaac and Jacob, as well as the God of the *philosophes et savants*. Perhaps then, the virtue of this collection is that it provides a model for the discipline of philosophical theology. And for those who have seen the theological pendulum swing, it is salutary to find in Farrer a mind that is fully aware and carefully concerned with traditional theism; and yet, or for that very reason, one that is fresh and invigorating.

As regards editorial policy, I have tried—adapting Farrer's metaphor about the divine initiative—to keep the hand of the editor perfectly hidden. Any change, apart from punctuation or spelling, was made in consultation with his wife and colleagues. Important alterations to the text are recorded in the footnotes; and the original manuscripts may be seen in the Bodleian Library, Oxford. Given the fact that Farrer seldom used footnotes, I have indicated where the footnotes are mine rather than his. In some cases I have added explanatory notes in square brackets in the text, and the numbers in the text refer to the Study Notes.

The condition in which I found the manuscripts varied. None was, so to speak, ready for publication (save the reprints). They would appear to be first-draft efforts: except that it is misleading so to describe them. For the manuscripts give as much indication of refinement and scholarship, as they do spontaneity or creativity. Quotations, when not simply a marriage of memory and originality, ranged widely: the classics, scripture, poetry, hymnody; and continental as well as English philosophers. (When I asked Mrs Farrer if those 'eloquent Promethean rodomontades', p. 21, was a reference to Shelley rather than Aeschylus, she replied, 'Well possibly, Austin did have a Shelley phase at about twelve.' Farrer was also fluent in Latin and Greek. Mr Ian Crombie recalls mentioning J. L. Austin's complaint that the entrance scholarship examiners, in asking schoolboys to put into Latin 'Another 2½ per cent would make all the difference' had expected too much, and Farrer's replying in a flash with a perfect idiomatic phrase.) In addition, there are no traces of piecemeal or laborious construction in the text; no interval or break in the flow of words or ink; and surprisingly few corrections, deletions or usual hints of writer's stutter.

There is an explanation for this spontaneous eloquence. It was supplied by Farrer's late wife and friends. When 'writing', Austin would sit deep in silent thought—occasionally thinking aloud, 'waking the echoes'—and if, after some hours, the incubation was productive, he would rise with the remark, 'Yes, I think I'll write that one.' Whereupon he would, in a single sitting—except that he mostly wrote standing—write out the piece from beginning to end. All the distillation was done before he set pen to paper, and perhaps this accounts for his uninhibited and fresh style.

To give the impression that these essays were easily prepared for publication would be unfair to those who worked so hard to bring them to their present state. Only some of the pieces were 'finished products'; most required considerable care. In their original handwritten state—nearly all were in longhand—some of the earlier manuscripts were difficult to read; others less so, and still others betrayed the most elegantly controlled quill. The first link towards publication was provided by Mrs D. Hopkins, who typed copies of the originals, as she had done for Farrer so often in the past. The final link was provided by Miss E. Gill, scholar of St Anne's College, Oxford, whose care for detail was inexhaustible. In between, I am indebted to Professor E. L. Mascall, Professor B. G. Mitchell, Mr Ian Crombie and others who generously lent their assistance. Of course, one does not publish without a publisher, and I cannot fail to acknowledge the cooperation and enthusiasm of Dr Raymond Foster, the Publisher, and Mr Darley Anderson, the editor, at S.P.C.K. I would also like to thank Mr R. D. Hewlett of the B.B.C. who opened archives and released typescripts of broadcasts; as well as Farrer's many friends in the States—especially Dr Edward Henderson who submitted

'The Prior Actuality of God' and Mr Philip Hanson for his help with the bibliography—who supported me in their letters and for whom, in the back of my mind, this collection was also prepared. Other acknowledgements belong to the Trustees of the Farrer estate, especially Mr Arthur Newton, for permission to carry on this project; and The Southern Fellowships Fund of the U.S.A., especially Mr Samuel M. Nabrit, Executive Director, for financial support in making it possible.

Finally, I am indebted to Mrs Katherine Farrer who, before her death on 25 March 1972, gathered the manuscripts, consented to my wish for publication, and checked the typescripts. She was not only a delightful co-worker, but a tangible link with her late husband. Ultimately, she would have our tribute go to him: a man whose reflective faith was not only transparent, but cast far-reaching shadows.

Mansfield College   CHARLES C. CONTI
Oxford

Foreword

This is an appropriate time for the publication of further essays in philosophical theology by Austin Farrer. For the theological scene, in the English-speaking world, has been characterized during the last two decades at least by an uncritical following of continually changing fashions. Every few years the imagination of the current generation of theological students has been captured by some new slant or slogan, which has been accorded the status almost of a revelation. Enough theological teachers (wishing to retain their student audiences) and enough reading clergy and ministers (wishing to be up to date) have followed each new direction, and produced articles, books, lectures and sermons expressing it, and making it for the time being the dominant fashion. One year God is 'out', the next year 'in'; God is alive, he is dead; he is relevant, he is irrelevant; now process theology is almost unheard of, now everything is seen as in process; now eschatology is a dirty word, now theology hinges upon the future and its central theme is hope; and there is political theology, black theology, environmental theology. . . . Each of these, it need not be doubted, has some value. But the way in which so much of the theological community has rushed after them in turn reveals a widespread bewilderment and lack of criteria.

Against this shifting background Farrer is an important figure, both because his work is a shining example of intellectual integrity and style, and because his theology has been shaped by a universally valid criterion.

The criterion to which Farrer appeals is rationality. But not rationality operating in the narrow channels of logical deduction and knockdown argument. Farrer does not profess, for example, to offer a self-sufficient philosophical proof of the existence of God. His method is not logic working in a vacuum, but rationality illuminatingly at work within the life of faith. For the religious thinker does not start in a world devoid of already functioning religious belief and experience. He starts within a religious tradition that is as old as mankind. As Farrer says, 'Many teachers have taught things they had not themselves been taught; Christ, for example, and Moses. But the novelty was never religion itself. The pioneer began with a hereditary system for interpreting things religiously, and in so doing found himself driven to innovation in religion—not to an innovation called "religion".' (*Faith and Speculation*, p. 4.)

And so, standing within the religious tradition, in its specifically Christian form, Farrer is concerned to test the rationality of the beliefs which he first inherited and then responsibly decided to live by. And this is, surely, the right approach. The proper question is not whether, starting from scratch, and without benefit of that religious response to the world which we call faith, one can prove the reality of God and the truth of the theistic picture of the universe. The proper question is whether it is reasonable for the religious man, experiencing the world as he does, to believe as he believes. And Farrer argues that when we look at the world with the perceptiveness of a poet, not imposing our cultural categories upon it but letting it affect us in its unique concrete particularity, our minds are led through the world by a rational path to its infinite creator and sustainer.

In his approach by way of the existing life of faith Farrer asks, as it seems to me, the right question and thereby puts philosophical theology on the right road.

Farrer is also important for the integrity and style of his thought. His writings disclose the mind of a poet, a poet who is using the resources of the English language to express exact theological insights and arguments. He is also blessed with the natural candidness of the really lucid mind. He can deceive neither himself nor others. This candidness shows itself, for example, in the often explicitly dialogue form of his writings. Having stated a position he puts himself in a critic's shoes and points out the difficulties. Then he moves back and forth, weaving a dialogue; and he conducts the critic's case as ably as his own. His work is so far removed from the realm of unanalysed slogans, vague metaphors, and all forms of sloppiness and imprecision, that to read someone of Farrer's stature is to lose any taste for the lower levels of theological writing.

To be influenced by Austin Farrer is not necessarily to be led to think as he thought, but to be led to think for oneself by the same canons of rationality. For Farrer was above all an independent mind, who followed no fashions, who thought and judged for himself, and who expressed the truth as he saw it in an inimitable style which also expressed the man himself. Although he was attached to no organized school of thought, he was a formidable figure, unable to be ignored. The sheer distinction and brilliance of his mind was backed by a vast learning that was never paraded but was always available. For Farrer was widely read in several languages, and was familiar at first hand with the works of the leading religious and secular thinkers, past and present. And yet he was never overwhelmed by his own scholarship, as mere scholars are; he listened to what each of the great thinkers had to say, reflected upon it, and then made his own path through the problems with which they were dealing.

This collection of Farrer's essays, ably edited by one who knows his writings well, constitutes an introduction to Farrer's thought such as many have wished for; and it will be important also for those who are concerned to study Farrer's work as a whole.

JOHN HICK

Prologue:
Theology and Philosophy†

I had a dream. There were Theology and Philosophy, clothed in both the moral and the academic dignity of female professors. Theology held several slips of paper in her hand, with a single sentence written upon each: 'God exists' on one, 'The world was created' on another. Philosophy displayed several baskets on a table, marked with tickets describing sentences of different logical kinds, 'Moral Commands', 'Empirical Statements', 'Truths of Definition', and so forth. 'Into which of my baskets, dear Theology,' she said, 'would you like to put your statements?'

Theology looked at the baskets and hesitated. 'Do I have to?' she replied. 'I mean, is it certain that the right basket for my statements is on your table at all? Of course, if it were demonstrable that all the possible sorts of logical baskets were represented here. . . .'

'Dear me, no,' said Philosophy, 'we can't claim to be sure of that. But don't you find some of these baskets rather alluring? Here is a brand new one, delivered only this morning by Logical Baskets Limited (limited, you know, or virtually so, to Oxford and Cambridge). It is called "Expressions of Attitude to Life". Isn't that what you want? Now be reasonable.'

'No, I'm afraid not,' Theology replied. 'You see, when I say, "God loves what he has made", I do not mean that John Christian takes up, or would be well advised to take up, a benevolent attitude to things in general or to his neighbour in particular; nor that he either does or should view them in the rosy light cast upon them by association with the creator-God image. No, I mean what I say; I mean that the actual creator is doing this actual loving.'

'Good God!' said Philosophy, 'you don't say so! Well, if that's how it is, Basket Four is what you require,' pointing to a basket

† A slightly abridged version of 'A Midwinter Dream', reprinted from *University*, Vol. 1, No. 2 (1951).

B

labelled 'Statements about Other Persons'. 'And in that case,' she continued, beginning to talk exceedingly fast, 'your statements will of course, be subject to the routine tests of empirical verifiability and falsifiab . . .'

'Please, please, not again,' said Theology, raising her hands to her ears. 'We've had this so many times before. Haven't I told you that statements about God are not statements about a person among persons, but about that transcendent subject to whom our personal existence bears only a distant, though a real, analogy?'

'And so,' said Philosophy, 'I suppose you are let off any attempt at relating your statements to real life.'

'Dear me, no,' said Theology, 'I don't get off that. Almost all religious thinking relates statements about God with statements or directions concerned with common life. Lots of people know how to do such thinking, but to know what its logical nature may be is a different matter. Perhaps you and I might hold a joint class, to find out how such thinking goes. I fear it will have to be an Advanced Class, for theological talk will turn out to be less simple in its logic, I suspect, than "It is sweet and commendable to die for our country" or "This garden is kept by a gardener whom no one has caught at work".'

'Ah, I dare say,' said Philosophy. 'But as it would be foolish to anticipate the findings of your Advanced Class, allow me to take up another point here. You were saying that you attach great importance to the literal sense of "God loves what he has made". But the next moment you were protesting that the divine person is only distantly analogous to human persons, and so, presumably, that his making is only distantly analogous to human making, and his loving to human loving. If so, you mayn't seem to be saying anything very literal, or very clear, when you say that God loves what he has made. Are such meagre dregs of meaning worth bothering about? You have conceded agnosticism already. Be an atheist and have done with it.'

Theology replied: 'It isn't only believers in an Unknown God who admit that their talk comes far short of expressing God or His doings. We should all be agnostics if our knowledge of God were our exploration of him; as though God sat there impassive as a rock-cut Buddha, and we tortoises vainly tried to scale his knees. We cannot aspire to talk about God in (as it were) divine language, but he can stoop, if he chooses, to talk to us in our language and to deal humanly with mankind. When, for example, for us men and for our salvation . . .'

On hearing these dogmatic words, Philosophy muttered, 'We will hear thee another time on this matter,' and faded away to tea, followed by the Stoics and Epicureans. Theology was left addressing the Empty Areopagus, except that I could see the Areopagite Denys skulking behind a column, and a woman called Damaris looking over the wall.

'Won't you come in, my dear?' said Theology to Damaris. Damaris entered, pulling on a commoner's gown. She produced a pencil and notebook as though from nowhere, but on being assured that the subject in hand was of no schools value she was persuaded to put them away again and converse like a human being. She had, in fact, thought of an Intelligent Question: 'I think I see what you mean', she began, 'when you say it doesn't matter so much our not being able to talk straight about God, so long as he talks straight to us. You would say he does that specially in the Gospel?'

Theology assented. 'But,' Damaris continued, 'doesn't that make God talk a terribly incorrect language? I mean, the Jews knew nothing about it really, did they, and they mixed up their logical types like anything. And we find Christ talking just like a Jew. And it isn't only the language, it's the ideas. He said he was messiah, and you can't understand what that means without a whole lot of Jewish history. And it's the same with everything else, for instance, how he meant the sacrament would be his body and blood.'

'I know,' said Theology. 'But we can't have it both ways, can we? If God comes down to our level and talks to us in our speech, it will have to be the speech of some one time and place. When he was fully grown he had the thought-forms of a bible-minded Jew; before that, he had used the broken speech of childhood.'

'That sounds all right in theory,' said Damaris, 'but the Jews' ideas were so queer, and it is all so far away now.'

'Queer, if you like,' said Theology, 'but expressive for the purpose. You could talk vividly about divine things and be understood in the streets of Galilee; just try at our street corners, or—or here in our Areopagus. And as to your "Far away"—two thousand years are two thousand years, but there is always a bridge. For those ideas you speak of have lived on and partly moulded, partly adopted the forms of every age from then till now.'

'What should we do then?' said Damaris. 'Should we try to strip away the Jewish stuff as much as we can?'

'No, I don't think so,' said Theology, 'my business anyhow is to understand the Scripture in its ancient dress and see what is signified to us through it. You don't understand Shakespeare by stripping away Elizabethan England: and it is a more weighty matter to understand God. Yet understanding Shakespeare is no unreal dramatization of yourself as an Elizabethan, and to understand Christ is not to dramatize yourself as an ancient Jew.

'The student of the New Testament need not say much about the modern world. He can open his readers' eyes to the way in which Apostles and Evangelists thought. He can describe, in our language, systems of imagery and implication which the ancients never dreamt of describing, because they lived in them. After doing this, he does not need to bring us back to our modern world. We are in it all the time, and if we have been seriously grasping the ancient speech and taking it to ourselves, we shall have been making the modern translation for ourselves—if, indeed, it is right to say that we do anything quite for ourselves in the sphere of revealed truth.'

Denys, feeling these remarks to be unfair, carried Theology and Damaris off to tea.

Rational Theology
The Study of Theological Reason

The Rational Grounds for Belief in God†

NATURE OF THE QUESTION

It is not possible, perhaps, to know altogether what we mean by God until we have found out the reasons for believing in him: for we cannot assume from the start what it is that we have to discover. Only discovery itself can shew us that. But it is useful to have a provisional definition, in order to know in what direction to look.[1] Let us say then that by the God we are seeking we mean a Being with whom (if he exists) we stand in an inescapable relation which is of practical concern to us.

From this provisional definition there follows immediately a conclusion as to the kind of question this is. There are two sorts of questions, those purely speculative, and those which are also at the same time practical. In the first sort of question, belief is judged of by an intellectual conclusion expressed in words, if expressed at all. In the second sort, it is true that we may form an intellectual conclusion, but the test of whether we effectively believe it is discovered by whether we act upon it when occasion arises. Not only so, but in the moment of action we often discover for the first time whether we really believe or not something which our mind has formulated and which we have supposed ourselves to believe; as the man who professed his conviction that the plank would bear discovered that he thought otherwise when it was a matter of walking across it. In the first kind of question there are three alternative answers—belief, disbelief, and suspense of judgement; and we do not make up our minds unless the evidence is sufficient. In the second kind there are only two alternatives, because the man who suspends belief about the soundness of the plank must in fact either cross it or not cross it; and the act is the expression of the practical judgement. Thus if our definition is to stand, it follows that agnosticism cannot in practice exist, since we either do or do not act responsively to the supposed relation between

† Date unknown: *circa FI.*

God and us. Suspense of judgement that results in refusal to act, is practical atheism. The attitude that is called 'pious agnosticism' turns out to be practical belief, but, generally, belief in certain of the tenets of the current theology and disbelief in others: as, one disbelieves in particular 'grace' given through conscious communion of the mind with God—for the man does not pray; but he believes in the immanence of God in the natural world—for he responds in reverence.

But not only is it true that all agnostics are either believers or disbelievers; equally is it true that all believers and disbelievers are agnostics: for the man who professes to have absolute knowledge of God in this world must be a strange beast. The question then is: Can I have fair assurance? and, Am I prepared to bet on my opinion by making my life answer it? Even though it is the business of a lifetime to resolve fully on the question: yet meanwhile I must have a provisional opinion to act upon, or rather, on which I shall actually find myself to be acting. For the question does not wait till the end of life to begin to be a practical issue, since I must answer it whether I choose or not, every day that I do or do not pray.

And if I cannot suspend my judgement as though the issue were merely speculative: neither can I let my mind drift into an answer, as though the issue were insignificant. For history, past and contemporary, shews that from sincere conviction about things divine there may follow consequences affecting the whole of life, and affecting it deeply. But for good, or ill? That is what we have to discover.

HOW TO LOOK FOR AN ANSWER, AND WHERE

A philosopher says that general culture lies in knowing what sort of treatment is demanded by various problems, and what sort of accuracy is to be demanded in the answers: and it is certain that if we begin by treating aesthetics by the standard of physics, we shall get nowhere. For there are, if not various sorts of truth, at least various classes of things that are true. The following may all be facts: my small dog is on her back in front of the fire; the atom is not indivisible; courage is a virtue of the spirit; the real is prior to the apparent. But the way that these facts refer to reality is very different. The first is a particular fact at a particular time verifiable by direct observation. The second is a timeless generalization not open to direct observation but based on it. The third is not about physical facts but about moral qualities and depends on an intuitive judgement of value from which there is no appeal to direct observation of any kind. The last is a pure matter of principle, and (supposing it is true at all) would, if there were no actual world, still be true about any possible world that might arise. There are, then, evidently various sorts of facts, which all have meaning and are capable of being true. It is a great part of the business of looking for an answer to our question, to keep oneself from a premature dogmatism as to the kind of fact it will have to be. It may even be a fact of a kind all its own. Investigation alone can show. But meanwhile we will not damn it out of hand because it turns out not to be historical fact, or scientific hypothesis, or judgement of value-quality, or whatever other class of idea we happen for the moment to have shut up ourselves in.

Another condition of success is, that we should consider what it is in the world that we know first, and with the greatest certainty. For it would be great good fortune if, having found this, we found further that we were able to base our answer upon it. And even if we cannot do this latter, we may at least be able to see how near to the basis of our best certainties the basis we actually adopt for our answer lies. This will be some measure of its probability or uncertainty.

Evidently, we first and most certainly know, immediate experience. I believe myself at this moment to be seeing a sheet of pink blotting-paper. Now I may be mistaken in believing that the substance there is that which is usually called 'blotting-paper'; I may be quite wrong in the opinion I hold of the physical constituents of blotting paper, even if this is blotting-paper; I may be wrong in supposing that the normal colour of this paper is pink, for it may be in a curious light or I may be suffering from distempered vision. Or I may be in a dream or a delirium, and there is nothing substantial there at all, of any colour or any sort. But in any case one thing stands firm: I am having the experience of seeing pink. Nothing can be more certain than these primary data. Our solidest scientific conclusions, being based on these, must always remain less certain than they, and plainly cannot be used to attack this basis of direct apprehension on which they are built. For example: if we have direct apprehension of the immediate experience of willing freely (that we have admittedly needs to be shown) then no attack could be made on this from the assumption of universal causality. For that assumption is at best a working principle of that scientific construction which we raise on the basis of immediate apprehension, and cannot therefore be turned to the overthrow of immediate apprehension itself.

But it is plain that the immediate apprehensions which are likely to concern us will not belong to the 'seeing pink' order; that is, they will not be apprehensions of the visual, auditory, tactual, or otherwise sensible. Nor, unfortunately, are they likely to be quite so obvious. Here a distinction must be drawn between the certain and the obvious. Every immediate apprehension, *if I am once sure that I am having it*, is, as immediate apprehension, quite certain, and thereby possesses an advantage over any and every scientific inference. In the case of the latter, even though I am sure of the logical correctness of my reasoning, yet the conclusion is not certain, because it is always possible that I have been reasoning along a false line. None the less, before I am certain of the immediate apprehension, I have first to be sure that I am really having it; or otherwise put, that what I am experiencing fits the description that I am giving myself of it. With some apprehensions it is fairly easy to be sure of this, e.g. in the case of seeing pink, and these we call obvious to apprehend, as well as certain when apprehended. But others, e.g. the experience of enjoying the exercise of free will, though equally certain if once clearly apprehended, are by no means so obvious to apprehend. We guess, then, that our search is likely to lie among these less obvious apprehensions, such as inform us not about pinkness, loudness, nor hardness, but about the essential character of our existence.[2]

WHAT KIND OF AN ARGUMENT WE CAN HOPE TO MAKE

In a boys' adventure story there is a vivid account of how a party of Roundheads, held up by a Cavalier marksman posted behind a judicious boulder in a mountain-pass, sent one of their number round by stealth to creep up on him from the rear, while they kept his attention occupied in front. It is commonly supposed by the public, as it used to be supposed by philosophers, that something

of the same sort should take place in our proving the existence of
God. Religion first sights the Object by something called faith;
but cannot by its own direct approach come up with It or make
properly sure of It. So, while Religion continues to keep It in sight
from the front by a direct, but distant and misty vision, she sends
Philosophy round by a quite different path, that of Pure Reason
arguing from quite different premises. So Reason (it is hoped)
having by this devious path reached the goal and discovered God
to be God, waves a reassuring signal back to Religion, who may
now continue to enjoy her contemplation from the front, but with
certainty and a good conscience. But we no longer now believe
that this mythical manœuvre can be executed. There are not two
lines of approach to God but one:[3] all that Reason can hope to do
is to trace over with rational examination the line which actually
joins God (or if you like, the phantasm of a God) to our ordinary
awareness thereof. It is a fact that the apprehension of God, or the
supposed apprehension of him, plays a certain part in the minds
and lives of men. But for the most part they use it without inquiring into its nature, as they use speech and reasoning without
inquiring into the nature of signification[4] as such or logic as such.
Reason, then, can only expect to look into the essential nature of
those functions which the (supposed) apprehension of God
exercises in our life, in the hope of being able to see either the
inevitableness and necessity, or the spuriousness and redundancy,
of that apprehension and those functions.

If this, then, is the kind of argument we can hope to make, we
shall not admit it as an objection that our argument is doing no
more than saying exactly what the ordinary believer obscurely
apprehends. For the objection rests on the supposition that by
some logical abracadabra or juggling with notions, philosophy can
establish God by a proof standing on empty air, or on some aspect
of experience which has nothing to do with God. But there is no
such magic power in philosophical reasoning, it can only examine
connections that are already there.

FREE WILL AND GOD

We turn now to our positive argument, and begin from one of
those immediate apprehensions which we have already described

as not obvious: the apprehension of freedom. Can we be sure that we have the immediate and interior experience of acting freely? Well, perhaps that depends on what one means by free action. Doubtless our thoughts and actions are very largely determined by causal forces; even beyond what we realize ourselves, as psychologists are from time to time able to show us. We certainly are not free at each moment to think and to do anything on earth that another mind might conceive for us. But can we be sure that there is some element of freedom in some of our activity?

We may at least be sure of this: the very experience of effort and search, as in the study of psychology itself or any other science, would be meaningless, unless we held the practical working belief that, by taking care and exercising conscious effort, we are able to bring our thought nearer to conformity with a standard of truth. If not: if we believed ourselves to be the mere playthings of psychological forces which guide us right or wrong without our having any say in the matter, then effortful search for truth would be meaningless. It is plain then that we have and, if we are to live, cannot help having, a working belief (a) that we can exercise effort, (b) that by so doing we can to some extent and on the whole—for of course in many cases we may be frustrated or deceived—conform our thought and our act to an objective standard of the true or right. Apart from the standard, the effort would be senseless; apart from the power to make the effort, the standard would be of no concern to us. The two things are correlatives.

Now it is the standard that we are interested in. Sometimes the standard consists of particular external facts, and then, perhaps, there is no great mystery about it. If I exercise my will in trying to judge rightly whose dog it is that is lying here on her back in front of my fire, then the standard to which I have to conform my judgement is nothing else but the identities of the animal actually there, and of the real person somewhere existing whose address is engraved on her collar. In another case, in mathematical reasoning for example, the standard appears to be something called the laws of thought; and it may be a little harder to say exactly what they are, and where they exist, for they claim to be valid for all minds, not only mine. But before we hasten to assume some Mind with a big M standing in a relation of intercommunication with each of our individual minds,[5] it may be sufficient to assume that each of our minds comes into being equipped with a complete set of the laws of thought as its working principles: these belonging to the nature of all minds as such, somewhat as tails belong to monkeys. But harder still to deal with is the case where we have to judge not about that which is, but about that which is not *yet* but ought to be. Where and what is the standard then?

For example: Aldous Huxley proposes to us in phantasy, and the Russian state sets out to realize in fact, certain new forms of human society and life. There is nothing we are more sure of than that we have got to make up our minds whether each such proposed spiritual revolution is for good or for evil. The question is not an easy one to answer, but, for all that, we know that it is a real and not a senseless question, and that there is therefore some standard of truth according to which the answer has to be given. But what is this standard? We might say, we just have to conjecture which order of society will make people happiest and, if we can't be sure of our guesses, experiment will show. But this won't do, for if by happiness you mean pleasure and absence of worry, then a pig or anyhow a piggish man can easily be happier than a poet, for it is not in the least demonstrable that the pleasures of poetry are stronger to the poet than those of gluttony to the glutton; and certainly the poet's distresses are likely to be more acute. But of course you will say that by happiness you mean the highest or best sorts of satisfactions, even at some cost of accompanying distress. But now by what standard are we to decide the highest and best sorts?—an important question, since we are bound to choose the order of society which will most promote their attainment.

People like to say: 'Those sorts of satisfactions which best express the true nature of human personality'. But the bother is that the nature of human personality is not fixed and therefore cannot be made the standard of our judgement. Human nature has evolved and is evolving, and what is of chief importance, its further evolution is placed more and more under man's own control. Doubtless we cannot do anything, whatever we may choose, with human nature; we cannot knock it into a cocked hat or a paper boat: but there is no reason why we shouldn't modify it a great deal. And the question about the system of society to be adopted is really a question about which direction human nature had best be modified in. This question cannot be decided by an appeal to the fixed type of human nature: that would just be a stupid appeal to the past, masquerading as an appeal to the timeless and eternal.

Well, but you may say, in judging what is likely to be the best sort of society (moulding the best sort of humanity to the enjoyment of the best sort of life) we do simply judge. That is, we can but think over the proposed systems as carefully as possible, and then assess their comparative worth by an intuitive judgement. Yes, admittedly that is what we do: but 'intuition' [from the Latin, *intueri*] means 'looking', and the question is, what the mind is looking at, when it makes its intuitive judgement? It is not merely looking at the proposed system, for if it were, it would merely apprehend the sort of system it is, but not its worth. For worth is not a simple quality spread through the system like greenness through grass and so grasped by direct inspection. On the contrary, it is a degree of approach to some standard or demand. What standard then: the standard of our ideals? But then our ideals themselves have to be judged in respect of their worth, and we are responsible for our judgement.

It is usual at this point of the argument to murmur something about 'values' and 'eternal principles' which have to be embodied by us in our lives as much as may be. But where are these alleged entities? You cannot have such supernatural furniture casually tumbling about the world of space and time. While we could still regard the nature of man as fixed, we could warehouse them in it; but now we cannot, where *are* we to deposit them? Some like to talk of the 'true self' of each man or of the race, which is trying, as it were, to realize itself by bringing the actual self up to standard. But since apparently everyone is to have a separate 'real self' distinct from his actual self, and since this real self will have constantly to be changing according to changing conditions, this theory would face us with a really formidable angelology, even if we succeeded in squaring our consciences about believing in a sort of things intermediate between actual present existences and possible future existences. It would seem a deal simpler to scrap this mythic host of real selves (not so real but that they must constantly be awaiting realization), and substitute one God who has a will about what the race and the individuals should from time to time become.

To sum up, then: when I try to judge and to will about myself or about the human race in practical things, I come at last to a point where I have no external guides or fixed principles; and my thought and desire are found aspiring out beyond and above myself or the self of the race, and yet this aspiration claims not to be random, but, with however much liability to error, to be aspiring after something objectively real. For if not, then the whole exercise of human freedom turns out to be nothing more than the careful choice of means towards a meaningless end—an irrational supposition, and not the working belief of any outside an asylum, although it is what cynics suppose themselves theoretically to believe.

But now what is this objective Good-for-men and Good-for-me after which thought aspires? It was suggested at the end of the last paragraph but one, that it might be the will of God, and that we are (whether consciously or unconsciously) exploring it whenever we sincerely attempt to make such searches as the one we were just now considering. Now this suggestion cannot possibly be supposed either to have been proved, or to be capable of absolute proof. We have merely shown at best that the objective correlative of moral freedom is very hard to find, and that all the easy and usual hypotheses fare badly under a quite simple cross-examination. But we cannot pretend to prove that the supposition of God is the only hypothesis that could possibly meet the case: at the best we can show that no satisfactory alternative is at present on the philosophic market.

RELIGIOUS AWARENESS

But then fortunately we are not left to decide between all conceivable alternatives by mere probability, because one of our alternatives has something particular to recommend it: that is, that it constitutes the object which the religious awareness believes itself to be aware of.

Now the religious awareness of a supernatural reality may, no doubt, conceivably be an illusion. Yet it is a curious fact that it occurs so widely and with such persistency, and if we are to explain it away we shall have to account for this; as also for the fact that on the whole the best men (by our ordinary judgement) have paid attention to it—though admittedly on the other hand it has been subject to great perversions, and, if we take it at its face-value, presents us with a bewildering variety of mutually incompatible theologies. But will it not be a satisfactory account of the facts, if from considering (as we have been doing) the very nature of our existence, we find there a function that the religious awareness seems exactly adapted to fulfil? We can then hold fast to this function, as giving us the very essence of what the religious awareness is; and as for the maze of conflicting theologies, we can see these as so many more or less clear and successful attempts of the human spirit to respond in actual vision to the God who presents himself as the final object of our aspiration. For plainly the mere notion of God is valueless as such an object, we must have an idea what sort of a God it is; the mere idea of his willing for us is valueless, we must have an idea what it is that he wills. This then becomes the supreme question in religion, how and where God is truly revealed, and the existence of many errors is no bar to there existing a true revelation.

All explanations given of the puzzling fact of the religious consciousness are bound, if they are going to be plausible, to show some pretty widely needed function which the thing fulfils; and, considering what religion is and has been in the world, the more universally required and the more respectable the function suggested, the more plausible the explanation. Thus we no longer think it plausible that this function is the self-interest of scheming priests, for this appears too narrow and inessential. The Freudian theory that God is a desire-image generated by a 'father-complex' is more plausible, because the function suggested is more essential and more likely to be a widespread need. It fails in not being either essential or widespread enough: for to make of all the heroes of faith neurotics, or at least psychic perverts and illusionists, is a view that fails of plausibility. But a view that can anchor religion in a function essential to our very existence is the most plausible of all. It has, besides, the advantage of accepting the positive testimony of the devout about the objective character of what they experience; and, other things being equal, it is reasonable to prefer to accept the positive testimony of sane men so far as their experiencing something real goes. Of course, we cannot always accept their formulation of what it is that they experience, because the preconceived ideas they apply to its interpretation may be false, or at least inadequate—as a scientist would not accept a child's account of the significance of a physical event but, if the child was sane, he would be wise to assume that the child had really seen something.

On the other hand, we have to account for the fact (which need not trouble Freud) that religious awareness is not the endowment of all. This looks like a difficulty, but turns out to be less of one, when we go back to our 'function'. Then we see that all men who have any sense whatever of spiritual values, are to this extent (though unconsciously) aware of the Divine Mind:[6] for that is, anyhow, the ultimate source of their intuitions, in so far as these are true. The advantage of the believer will then be, that he has a view approaching truth about a function exercised by unbelievers in ignorance or misunderstanding of its nature. So that we do not attribute to the believer a whole realm of experience closed to others, but only the clearer understanding and more vivid realization and appropriation of a realm through which others blunder in a half-light; or even, on which they draw without knowing that they are drawing upon it at all.

The knowledge of God is not, however, a mere speculative theory about a function which fulfils itself just the same whether we have the knowledge about it or not, as the healthy man's blood circulates just as well whether he knows anatomy or not. For in matters concerning our spirit a true understanding helps and a false understanding hinders functioning, just because the function itself works through understanding and not (as in the case of the blood) through other organs. We see this in experience, and most clearly by negative examples. Thus extreme cynicism, a disbelief in the possibility of man's disinterestedly following an objective Good, or even in the existence of that Good—such an attitude is, if you like, a speculative theory about the functioning of human aspiration, and one which does not prevent the cynic himself from having aspirations, nor prevent these aspirations from being drawn towards real values. Otherwise the man would soon be in an asylum. But for all that we easily see that the opinion, the cynicism, can clog the functioning of aspiration, and therefore all the activities that follow therefrom: if only because the cynic's theory excuses him from making effort, when to follow his best aspiration

c

requires it; or because prepossession distorts vision and prevents his seeing many of the less obvious sorts of good.

It is the same with religious belief, but in a positive direction. Thus Jesus evidently regarded it as most important that men should realize themselves to be offenders living on God's mercy like beggars on charity, because then their whole attitude to the source of spiritual knowledge and strength would be other than if they lived in Pharisaic pride: their receptivity would be vastly increased. So it is the claim of religion that a true knowledge of, and attitude towards, the spiritual good is a main factor (alongside the honest exercise of will) in enabling us to receive therefrom; and the experience of objectivity in religion, as the ordinary man has it, is best thus expressed: that when his mind settles in an attitude of belief he has a convincing experience of getting through, of opening up the true sources of his being, that is of the being he is called to be. The attitudes and opinions that compete with this one are no more to be compared with it than the various false shots one may make in trying to put the key into the lock at night can be compared with the shot that gets the key home; and this though many of them are quite close to the truth, and much closer than many others.

GOD AND MORAL INTELLIGIBILITY

We have followed the point we made in connection with the Cavalier story, by looking a little philosophically into that very line of connection which binds the existence of the religious life to God most essentially and obviously. But there are other (of course connected) functions which the apprehension of God plays in life, and we could examine these also. In fact we will take two: the moral intelligibility of experience; and the contingent or dependent nature of the world.

As to the former: the serious man wants to take long views, and to see what he chooses to do among the alternatives open to him as a valuable part of the greatest whole his thought can embrace. Thus this activity of mine is not good at all unless it forms a good element in my life as a whole; nor is my way of conducting my life as a whole good at all unless it forms a good element in a further whole which is good: that is the good life of the society of men in which I am. This again must stand judgement. Now it seems that the absolute value which the honest man's moral sense assures him of as belonging to the really good act, involves that there is an ultimate and final whole of which it is a part; and this would be the whole constituted by the purpose of God for the world. And it is this consideration which above all others begets faith in God as re-creator of the dead, that only so is the whole spiritual activity of the human race prevented from being a cul-de-sac, a flower that blooms a day on a dying bush on a blasted heath, with the current of life not running on through it into any future. Now our assurance that our existence is not thus senseless, but that the life we now live has a quality only explicable by its being part of the final whole of an intelligible divine purpose, is once again no more than an intuition, and an intuition by no means 'obvious' in the sense we defined. Yet I believe that the more we think, the more this intuition comes to light; and anyhow, it is not left to bear alone the weight of the evidence for God.

That the development of this intuition, and the consequent strengthening of the sense of life and value, plays a part in all civilized religion, is a truth that does not need to be argued for.

GOD AND THE COSMOS

If religion finds herself constrained to such beliefs as we have touched upon, it is plain in reason (as it has always appeared in history) that she will need to hold also that God is the final ground of the existence and development of the world. Now first of all, is this conceivable? And second, if it is conceivable, have we any positive reason to believe it true?—any reason, that is, belonging to the nature of the cosmos, for other reasons we already have.

First, as to whether it is conceivable, there comes in that principle we placed among our principles of investigation, namely of remembering to consider what it is we know first and best among the many sorts of facts there are. Now first and best we know our own existence, and that of other selves; and (which is the point here relevant) there is a sense in which we know this only and nothing else whatever. I know myself interiorly; that is, I know what it is to be a man. But I have no such knowledge of anything else. I know a little what it is to be a dog, but that is by the rough and ready method of cutting down my intuition of my own being until it looks like making a plausible fit to the behaviour of the dog. I do not pretend to know what it is to be a snail, least of all what it is to be an atom of any substance. Though I analyse my atom to its last constituents, my knowledge is at best only about the measurable aspects of its activity as externally experienced. Physics is an exact science and perfect in its kind, but this is the limit within which it works.

Now this is a fact of great importance, since my knowledge of God from my knowledge of myself depends on my *interior* knowledge of myself. It is in looking at the essence of free and purposeful activity (that is, an aspect of 'what it is to be a man') that I discover such activity to be necessarily a response to a demand, and thus dependent on God the Word, to borrow a phrase from Christian dogma. But since I have no such knowledge of the sub-spiritual universe, I cannot expect to see the manner of its relation with God, in the way that I can my own. Jeans, Eddington, and suchlike persons, assuming that the exterior knowledge of physics is true interior knowledge of the 'what-it-is-to-be . . .' of things, have gone on very naturally to conclude, that things just are measures and relations in somebody's mind: God's presumably— for, of course, if you once assume that there is no more in things than a physicist sees, you will have to conclude that there is no more there than a physicist's seeing; and then, to account for the fact that not even the most able physicist can see the world that he chooses to see, you have to suppose a Physicist with a big P, with whose seeing ours has to agree—let us call him 'God'.[7]

This appears to most of us an argument contrary to common sense, and to result from taking abstraction for reality, exterior for interior knowledge. We shall say on the contrary that the manner of the physical world's dependence on God must remain a mystery to us. If we think of it, we shall inevitably use the analogy of the (limited) power that our wills can exercise over the physical world, but with the consciousness that the analogy is pretty poor.

But this ignorance of the 'what-it-is-to-be . . .' of the physical universe has its compensations, for it frees us from oppressing our imaginations with thoughts of the limitless waste of a dead and indifferent universe. We have no reason whatever for believing that the universe is lifeless or meaningless for the world of spiritual value: all that we know is that our acquaintance with it, outside the infinitesimal area constituted by mankind and the higher animals, is exterior only. So that those eloquent Promethean rodomontades about the indifferent stars, in which some take so much pleasure, are not only without philosophical justification, but strictly meaningless. For all we know, every star may be a phenomenal aspect of the being of an archangel (whatever an archangel may happen to be).

We are bound, then, to understand the 'being' of the universe by the clue of our own—a bad enough clue if you like, but it's all we have.[8]

But have we no positive reason for supposing the cosmos to be grounded in God? Well, yes, just about as good a one as the circumstances allow, but no better. Since any exact vision of *how* it depends on him is excluded, we cannot have more than a vague awareness *that* it does so. And it is an undoubted fact that one of the things that has most moved man to belief at all times is the contemplation of the unity in complexity of the world; its adaptation to our minds and senses, and the manifold experiences of beauty and delight that are struck out by our interaction with it. It is easy enough to show that no strict proof can follow, and yet it is next to impossible, as Hume confessed, to consider these things without being moved to belief. And if it is more an intuition than an inference, then the same is true of my apprehending your meaning from your words. I see your mind in your utterance,[9] and there is no reason why this other constant and invasive certainty should not be similarly grounded—why we should not be hearing a word spoken to us by God through the world.

It is the same if we consider the contingency of all things— they might be there, they might not be there, all might be otherwise, and we are impelled to see the Eternal and Necessary behind them. Yet the conclusion is not logically inevitable—with our ignorance of the 'what-it-is-to-be . . .' of things, why should we suppose them other than merely contingent? And yet the mind is impelled to the step. Short of supposing a universal deceiver let loose in the world—in which case goodbye to philosophy!—why are we not to believe that this impulsion also is due to the divine 'word' through things?

These cosmic considerations also we find to have their place in actual religious thought, which has always turned to nature for a vision of the might and riches of the Divine Activity. And it is significant that the non-religious are impelled to personify nature, and import into their actual thinking a quasi-personal unity in things, which their theory should deny. Apart from God, there can be no unity in things except that constituted by the laws of physics. But when we talk of nature, we are unconsciously thinking of a unity based on the *interior* being of things, a sort of 'life' transcending mere individual objects. But if we are honest we must either deny this or admit God.

HOW CAN GOD BE CONCEIVED?

It is here that it is above all necessary to remember that there are various sorts of facts, and that we can't determine beforehand what sort of fact we are going to find. For it is plain that if we have knowledge of God, it can be forced neither into the mould of our interior knowledge of ourselves (for we are not God), nor into that of our exterior acquaintance with things (for we do not have sense–experience of him). It remains, then, that our immediate touch with the Divine Spirit should, in order to become intelligible to us, express itself in appropriate *analogies* drawn from the two worlds that we do understand; above all from our knowledge of finite spirit. Thus, whereas our contact with God is direct, our conception of him cannot be other than *analogical*. But this does not prevent the analogies from being true in so far as they go: for the experience itself refuses, as it were, some expressions of itself and admits others, though accepting none as adequate. How could they be?

Our conceptions of God then, are, in so far as they are true, a curious and unique sort of fact, appropriate to this realm of our experience and to no other. Being analogies that can never quite fit, they fall necessarily into paradox at last. But through them we are aware of grasping something wholly unique, wholly one, and not at all meaningless—the notion of the Absolute, of the First and Last, of God.

Still, we do grasp this through figures that can never be exact— an admission which religion itself has generally been more eager than anyone to make. And from this follows all those refutations of theism which are so well known. They all have the same general form, for they take some alleged fact about God and his relation to the world and show that, if examined by the logic of exact statement, it falls into contradiction with itself; or with some other necessary position of theology; or with known fact. But, if what we have just been saying has any truth in it, this is just exactly what we should be led to expect. Those, then, who make such refutations are behaving like men who should rack the judgements of aesthetics with the criteria of physical matters of fact.

The evidence of religion, then, does not rest on the ability of theology to draw (so to speak) a convincing inch-to-the-mile map of the supernatural sphere, but on the fact that the whole world of our experience becomes intelligible and luminous only when it is recognized as derivative from and aspirant towards a supernature which lies on the very verge of our conceiving.

On the verge of our conceiving, but at the heart of our being; not eluding our sense by distance, but overwhelming it by presence, universality, and depth of actuality. 'Our intelligence is to the divine perfection, as the eyes of a bat are to the sun.'*

CONCLUSION

We began by asserting that the question about God is not speculative only but practical, because belief or disbelief is measured by our actually making or not making some response. And now it appears that this response will be an opening of the mind to the drawing of that Divine Reality which evokes our aspiration about the things that concern us, and this is prayer; and action upon it is obedience. But it is when this point is reached, that the demand becomes insistent for a knowledge of more than general reasoning can give us; for a positive vision of God that has content—if any such has been vouchsafed to the world. But this is a different question, the question after revelation.

---

* Adapted from Aristotle (*Metaphysics* II. 993b 9–11), where Aristotle uses the comparison to argue that our minds are feeble in apprehension—Ed.

Poetic Truth†

Let me begin with characteristic donnishness by explaining what I am *not* going to talk about: a mere confession of incompetence to find a title that would not mislead. I call this paper 'Poetic Truth': but I am not going to dogmatize on the famous question, 'What is the essence of poetry, and what kind of truth does it have?' That is what I call a silly question. There are so many types of writing to which the name 'poetry' is applied by a slipshod public, and it seems quite unlikely that there is a single essence common to them all, or that they are all true in just the same way. Even if, by a miracle of verbal skill, I concocted a formula that would cover all the poems already written, would you be satisfied? You would not: one of you would go straight home and write a poem to fall outside the formula, and then I should be wrong, even if I was right before.

But here is what I am going to do: I am going to examine a feature that is in fact very common in nearly all poetry, and see whether it may not throw some light on the way in which we have to think about the soul and about God. But please don't think that I am going to tell you that theology is just figurative poetry: that is a very wicked thing to say, though some people have not shrunk from it. The relation between poetry and theology is not so simple as that. If it were, I should not be wasting your time with the matter now.

The feature of poetry which I propose to take is nothing more nor less than metaphor. Of course, we all use metaphor all the time: you'll hardly find a word in any language which has not got a flavour of metaphor about it. But this strange human passion for never saying what one means but always something else finds its most extreme and absolute development in the poets.

† The similarity of the definition of God, p. 37 below, to that of *FI*, 58; and the fact that it was written on the reverse side of *FI* manuscript, suggests closeness in date.

What is the sense of this habit? 'The curfew tolls the knell of parting day.' Why say it? The day is a space of time in which light and warmth prevail, and we are no doubt sorry sometimes when it is over, but that does not seem to be a good reason for describing it as a Christian invalid *in extremis*. Even if it were, it would be somewhat callous to begin tolling the bell before the patient had expired, as with the woman who began cooking the funeral ham. To multiply instances is unnecessary: this one will do for all.

Why use metaphors? One answer might be, that it is more amusing, and this is the view perhaps wrongly taken by the journalists who report sporting events. Sport is in itself unspeakably dull: it is just possible that someone may bear to read about it if you write your account as a sort of crossword puzzle for tiny tots, substituting easy clues for natural words, and taking pains never to call the ball a ball. The reader is kept awake by his own exercise of mild ingenuity in figuring it out. On this view a poem would be an elaborate riddle on the model of, 'Why is a lazy dog (more offensively, Why are you?) like a sheet of foolscap paper?' We divert our minds and congratulate our cleverness in getting the point of the poet's comparisons; and the more surprising and complex they are, the better the joke, until, of course, the thread completely eludes our grasp. This was the mistake of the Alexandrian poet, Lycophron, who wrote his *Alexandra* in order not to be understood without a full-length commentary: he turned with a sigh of relief from the last line of his arid poem to the first paragraph of his juicy footnotes.

But the trouble about this theory is not that bores like Lycophron have overdone it: it is, that the best figurative poetry speaks not to the frivolous intellect, but (if anything does) straight to the heart; and does it better than plain prose. There seems then to be something which is better said with metaphor than without, which goes straighter to its mark by going crooked, and hits its aim exactly by flying off at tangents. An odd fact, if true.

I shall now keep you gasping for the true answer as a thirsty land gasps for rain, while I inhumanly interpose the refutation of two heresies. The first says: metaphor is the language of emotion; the second says: metaphor is the language of the subconscious mind.

First then: metaphor is the language of emotion. Why should it be? If you wished to inspire me with the emotion of terror and the motion of flight, you would find the words, 'A bull is charging you from behind' just as effective as any poetical circumlocution. 'The playfellow of Europa' or 'a pint of Bovril unreduced' would be not more, but probably less, effective. But, of course, that isn't the point. The poet does not wish to set going in us a high horse-power (or even bull-power) of crude and simple emotion but (it is supposed) to evoke a delicate balance of recherché emotions, to tap out an elaborate melody on the piano of our hearts, and not just loudly to thump the baser notes. It is only cads like Euripides, with his detestable pathos, who plan this sort of spiritual assault and battery upon us. But, if subtle emotion is to be stirred, it seems as though metaphor is what we want. For we cannot be trusted to react to the failing evening light just as the poet does. He will not convey to us his feeling about it merely by stating that it is failing in fact, nor would we get at all a clear idea of his sentiment if he said: 'The light is failing, and how sad I feel.' But if he says: 'The curfew tolls the knell of parting day', he presents to us the dying day in all those colours of sadness and solemnity which he reads into it. There may not be a great deal of similarity between an expiring invalid and a late evening, objectively considered: but there may be much affinity between our feelings about the two. What the poet seems to be saying to us, is this: 'Find an emotion, such that it might be felt *either* about a dying man *or* about a late evening.' Either of these subjects considered in isolation might have a great variety of emotion attaching to it, but if we have to find one that could do for both, we are supplied with a direction which is more precise. It is as though we had to find a point upon a map. If we were directed to find it along a single line, it might be anywhere on that line: but if we are given two lines, and directed to the place where they intersect, then we shall find our position well enough. So the poet seems to direct us to the place where our feelings about dying men and late evening coincide.

Well, but this seems to be a convincing theory: surely then, metaphor *is* the language of emotion, for it enables us to describe or convey emotion more accurately than anything else. Why then have we called this doctrine a heresy? I reply: not because it isn't true in itself but because it isn't that whole truth which it pretends to be. Metaphor is, among other things, the language of emotion: but it has other functions beside; and it is a heresy and a damnable heresy to limit the function of figurative poetry to the description of subjective emotion alone. Of any true lover of poetry I will ask the question: Do you really think that figurative verse or prose does nothing but play a tune on the strings of your heart, in unison with the tones of emotion that you suppose the author himself to have felt? Do you really think that such writing never illuminates the real object which the poet is professing to describe? Do you think that from reading or hearing such poetry you never come away with a livelier sense of what exists, exists not in your heart or in the poet's heart, but out there in the world which is his world and yours?

It is no use arguing about this: you either think it or you do not think it. Take any instance you like. Take Housman *en bloc* as a convenient example, because he is so uniform. Will you tell me that to read him is only to find out how Housman reacted to certain aspects of human destiny? Is it not also to apprehend more strongly what those aspects of human destiny in fact *are*? What is, on one face of it, man's position in the universe and setting in the context of inhuman nature? And does he not tell us these things by figurative discourse?

Perhaps it would contribute towards the clearing up of this matter if we state a distinction between two senses that can be given and are given to the word 'subjective' and the word 'feeling'. For we do think that there is something subjective about poetry, that it expresses what is felt about things and not just what they are; and yet when somebody draws from this the apparently logical conclusion that poetry tells us nothing about existence but only about a poet's emotions, I for one feel myself unsatisfied. And perhaps the trouble lies in the words 'subjective' and 'feeling'. If we think that they do apply, and yet can't swallow the consequences which follow from applying them, it is most likely that the words have a double sense, and that the sense in which they apply is not the sense which yields these unpalatable consequences.

You will be thinking now that you are in for a philosophy lecture: you aren't; you are in for a visit to an aquarium. It is a provincial aquarium, and it is not very well-lighted, well-glazed, or well-kept. Let us flatten our noses against the glass, and spy. What is that curious and fishlike shadow undulating there behind the unconvincing rock and mangy seaweed? Can the creature really be so odd as it looks? Does it swell in and out as it moves, or is that a distortion due to a twist in the glass through which we are viewing it? Is it really that remarkable colour, or is that due to the lurid lighting and the dirty water? Now of us two who are flattening our noses against the glass, the philosopher—say me—will be busy with these questions, trying to separate what really belongs to the fish from that which belongs to the glass, the water, and the lamps, while the poet—that's you—will begin without more ado describing just what he sees, reckless of all distinction between the fish and the complicated medium through which it is seen. You will be expressing to yourself, or anyone whom you can buttonhole and bore, with those telling literary phrases of which you have such a mastery, the block-effect of what is in front of your eyes. You see it as an astonishing sea monster: how much of it is really sea monster, how much bad lighting and worse water, you have not paused to consider.

Such, I submit, is the so-called subjectivism of the poet. He describes the block-effect in front of his mind's eye, as he presses that metaphorical organ against the window pane of experience. In the block-effect that he sees, how much is the genuine object as it is in itself, and how much the haze of emotion or instinctive mis-interpretation through which he views it? In the picture in his mind's eye, not only has the object got mixed with his own reactions, but several objects, perhaps, have got mixed with one another. Never mind, he does not sort them out, he describes as he sees.

Now this is subjectivism of a sort, because criticism has not been introduced, and criticism is necessary for making sure that we have separated out the object from other objects and from our own reactions. But it is not subjectivism in the sense that the man is concerned with conveying his own emotions alone; or that what he thinks he sees and describes is his own emotions. On the contrary, he is, very likely, concerned primarily with the object; and if it happens that the emotions are appropriate and don't distort the vision of that to which they react, then there is nothing to prevent him from seeing and describing the object as it is. To return to the aquarium: there am I, with philosophic caution, trying to sort out the real fish from the distortions of the medium through which I see it. A waste of time, for it happens, perhaps, that the water is clear, the lighting good, and the glass true: so that you who with poetic recklessness have dashed straight off into description, are describing the object just as it is, with your inimitable felicity of phrase; while it is I who am making a fool of myself, nasty, suspicious fellow that I am, and one that doubtless began life by suspecting poison in the feeding-bottle. I say that it is just your luck, to have trusted your eyes without reflection and got away with it. It may be so, but that does not alter the fact that while the luck holds you are seeing and describing what is there.

Very well, then: the poet's subjectivism has no need to be a concern with his own reactions or emotions, though of course he may describe those if he chooses. But more often he is concerned with objects outside him; and then, given luck, he may get them right, and so be 'objective'. Or even, given different luck, what he describes will be a hodge-podge which is not all emotions, but in which qualities really belonging to the object will play a large part. We may sum it up by saying, that while the poet undoubtedly describes things just as he feels them, he does not describe what he feels *about* the things.

We must conclude, then, that metaphor, the poet's chosen instrument, is not the language of emotion, but the language of description. It may describe anything you like, emotions, phantasies, realities. And we say that it is good and true when it effectively describes what the poet sees, whether he is looking at his own heart, or his own dream, or the real world of things, or a mixture of them all.

And now we are free to open up the main question—Why is metaphor the best means of description? If there is anyone here who wants to follow my argument I ask him to listen carefully to what I am now going to say. There are two main uses of language: one is to analyse things; the other is to describe them. Analysis is the work of scientific language. As grammarians may break up sentences into words and words into letters, so the scientist analyses the world into the factors which in his view compose it. When in science we ask, What is such-and-such a thing? we really mean, into what pattern of parts or system of factors can it be analysed? For this purpose metaphors are not particularly useful. Many technical scientific terms are metaphors, but that doesn't really help the scientific quest. When the scientist goes further and substitutes English or Greek letters instead of the names of his physical elements and functions, these letters do just as well as the hideous words for which they stand.

But when we are not being scientists, we do not use language to break things up into factors, we use it to describe the quality they have. I do not now want to know how a thing can be analysed, I want to know *what it is like*: I am interested in its individual character. But now whatever can one say about the individual character of anything? Suppose, for example, that a lover wishes to describe the object of his passion: an urge incident to that pathological condition. It is no use saying that she is a girl: it is true, but there are plenty of those. Get out your whole paintbox of adjectives, and splosh them on, it will not help much; no array of superlatives will content you. And certainly no scientific analysis of the texture of her skin or the system of her psychology would be any better. You will have to compare her skin to flowers and her eyes to pools and all the rest of it. Until you were in love you regarded such poetical comparisons as nonsense, but once you are in, you see that they are exactly what is wanted.

While we are on this tender and interesting topic, I would like to raise a question about it, because it illustrates what I was saying just now about poetry and emotion. The passion of love is accompanied by a deal of emotion: but does his emotion blind the lover's eyes? It seems to the onlooker that the lover makes a fool of himself for getting so worked up about a perfectly commonplace girl. But I am inclined to take up the lover's defence. In the name of the philosophical lover I reply: 'That isn't the point, I am not unaware of the girl's faults, and I am not pretending that she is actually more virtuous, more intelligent, or more sculpturesquely beautiful than other girls. What I say is, that scales have fallen from my eyes, and because of some inner sympathy between this girl and me I am able to appreciate the miracle of a woman's existence, something so vivid, so real, and so sweet, that there is no end to the delight of it. Other girls may have something like it in them too, but I'm not interested in them just now, thank you all the same.'

The emotion, he claims, does not blind his eyes, but opens them. It would be a strange fact if being passionately interested in something were always a bar to appreciating it truly; and, he says, 'I am passionately interested in this woman. Every woman and every man, and I dare say every beast and every blade of grass, is the work of an almighty hand, which has poured into it an intensity of life, and an individuality of being, and a variety of perfections above what the angels of God can ever hope fully to grasp. We go about most of our time with our eyes glued to the floor, or looking up only to take in a dull façade of things, unable to penetrate and seize the living being in which the Creator himself is expressed. It takes the violent passion of love to break down the dull custom of incomprehension, the blindness of the eyes and the hardness of the heart. And then you tell me that because for once I care about the creature of God with all my mind, for that very reason I am seeing nothing. Go and sing that song in another street: I am tired of you. My mind is a vessel, having a certain capacity of vision, and just now it is filled to overflowing with the contemplated being of the women that I love and I am only sorry that I have not room to contain more.'

Enough of this young gentleman's ecstasies: he has taken an embarrassingly solemn line, but I must say that I accept his case in the main, even though it is unpleasant having to agree with such a heavy talker. And I call upon all those of you who have suffered from the amatory passion to concur: if you don't, I shall delate you to your ladies. In poetic vision, then, and in amatory passion we are convinced that the object of our contemplation has a vividness of being, a distinctness of incommunicable individuality which scientific analysis would in vain hope to express—we are driven into metaphor. Science considers things in so far as they are the same; poetry, in so far as each is irreducibly itself. But what can we say about that which is truly unique? We may say that it is itself, but that's not very illuminating. One can get a certain pleasure out of it, as lovers from the repetition of the beloved person's name, or even from an excessive use of the second-person pronoun: the over-emphasis of the word 'you' in amatory ditties is not only due to its suitability to be sung as a top note, it is also because it is germane to the subject. But if we want to get beyond 'Daphne Daphne Daphne' or 'you you you', and say something *about* the shepherdess, there really seems nothing left but comparison, metaphor and simile. And this seems to be indicated by the ordinary man's form of speech when he asks for information about the nature of anything. He leaves to philosophers and pedants such questions as 'What is its nature?' or 'What kind of a fact is it?' and says simply 'What is it *like*?' which literally means 'What other thing does it resemble?' and show that he expects an answer in the form of a comparison.

We now take the next great step in our argument. If metaphor and comparison can really illuminate, it must be because the things compared are really alike in the required respect. Behind verbal metaphor stands real analogy. The blind man who had never seen, guessed from the talk of men with eyes, that scarlet must be a sort of trumpet note among colours; and there is a real sense in which he was not only poetical, but right. The two things are alike: there is analogy between them.

All the unique creatures God has made resemble one another, at greater or less distance; for all reflect in diverse manner and degree their one creator, and imitate his existence, as far as their lowliness allows, by being each themselves. But if they have a family resemblance, they have an unlikeness too. I don't know whether your aunts play over you the tiresome game of family faces: I mean of sharing out your eyes, nose and chin among your direct and collateral family elders, who are supposed (frequently by a causal connection which would baffle the student of genetics) to be responsible for these several features: you begin to feel that your face is nothing but a heap of mixed genealogy. And when they have finished with your face, they start on your mental and moral qualities and failings. When the nuisance has subsided and the aunts are gone, your mother says: 'Never mind, dear: they have to talk like that. But it's a lot of nonsense. You are just yourself, and very nice too.'

Still the aunts and the poets have their justifications: Uncle George and you, girls and fresh flowers, scarlet uniforms and blaring trumpets have real resemblances, although their individual natures defy the power of any number of comparisons to state them exhaustively. It is only by comparison and contrast with other things that we become aware of their individualities, and find out, as the saying is, what they are like.

Now the poet is the man who has a gift for grasping fresh and profound resemblances, and that is why he works with metaphor, and why his metaphors illuminate the nature of things. This gift can only work by inspiration. There is no technique for finding out

the analogy of scarlet to the trumpet-note: it has just to be seen or
not seen. Like the slave of Aristotle, who could not find reason for
himself, but could see reason when handed to him by his superior
and master, so are we related to the poet: we cannot divine the
analogies ourselves, but we can follow him when he points them
out. But he divines them; and it is because he works by divination
that the poet necessarily falls into that so-called subjectivism
which I was explaining just now by the fable of the two visitors to
the aquarium. We cannot regulate, control or direct by critical
method that mysterious gift for catching a likeness, and so the
man who is engaged in critically sorting out the fish from the seaweed, the discoloured water, the false light and the twisted glass
will not be in the same moment appreciating the revealing likeness
of the strange apparent creature to some other thing. And so, to
apply the parable, the poet must go where inspiration or divination
leads, and see what likenesses suggest themselves: he cannot afford
to distract himself by a philosophical criticism, or to separate out
the object from the medium in which it is seen; and so, as we said,
when his view does happen to be purely objective that is just his
luck.

People sometimes say of this poetical divination, this miracle of
metaphor, that it is the work of the subconscious mind. If so, we
may congratulate that dark divinity upon her skill, and go for
oracles to her prophetic cave. An older generation called it Phoebus
or the Muse; and, by whatever name, it seems to the poet a power
from within him, other than the mind he consciously manipulates,
something by him uncontrollable and very different from the
methodical application of scientific reason. It is not because the
poet wishes to be subjective that he is so: he is interested in grasping real being, but because he grasps it by way of divination, he is
unable to reason, criticize and sort out.

I promised you some theology, so now we had better turn to
that. We have said that metaphor is our way of describing what is
unique, because there is nothing proper or exact to be said about it
but that it is itself; so we fall back on its always imperfect likenesses to other things. But now of all things known to us, the most
simply and absolutely unique is God; and next to him, the human
soul. The soul is not much like anything else, and so men have
always been forced to talk about it in unconvincing metaphors: a

D

flame of aspiration, a light of consciousness, a force of will, a weighing-scale of choice—these threadbare physical analogies serve their turn, and we recognize our very self by the means of them, apprehending not only the likeness but the difference that there is between our soul and all such things. Without such comparisons, no one has ever been or ever will be able to recognize the soul, or say anything about it even to himself. Whenever we think of the soul we use some such figure half-consciously, as you will be able to discover by analysing your own thoughts. And when we see through one such figure and wish to correct it, we can only do so by calling in another to balance it.

When we were considering metaphor as the language of emotion, we said that understanding the metaphor was like solving a riddle, as though the poet had said: 'Find an emotion that might be felt *either* about a dying man *or* a late evening.' So with our mixed metaphors about the soul. They suggest the problem: find not the emotion, but the real being which is like a flame, a dynamo, a weighing-scale and an illumination, and which is also the centre of your own existence. I reply: 'That is easy. It is what I have and what I am.' But the riddle is not a mere riddle: by suggesting both contrast and likeness it gives us a vivid perception of what the soul is.

Some hard-boiled men, too dull to understand poetry or too proud to learn from riddles, or too obsessed with scientific method, have roundly declared that the soul does not exist, because we cannot speak plainly and properly of it. They have denied that the mind is anything but a heap of mental events, connected by psychological laws. But the soul does exist: there is nothing of which we are more aware, for it is we ourselves; only its uniqueness and singleness prevents our talking prose about it, and that's the whole of the mystery.

The soul is unique when compared with that which is not a soul; for if we are classifying created things, we must put the soul all by itself on one side of the main division, and on the other the whole host of things which the soul knows, loves, hates, feels, manages, copes with and exploits. But though the soul is unique by comparison with all that is not soul, it is in this respect not unique, that there are many souls, yours and mine and the next man's, and these have a common nature, and I can know something about

several such. But God is uniquely unique. There is not a class of
Gods, but one alone. The philosophers have rightly said that
God can be placed in no class with anything else. We cannot even
say, for example, that he and we fall into one class, the class of
persons or spirits; for though we are certainly nearer to God's
personality than are the beasts, yet we do not come up to it, any
more than the minds of the beasts come up to ours: we are not
persons really in the same sense, but only by some faint approach
to it.

Now God is a reality as is our soul, absolutely present and active
in the existence and operation of all the creatures; for they are the
expression of continual creative power. But though we had the
eyes of angels to see his work, though we enjoyed that vision of
him face to face reserved for those who have put off mortality and
passed the purging fire, our inability of speech would still remain.
It is his uniqueness and not only his hiddenness, which prevents
our saying anything perfectly exact about him, except that he is
himself: that God is God alone; and the very hymn of the angels,
scripture divines, is not an expression of what he is by himself,
but an appeal to the various similitudes in which the creatures share
and imitate his being: *pleni sunt caeli et terra majestate gloriae tuae*
['Heaven and earth are full of the majesty of Thy glory']. Of himself, they can only say that he is, and that he is exalted: 'Sanctus,
Sanctus, Sanctus, Dominus Deus Sabaoth.'

It is therefore not a scandal, but something every hearer of
poetry should understand, that all the statements we make about
God are similitudes, as it is written, *per speculum in enigmate*
['Through a glass darkly']. I will appear to man through a glass and
in a riddle. All words about God pose a riddle, as we saw about
descriptions of the soul. Let us call him the *eternal spirit*. That is as
much as to say, 'Find a being in whom the living act of personality
and the changelessness of mathematical truth meet and coincide.'
The personal life that we know is above all in movement and
changeable, and the eternal truth we know is neither personal nor
alive, but God is the unimaginable being in whom these two are
one. To object to such paradoxes is just to be silly and to ignore the
point—the uniqueness of God. To say 'God is alive, and therefore
not changeless' is to stop talking about the unique being, God, who
has some slight analogy to the living things we know, and to begin

talking about these finite living things instead. We fall into the same error if we say: 'God is changeless, and therefore not alive.' Then we are talking, not about God, but about the class of changeless things such as mathematical axioms.

Well now, 'But,' you may say, 'this is to reduce theology to poetry, and that you promised us you would not do. If the prophets and apostles were just poets, who divined likenesses between God and his creatures, between God's acts and purposes, and human acts and purposes, then, like other poetic divinations, the scriptures will present the same unreliable half-subjectivism to which the poet is condemned. In the case of the poet, it does not matter, we do not go to him for reliable objective truth; but in the case of theology, this is vital. We cannot do with a hodge-podge of the real deity and every kind of emotional and subjective illusion: we may have to put up with similitudes about God, but they must be similitudes about *him*, and not about a confused mass of experience in which he plays we know not what part.'

If that is your objection, your objection is just: Theology is *not* identical with the subjective poetry of devotion but strives after a higher exactitude. How can it achieve this? It cannot go right beyond the language of similitude and achieve a science of God as we have a science of mathematics or even physics. For against the possibility of such a science there remains the impossible barrier: God is not an analysable system but a single being; nor can God be placed in any class of beings. He is unique.

What then does the theologian do? You remember that we said about the poet, that if his metaphors illuminate, it must be because there is some real likeness or analogy, however incomplete, between the things compared. But the poet does not bother his head about this: he goes on divining his likenesses as the spirit moves him. We, however, if we wish to do so, may take him to pieces and try to get back behind the metaphors to the real analogies on which they are based, as we did in the case of: 'The curfew tolls the knell of parting day.' To do that in the case of poetry is on the whole a thankless task; for in reading poetry we do not want to attend to the comparison, we want to attend to the object which the comparison illuminates: we do not want to think about the dying invalid, we want to think about the failing daylight. In theology it is otherwise: we must get behind the poetry to the real analogies.

And so, with agonizing care, the great theologians have strained their minds to grasp the actual relations of likeness in which things stand to God. By this they have been able to determine which are the closest and most appropriate analogies to use about him; and beside this, which aspects of the things compared with him really apply, and which are irrelevant—a problem which of course confronts us in interpreting any parable. There are always details in the 'earthly' story which do not apply to the 'heavenly meaning', and to force which is to miss the point. By these methods we can know many things with certainty: for example, that personal analogies are the closest and best; that God can be compared with our will and intellect, but not with our passions; that though the acts of will and intellect in us are distinct, this division has no counterpart in God, who wills all that he knows, and knows all that he wills.[1]

It would be absurd to run on in this manner. I fear I have become compressed and obscure, and have fallen between the two stools of wanting to say something about the method of theology, and wanting to spare you a professional diatribe. Let me compress the single point I really wish to make here. Theology shares with poetry the method of comparison, but that does not mean that the comparison is wild and irresponsible: we need not plaster the idea of God with every kind of analogy till we are tired, merely in order to conclude that he is after all equally unlike all these things—the method, I believe, of some Indian pantheists. No, we can range things scientifically in degree of approximation to him, and know by what comparison we are nearest, by what furthest; and so purge our thinking of subjective bias.

I have said too much about the *form* of poetry and of theology, and I should like to conclude with a remark about their substance. I count poetical vision and even amatory passion the friends of religion, in spite of the fact that their abuse may easily tend the other way. But though poetry often breeds an attitude of fancifulness and egotism; and love, heaven knows, of animality and complacency; yet we have on the other side to set this—that the lover and the poet at least look at something and see it. And the chief impediment to religion in this age, I often think, is that no one ever looks at anything at all: not so as to contemplate it, to apprehend what it is to be that thing, and plumb, if he can, the deep fact of its individual existence. The mind rises from the knowledge of creatures to the knowledge of their creator, but this does not happen through the sort of knowledge which can analyse things into factors or manipulate them with technical skill or classify them into groups. It comes from the appreciation of things which we have when we love them and fill our minds and senses with them, and feel something of the silent force and great mystery of their existence. For it is in this that the creative power is displayed of an existence higher and richer and more intense than all.

Does God Exist?†

INTRODUCTORY REMARKS

I am asked to state an argument for the existence of God which
appeals to grounds of general reason. I will do what I can, even
though it is my experience that such arguments are about as likely
to weaken as to strengthen belief. For, even granted that the argument is convincing in itself, its force lies in many presuppositions
which cannot themselves all be stated, still less established, except
in a big book. These presuppositions are (in the theist's opinion)
natural, and so he puts forward his argument, hoping that the
presuppositions will awake in his hearer's mind. But he knows that
they may be buried, lost, or distorted: and in that case the argument will fall flat and discredit theism by so falling.

In any case, theistic arguments are not formal demonstrations.
Since the Divine Being is unique, he can only be known by a sort
of acquaintance: he must impress us *in and through* finite things,
very likely without our fully conscious appreciation of the fact. We
can never know the unique by mere inference from other things,
nor God by mere inference from the world. What we suppose, is
that finite-things-enacted-by-God form the proper object of a
fully awakened understanding. For a thousand practical purposes
we neglect, we abstract from, the God-dependence of things: we
may never, even, have become distinctly aware of it. But because
it is there for us, we can make ourselves aware of our neglect of it,
by making ourselves see that a Godless account of things is incomplete. The incompleteness is not logical: what it falls short of is the
ideal completeness which is, in fact, present to our minds, however
neglected or misunderstood—the activity of God everywhere
supporting and inworking his creatures.

So without more ado, let us set forth an argument through
which the dependence of the world on God may make itself felt by
our minds.

† A paper delivered to the Socratic Club, Oxford; 13 October 1947. Reprinted
from the *Socratic Digest*, No. 4 (in essence, a précis of *FI*).

THE ARGUMENT

The world, so far as I can see, appears to be made up of systems of active process. My conscious being is a system of active process anyhow, a wonderfully balanced interplay of willings and reactings and doings. The existence of living things, my own body for example, is also an interplay of active processes: my body lives as a body only in so far as the heart beats and the blood circulates and the lungs expand and contract and all sorts of other rhythms of digestion and distribution go on, such as physiologists study. There are living bodies of all kinds in the world, vegetable as well as animal, and all are systems of active process. But, if we are to believe the sciences, active process is not the being of living things alone. The apparently solid and stupid lumps of physical matter are, in fact, nothing of the sort: they are really made up of infinitely complicated, minute rhythms of active process, without which process, nothing would exist at all.

Active process, then, is a sort of common denominator of all existence known to us, from the lowest to the highest. It seems to be capable of existing at various levels, and in various forms: moreover, it is capable of passing from one level and one form to another level and another form. I am a living and active process when I am half awake, but it only requires someone to apply a suitable stimulus to me, and the slumbering activity which was me a minute ago becomes the highest degree of active attention and perhaps the highest energy of physical action. Lazy day-dreaming may transform itself into philosophical contemplation in a moment, so that the active process which constitutes my being may vary its form, e.g. from thought to action, and it may vary its level, e.g. from feeding to reasoning.

These transformations take place within my own conscious life; but consider the transformation by which my conscious life itself arises out of the elementary active process shut up within a germ, or the transformation by which, according to the evolutionists, the rudimentary system of action called an amoeba becomes at last a mammal. We must not, of course, imagine that the transformations are all for the better. On the contrary, species of animals degenerate, individuals die, moral character decays, and as I awake out of sleep into consciousness, so I fall away out of consciousness back into sleep.

I have two points to make here: first, that the common and basic something, active being, takes on an infinity of forms; and second, that all these forms appear to be in a sense arbitrary. None of them is the form of active being as such: they are all particular forms, and they might have been otherwise. We might have had a universe in which physical matter was not organized in the manner in which the atomic theorists say it is, in which there were no oak trees or daisies, no dogs, horses, or men, but completely different systems of active being.

Thus we seem to require an explanation for the fact that existence has taken the shape that it has. In the ordinary way, when we ask for explanations, we simply go one step, or several steps, back into the history of the process; if we want to know how there came to be those active systems which we call giraffes, we take for granted antelopes, a habitat providing the best fodder on the tops of trees, and the fact of chance-variation. From a certain state of affairs we can see another state arising, and we call this 'explanation': but the explanation is limited, for there is always some state of affairs presupposed. If we presuppose no state of affairs, no organization of active existence already operative, we can explain nothing. We cannot say: let it be supposed that *active existence as such* is loose in space, and you will get a world. You have to suppose, not active existence as such, but active existence already organized in a particular way: but why in such a way? We always have to suppose active existence running on certain lines: what put it on those lines? If we say, some other finite organization of active existence, the same question crops up about that. We can arrive at no answer which gives final satisfaction, except one. We must step right out of the finite sphere altogether, and conceive of a being who is not just one possible form of active existence, for then we should have to ask 'why *this* form rather than another?'—but who realizes in himself the fullest possibility of active existence, in whom Reality has the full stature of which it is capable.[1] The notion of such a being is self-explanatory: we do not ask why he is *so*, rather than otherwise: he is just himself. Such a being it must be, therefore, who has laid down the particular lines on which active existence runs in the world we know. He has, to use an

ancient phrase, *ordained*² it thus. The processes which make up
the world cannot be what they are, they are not capable of existing
at all, without an infinite ordainer who wills that they should be so.

The argument which I have sketched is based on a survey of
everything in general, it argues from the most general facts we can
state about the whole range of existing beings in our world. I will
now support it by an argument drawn from one very special sort of
being, the being that we ourselves are. We can become aware of a
whole universe of creatures objectively, but there is only one
creature we can experience subjectively, and that is ourself. I can
become aware through outward experience of the patterns of
activity which make up many levels and sorts of being, for example,
a biologist can examine the activity-pattern of the body of a frog.
But one cannot taste what it is like to be a frog, one can only taste
what it is like to be a man.

Therefore, when we have concluded on grounds of general
reason that an infinite and absolute being must have ordained or
appointed the forms of finite being, we naturally turn to our own
being, in order to ask whether, in our own case, finite being tastes
as though it had been appointed or ordained: whether we experience our own existence as something for which the lines have been
laid down by a higher power. And, I maintain, this is in fact the
case. I shall argue as follows:

We experience our own existence as an activity of self-
determination. To be a man is to be the architect of one's own life.
We do what we choose to do. The astonishing and almost terrifying
fact of our own freedom only throws into higher relief the fact of
its limitations. These limitations are of two kinds. On the one hand
there are limitations imposed by brute fact. I may try as hard as I
will to see into the essential nature of physical being, but I can get
hardly any way at all, and never shall, because my faculties don't
allow of it: I am a man, and not an angel. I may try as hard as I like
to think as well as Aristotle or Kant, but I shall not do it, because I
am only Austin Farrer and I haven't got it in me. I may do my best
to be in Trinity College to keep an appointment at 10.00 a.m., but
even if I defy the traffic lights I can't do it, because it was 9.59 a.m.
when I mounted my bicycle in Manor Road. I may resolve to
remember and do something at a given hour, but for all my resolu-
tion an intervening train of thought washes the memory out. All

these are cases of brute fact limitation, and they really add nothing to our argument, for we have already seen that every finite existence is limited by the hard fact of its nature and its place. When I find how many things I cannot do, I am simply realizing that I am Austin Farrer, and not God Almighty, not even the Archangel Gabriel, nor even Immanuel Kant, nor even the captain of university athletics.

But there is another set of limitations which are of more interest here. My free activity is not merely limited by the things I can't do: it is limited also in the doing of the things I can do. All serious men know that they are limited not only by what they are, but by what they are *called to be*: not by what the human race has attained (which isn't, on the average, anything very grand) but by what the human race in general, and they themselves in particular, are *called* to attain. *Called* to attain: and who does the calling? It is, fundamentally, as simple as that. There is a pattern³ of our true destiny to which we know that we are called, and to which we are bound to show a measureless respect. Now the more evolutionist we are, the more sceptical about any fixed form called human nature, the more ready to admit that all the forms of finite existence are mere temporary phases in the process of the world—the more we admit these things, the more we ought to be bothered by the question, who or what calls us on into one destiny rather than another? It is vain to talk about 'ideals', as though ideals somehow floated about in space or inscribed themselves in the colours of the sunset. Ideals are made by men, or else they are evoked by God. If they are made by men, why cannot we make them what we choose? But we cannot. Old-fashioned philosophy based the stern call to the quest for perfection on a fixed form called human nature, the same in all men from the beginning of the world and on to the end of time. Darwinianism and Historicism have knocked that on the head fairly effectively.⁴ Human nature is the form of one particular emergent process. Yet we all know that we are called—not by what man just essentially always was and always will be, nor by what in fact he is going to become in this world, for he may be going to become something not very creditable. Then by what, or rather, by whom, are we called?

Are we not here experiencing God's ordaining in its actual happening? We were previously arguing that it was necessary to suppose that all finite existence is ordained, because it is finite. Then we turned to our own existence, the only existence which we can taste from within, to see whether being a man feels like being under divine ordinance, or no. And it seems that it does, even in our most human, most independent, most godlike aspect, our free will. Precisely at this point at which we are able to make the experiment of playing at being God Almighty, and decreeing what we choose, we find that we cannot, but are under mysterious ordinances. Our free will certainly has great play, it can even reject its true destiny: but that, we know, is a sort of suicide.

Now what can we say of the nature of the being who ordains for us the perfection after which we have to strive? We can say that he is a being to whom none has (in turn) measured out a perfection after which *he* has to strive: he is one who has caught up with his own perfection, who is all the good he sees, and sees all the good he is.

I have put forward these arguments with extreme crudity, and without any of the philosophical caution the matter requires. But I think that some such crude statement may suffice for my immediate purpose, which is not so much to prove God, as to show you what the method of argument for God's existence is. They simply show how the incomplete and Godless view of the world is supplemented with what it needs by that which believers think God to be. I am well aware that unbelievers can get rid of the whole force of the arguments by denying the meaningfulness of the whole basis from which the arguments start. It is easy, for example, as you very well know, to challenge the whole account of our free will and the claim of our true destiny upon us, which I have so roughly sketched. To which our only reply is, that serious men are forced to think like that in practice, whatever they may pretend to hold in theory. Still, if you deny, you deny, and there is nothing to be done about it, except to cultivate the power of contemplating your own spiritual being, a power which in some otherwise very clever men remains at a rudimentary stage. Cleverness will not take us to the knowledge of God, but wisdom will, and wisdom is a rarer gift.

But the most serious sceptical objection to all arguments for God's existence is that we have no intelligible notion whatever of God, nor therefore of the way in which the world depends upon

him. To return to our first argument: if we argue that finite existence as such is an arbitrary sort of fact requiring explanation, we
are tacitly comparing finite existence, to its disadvantage, with
some other sort of existence which would *not* be an arbitrary fact.
But this other sort of existence can be none other than the existence
of God. The argument cannot stand at all, unless we are catching a
glimpse of the Divine Nature out of the corner of the mind's eye.
We are really saying: since Divine Nature is the standard of what
one might expect being simply to be, how does it arise that what
our senses meet on every hand is not God, but finite things? And
the argument goes on to answer: it is because the finite things have
been ordained by God.

This is perfectly true. If you feel the force of the argument, it is
because you are catching sight of the Divine Nature out of the
corner of your mind's eye. So much the better for us: that does not
help to discredit the argument: it rather helps to suggest that God
is there in fact.

Still, if the most rudimentary analysis can show (as many people
say) that the idea of God is completely bogus, a piece of unintelligible nonsense: if 'infinite spiritual activity'[5] is the description of
God, and if 'infinite spiritual activity' is a piece of contradictory
nonsense like 'square circle' or 'perfect wickedness', then, of
course, the whole argument collapses.

I mention this question because it seems only honest to do so,
but I can scarcely handle it here. The most subtle point of theist
philosophy is the definition of the sense in which we can think
about God. The theistic philosophers are well aware that all our
thinking about God is infinitely short of his real nature, and yet
they have thought it possible to find a middle position between
adequacy and complete frustration. I will not enter into the subtleties of this question: but I will just put before you a train of
thought which makes a great appeal to my own mind, and which
may show you that the thought of an absolute spirit is far more
natural and usual with us than we are inclined to suppose.

I ask you simply to reflect for a moment about your own understanding and will. Simply ask yourself, what you mean by understanding, and what you mean by willing. And I think you will find
that the first and simplest thing you tell yourself about understanding is that it is a sort of seeing with the mind of how other

things are in themselves. But when you turn to look at your own understanding, you will find that it never is in fact this, but at the best, a distant approximation to it. When have you understood any being as it is in itself? So you have to say, 'My understanding is not a pure or proper understanding; it is a limited or diluted understanding.' What have you done? You have found it natural, when you begin to think about understanding, to start with what believers suppose the Divine Mind to be: then you have gone on to make the surprising discovery that your mind isn't the Divine Mind. An odd way of thinking, but one which suggests that the idea of absolute or perfect mind is not so completely foreign to us as we were inclined to suspect. So again with will. What is will? A power freely to frame projects seen to be good, and to execute them because they are seen to be good. What could be simpler—and what could be more divine? We have hardly, ourselves, more than the shadow of such a power. Our rational choice is invaded in every part by irrational impulse, so that we can never perfectly separate the two: we never fully understand the business that we bring about; and we cannot choose what is simply good, but only the best of the possibilities that circumstances open for us. It is because our will is only half a will, that the determinist case has any plausibility. So natural it is to us to measure the modicum of will we possess by the standard of this absolute, creative freedom which is what we mean by God.

What I have been saying about understanding and will is no sort of proof that God exists: it is only some indication that the notion of such a being as God is believed to be, plays quite a natural part in our common thinking. If this is so, then we must be overdoing it if we say that the idea of God, or of his creative act, is just meaningless. We measure ourselves by our approximation to the divine. That does not mean that God exists: but it should mean that the idea of God isn't nonsense.

On the other side we must not overdrive the argument. We haven't got 'a clear and distinct idea of God'[6] or anything approaching it. If you take the notion of a pure understanding or an absolute will and try to work it out, to conceive such a being in the round, you will quickly fall into an abyss of darkness. But after all, that is what we have to expect. If God might be comprehended, he would not be God. An over-confident dogmatism is as fatal to theistic belief as scepticism itself: it pretends to prove and to define, only to discover that what it has defined and proved is not its Lord and God. You can no more catch God's infinity in a net of words, than (to misapply Housman's poem) you can fish out of the sea the glories of the dying day.

Faith and Reason[†]

The object is, to define faith in so far as it is the name of a cognitive act: to determine its relations with other acts of intellect, and the scope of realities with which it is concerned. For this purpose we must consider:

1. The fundamental constitution of the human mind as an apprehensive power.
2. Several levels of realities which it contemplates, and how they are mutually related *qua* cognoscible by it.
3. The formal subjective character of the act of faith.
4. The opposition of faith and reason.
5. The supernatural character of faith.

1 THE HUMAN MIND

There is not a Christian or theological theory of knowledge, any more than of aviation or potato-culture, and those who have introduced God as a bridge between the finite mind and its natural objects have done no better than those who made him the link between physical causes and physical effects. But there are truths about the nature of knowledge which a Christian is better placed for recognizing than is an unbeliever. His theology gives him the proper frame in which to view things and diminishes the probability of his misinterpreting them. Such a truth is this double one: (a) Knowledge is the simple apprehension of existent being, such that the character of the real object comes to exist in the mind in a state of understoodness; (b) Human knowledge is a very imperfect instance of knowledge in general: it apprehends the realities through a thick veil of sensation-signs and abstract mental interpretations. From these interpretations and signs it can never

† Date unknown; the footnote p. 56 suggests it is early.

perfectly separate that which it grasps through them. Therefore the character of the object comes to 'exist in the mind' only in a very qualified manner, when that mind is human.

The Christian, we said, is especially well placed for seeing this double truth. He cannot doubt that the divine mind knows all things just as they are in themselves: nor yet that the human mind falls utterly short of the divine, as well in the scope as in the fashion of its knowing. The divine mind sets for him the standard of what it is to know. The creaturely mind, being a diminished expression of the divine image, is not a pure case of knowing, but a participation in what knowledge truly is, in the degree that its lowly estate allows: for we know, says the Apostle, in part, and not by any means in the manner in which we are known by God.

It must seem a strange thing, and especially to disbelievers in God, that the only way to understand the human mind straight, should be to establish an ideal description of what that mind never attains, and then to water down this perfection to the required degree of alteration. It would seem more natural to set about describing just what the human mind is in itself and how it works. Yet if we take this latter course, we lose our way and do not arrive: so true is it that the attempt after knowledge is always and of its essence an aspiration after the exercise of a divine function never attained. This paradox may be realized and has been realized by unbelievers; for while they denied all ultimate attainment of adequate knowledge even by an existent divine being, they could recognize that the will to know was always an aspiration after this unattainable and unactualized divinity.

The ignorance or neglect of this truth leads straight to the opposite absurdities of crude realism and negative idealism. For we cannot help recognizing, at the bottom of our hearts, what knowledge consists in; but since we fail to recognize that the human mind merely participates in such knowing, we try it by the absolute standard and ask a 'yes or no' question. Does our mind know existent reality or not? Yes, say the realists: things are in themselves as odorous as our nose's smell of them, as green as our eye's vision of them, and as notional as our thought's conception of them. No, say the idealists, with equal justification: things cannot be in themselves as the signs and concepts by which we suppose ourselves to know them. Therefore we cannot know existent

E

being: we can merely introduce order into our own mental being and make it to be other and tidier than it was.

Such errors do not concern us here, but a different one, which idealists and realists may share—that reason, in the sense of reasoning or ratiocination, might be supposed to be a source of knowledge. Realists may think so, because it is hardly plausible to maintain that all we suppose ourselves to know is pure apprehension. The rest, then, must arise through reasoning upon our limited apprehension-data. Idealists will naturally think so, for what is called knowledge is for them the tidying up of the matter of experience by a form or order contributed by the human mind: and to impose such an order is to reason. But the Christian philosopher will not think so. For if our apprehension is partial, dim, uncertain, we have continually to be steadying and confirming our darkened vision by comparing what we suppose ourselves to see here with what we suppose ourselves to see there, until we gain both confidence and precision. If we had clear vision to start with, the process would be superfluous: but we have not. Hence the continual cross-reference, mediated by verbal signs, which we call 'reasoning'. Without reasoning there is no knowledge for such as us. But this does not alter the fact that apprehension is both the beginning and the end of our subjective coming-to-know, and also its sole objective control throughout. Reasoning is not a source of knowledge but an instrument to clarify apprehension: and what we apprehend we accept in the last resort in the evidence of its self-presentation.

Knowledge from reason cannot therefore be properly contrasted with some other knowledge or belief that is simply accepted. There may be, and of course are, spheres of knowledge—or should we say, of belief, if no human 'knowledge' has a firmness sufficient to justify the name—where ratiocination plays a greater part than in others. But in no sphere is its part more than an instrumental one.

2 THREE LEVELS OF OBJECTS

In order to take the next step, let us return to our original position, that the human mind participates in the true nature of knowledge but is not a perfect instance of it. Now of a pure knower we may say two things: (a) his mind is an instrument for the apprehension of all being equally—it is 'connatural with existence as such'; (b) he knows what exists just as it is in itself, not as it appears in the glass of sense and the riddle of abstract conceiving. Merely to make these statements is to recognize that our own mind falls short in both respects. We are limited by brute sense and abstractive thought; and we are limited by a certain range of objects, namely such finite beings as enjoy a bodily mode of existence. As sense and abstraction are the means by which we take hold, so corporeal being is the place where we take hold, and these two facts define the human mind.

But if our minds are a mere participation in knowledge, they are a real participation none the less. We do not merely see the glass and the riddle without power to decipher: through them we see existent things. And because corporeal being is where we take hold we are not for that reason simply confined to it. As through sense and abstraction we have some grasp of corporeal being, so through corporeal being we grasp spiritual and infinite being, thereby vindicating even in ourselves the intrinsic universality of intellect.

Now it is not for us here to consider how many distinct levels of knowledge and knowables there are for the human mind: far less to raise the intricate question, how we come to know the higher level through the lower. It is sufficient to indicate (a) that there are certain distinct levels, (b) that there are certain simple principles of order in our knowing them.

(a) When we grasp that finite being which is the immediate natural object of our understanding, we do not merely grasp its particular character, we grasp also the fact that it, being finite, exists. And one aspect of the existence of the finite is its being an expression of the creative act of the infinite: whom we therefore apprehend just in so far as he and his agency are expressed in the existence of the finite. The finite, then, is first known and our knowledge of it is the place where we recognize the second fact of infinite being and agency. Remove the knowledge of the finite, and all knowledge of the infinite is removed: remove knowledge of the infinite, and knowledge of the finite remains. This is what is meant by saying that knowledge of the finite and the infinite constitutes two levels of knowledge.

Granted knowledge of the finite, and of the infinite as its active ground, we may have presented to us, in the detail of finitude and

the field of history, particular events in which this infinite acts
with particular purpose concerning mankind. Remove the knowledge of historical facts and there is no field left in which the
revelation can appear; remove the knowledge of infinite being and
there remains no understanding of who or what is revealed: the
story of Christ becomes a mere fairy-tale about a spirit who performs just these miraculous actions and is otherwise unknown.
Christ may indeed declare himself to be the expression of the
infinite and absolute. But the notion is one whose very meaning
can only be understood by an apprehension of the creative act and
agent in the very fact of the creature's existence. We might not
have heard of God or creation until Christ spoke of them, but we
should still need to see there and then the reality to which he was
directing our attention. On the other hand, the special revelation
in Christ may be removed, and knowledge both of historical reality
and of divine existence still remain.

(b) The first principle of order between the levels is one that has
already appeared in what we have said—that knowledge of what is
further from us is always secondary to knowledge of what is more
immediate to us. The opposed absurdity is committed in the
sphere of the relation between the first two levels, by those who,
for example, conclude from God's absolute and free activity to the
denial of our own freedom. For the knowledge of our own freedom
comes first, and it is through this and this alone that we can reach
any awareness of God's. And the same error is committed in the
sphere of the relation between the second level and the third by
those who deduce from Christ's passion the intrinsic passibility of
the divine nature, overthrowing thereby our very notion of what it
is to be God and so removing the very subject about which they
pretend to be making their assertion.

We are not concerned to say that knowledge at the lower level is
always in fact obtainable without the guidance and assistance of
knowledge at the higher level. For example, it might well be that a
man had a very confused idea of human freedom until he came to
understand man's responsibility to God and God's grace to man.
We must distinguish here. First we strip away those added truths
about the fact of human freedom which are concerned with its relation to God himself. It is plain that to know these we must know
both man and God. But there remains the mere formal character of

human free choice, as it may be, and often is, acknowledged by
unbelievers. We must now distinguish again. Our apprehension of
God is mediated by some knowledge of the finite, and this finite
knowledge being its basis must precede it, at least in an implicit
form. But this knowledge of the finite which is the actual foundation of my imperfect apprehension of God at this moment, may
not include even implicitly that piece of knowledge about the
finite which is under discussion: not, for example, knowledge of
human freedom, for freedom may not have entered into my conception of God himself. Then my discovery of God, not under the
form of the absolute freedom, but under that, say, of the absolute
good, may open my eyes to my own freedom. For an absolute
good set over against the human mind calls our attention to that
freedom in the mind by which the good is embraced, and whose
good the good is.

But however much the knowledge of God may act as a pointer
for the discovery of some finite fact, that fact must be discovered
in and as itself. It is not logically dependent upon the knowledge of
God: it is not known through God, but God through it. And it is in
principle the same, even when revelation—e.g. the word of Christ—
instructs us of something in the finite order, say, our responsible
freedom once more. This is a statement about the finite; and we
can apprehend its meaning only by some apprehension of the
finite fact. Then can revelation serve no purpose, in such a case,
but to direct our attention? Indeed it can, for it can supply conviction. Though to understand what freedom means we must in
fact 'read it off'[1] our own existence, we might still doubt the
correctness of our 'reading' and incline to disbelieve it. Then our
confidence in God's veracity through Christ might supply the
necessary faith. But not with any justification, if we had *adequate*
finite grounds for disbelief.

So much for this principle of order between the levels: knowledge of the higher and second depends on that of the lower and
first. There is another principle the reverse of it: that the lower
cannot be made the measure of the higher. As the former principle
defends the rights of the primary against the secondary, so does
the latter those of the secondary against the primary. Divine freedom (or anything else divine) cannot be known but through
creaturely freedom, the diminished offprint through which alone

we know the perfect archetype. But neither can it be made the measure of that divine freedom, which infinitely surpasses it. How, through finite categories, there comes to be known an infinite being which distends and bursts them, may well seem a wonder: but it is so. We cannot say *a priori* that the finite sign is bound to limit thus and thus the divine truth signified. We can only know that the divine truth must be known through the sign: but just how much can be known, we can only discover by seeing how much in fact gets known. We shall indeed find that the rational knowledge of God is limited, and limited by the finite things through which it reaches us. But just how they limit it we shall not know by looking at the finites themselves, before we begin to theologize: but only by the theologizing.

So, too, is it with the relation of rational theology and the revealed. The rational is not the measure of the revealed except in the sense that the revealed must not overthrow its own rational foundations. To try to deduce *a priori* from the rational concept of God just such a self-revelation as he made in Christ is a waste of time.[2] It cannot be done. We can only see after the event the agreeableness of the revelation to that rational knowledge. But the historical self-revealingness of God is, for our minds, a character simply additional to his metaphysical perfection, consonant but not implied. And as it cannot be measured by rational theology, still less can it by historical reality. The revelation employs an historical vehicle—granted—and must respect its historical character. But it employs that vehicle after its own manner, not after that of the historical reality. We could not discover from the vehicle *a priori* what revelation God can make it carry.

This is the sense of that famous theologoumenon—we cannot judge the word of God—not, that is, by a measure other than its own. We compare the spiritual with the spiritual, we do not measure it by preconceived standards whether of the 'carnal' or of the (theologically) rational. In another sense, of course, we do judge it: we ask ourselves whether we are in fact apprehending it, or indeed, apprehending anything. Yet in another sense 'we' cannot judge it even so: for it is not 'we', our neutral selves, that judge; neither is it our natural selves that apprehend, but the Holy Spirit in us. But this is a dogmatic and not an epistemological consideration: for the Holy Spirit then apprehends and judges not only in us, but through us. He is not an element in the situation distinguishable by analysis.

3 FAITH

For a perfect mind, the only condition necessary if something is to be known is that it should exist. By a purely intellective or spiritual act he sees what it is to be that thing in itself. Now in so far as we do come to know what it is to be any real existent thing, we likewise perform a spiritual act. But for us to know, other conditions are necessary than that the object should exist. For first, it must be signified to us by sense; second, it must be itself in type analogous to our own finite being, or we should have no clue to its nature—it must be 'connatural with us'. And two other conditions seem almost indispensable props to our knowledge, even if not so demonstrably essential: we expect to be able to comprehend that character in the object which we apprehend, and to give ourselves a clear account of it; and we expect to be able to confirm and fix our knowledge by strict analogy and comparison with a host of other like objects elsewhere known.

Now the singularity of faith as a way of apprehending is simply this—that because of the object's peculiar nature, all these favouring conditions are, if not absolutely denied us, at least reduced to a minimum. And so, in the act of faith, the mind approaches, in a sense, most near to the divine way of knowing, for it then comes nearer to knowing an object, not because of favouring conditions fulfilled, but because that object most truly exists.

Yet equally, and in another sense, the act of faith takes us farthest from the divine way of knowing. For the divine knowledge is, above all, adequate: but faith is a most inadequate apprehension. For knowing another man, I am tolerably equipped; for knowing God, most beggarly. Faith is a shivering, naked apprehension, stripped of the warm flesh and blood of its natural condition. We may compare the case of the soul. The soul may seem to depart from the divine likeness by being incarnate. By release from the body she approximates to that pure being which needs no bodily prop and feels no bodily confines. But then again, she precisely does herself need that prop. Divorced from it, she falls farthest from the divine likeness by becoming incomplete in her own kind, so that she can only find her 'perfect fruition and bliss' in a spiritual body which completes without obstructing her. So faith, the naked apprehension of the soul, hopes to be 'clothed upon' with a knowledge and sight as clear and firm as that of her own sensuous being, but not so discriminatory against the noblest objects.

If we do not describe faith negatively, by stripping apprehension to its spiritual core, we must give paradoxical definitions: we must say that the sheer reception of the object plays the parts usually played by the several favouring conditions. It does duty for 'sight', whether in the literal meaning of sense-experience, or that of conceptual clarity: and it is its own 'reason'—for it cannot seek confirmation without a manifold analogy. Again, as dispensing with these props, and leaning on the mere self-presentation of the object, it resembles 'trust', and gets confused with belief upon testimony, when we take a man's mere word for what he says. Of course, we do also trust divine testimony: yet this is secondary and presupposes the act by which we apprehend God speaking to us. But, in another sense, faith *involves* a sort of trust and especially when it is first exercised, for there is a kind of moral virtue resembling trustfulness* in the readiness to use a supernatural faculty and grope for a supernatural object. And besides all this, faith must find an *expression* in some degree of practical trust—in some preparedness to act upon the basis of it—for the understanding and the will cannot be absolutely divorced. Even St James's devils that 'believe and tremble' express their faith in their trembling and in their conscious efforts, however vain, to oppose and shun the divine will. But the *cognitive* faith is to be distinguished from them as merely analogies to trust, in as much as it throws itself upon the self-presented object alone.

Still the negative description is the best: faith is unsupported apprehension. The lack of support is not, of course, absolute. The object of faith is mediated through sense—'That which we have seen, that which we have heard' of Christ walking in Galilee; and it is presented through finite being, connatural with ours, and immediately declared by the sense signs—for Christ, in his manhood, is very man indeed, as we are. And even his deity we are

* Adventurousness, according to Dr Streeter and his friends. [A reference to the joint publication by B. H. Streeter, C. M. Chilcott and others; *Adventure: the faith of science and the science of faith*, 1927—Ed.]

able to think about through some kind of analogy with finite spirit. But—and this is crucial—we have seen that his manhood does not simply *qua* manhood express deity, nor do the creaturely analogies by which we think that deity to ourselves. These are mere instruments through which God declares that which is ineffable. It is the act of reading in the history, in the verbal signs, this ineffable reality, which constitutes the distinctive operation of faith.

Again, ratiocinative comparison is not completely absent from faith: for, though the 'higher order' cannot be subjected to rules or laws drawn from the lower, we may compare one element in the divine economy itself with another. St Paul was not prepared to allow the 'wisdom of this world' to set up carnal measures for the spiritual, but he was ready to compare 'spiritual things with spiritual'. And after the event of our apprehending the spiritual revealed order, we may grasp some vestigial analogy of it in a lower sphere.

4 FAITH AND REASON

The easiest way to settle the opposition of faith and reason is to choose a definition of reason which makes it unopposable to faith. This is known to the gods as *ignoratio elenchi* and to men as *rotting the question*. It is a method which, handled with dexterity, will obtain you a second class degree at Oxford, but it is not a key which will open to you the door of knowledge. It is possible to play the same trick with the definition of faith: for example, if we describe it as what natural scientists do when they confide in their hypotheses. The most amusing results would be obtained, if we were to play the trick on the definitions of faith and reason both at once; when the two terms might be discovered actually to have exchanged places. But no one seems to have thought of this.

We recommend beginning with reason, however, as more radically ambiguous and speciously simple. You can usually get away with any of the following.

(i) Reason is the process of arriving, with reflection, at that which it is reasonable, or worthy of a mind, to believe. Faith itself will evidently fall within this definition.

(ii) Reason is the opposite of sense: in proportion as a correct mental act is more intellectual and less sensual it is more 'of reason'. And so faith is rational above all other acts whatsoever.

(iii) Reason is the process which seeks a satisfying completeness in its total view of the world. But faith, since it alone truly puts the keystone to the arch of philosophy, is the highest reason man can exercise.[3]

But we, who are not just now interested in rotting the question, prefer to ask, in what sense of the word 'reason' is reason opposite to faith? And, in view of the description of faith just given, it is not difficult to find an answer sufficient for our present purposes. Reason is to be identified with the second pair of favouring conditions for human apprehension: (a) ability to comprehend that in the object which we apprehend, and to give ourselves a clear account of it; (b) ability to confirm and fix our knowledge by strict analogy and comparison with a host of other like objects elsewhere known.

A slightly enlarged definition arises if we consider that it is by these processes our natural faculties arrive at all serious knowledge in excess of a mere animal recognition of things: so that reason becomes synonymous with the knowledge-acquiring powers of the natural mind. It then follows that reason and faith exactly divide the field between them.

If faith and reason are thus defined by opposition, it is a waste of time to discuss at length how they are opposed. The real question is, what range of objects falls within the province of each. Now it has been traditional to defend one of the three following positions:

(a) The province of reason includes not only the natural and philosophical sciences: it includes theological science, i.e. rational theology, that part of metaphysics which assures us of God's existence, attributes, and creation of the world. The province of faith is that of special revelation alone.

(b) The province of reason is confined to natural and philosophical sciences. There is no 'rational theology'. All knowledge of God is the object of faith and the subject of revelation. So far as there is any substance in 'rational theology', it is a sorting out and a comparison of the revealed truths.

(c) Everywhere and in all things God is actively revealing himself and man's reason is active in attempting to describe and sort and compare the revealed truth, both in relation to itself and in relation to the whole of existence. So there are no distinct provinces of faith and reason, but just two factors in a single process.

(c) savours strongly of rotting the question, and we do not propose to discuss it. But assuming that the question is not to be rotted, the mind can hardly dwell upon (a) and (b) above without at once seeing the possibility of a mediating position and suspecting strongly that it is the true one. It runs as follows.

(a) and (b) appear to get into difficulty and mutual contradiction over the adjustment of a two-fold scheme (reason and faith) to a three-fold division—sciences of the finite, 'rational' theology, revealed truth. They seem to be assuming that reason and faith are opposed as black and white, with no possible gradation of shades between them. But the account which we have given of them suggests nothing of the kind. The suggestion was rather that in so far as reason falls away, faith takes its place. The two are polar opposites like hot and cold, and there is no difficulty in fitting them to a series of three, four, five or any number of terms. This 'rational theology', if there is such a science, may perfectly well be 'rational' compared with the theology of revelation, and 'of faith' when compared with the sciences of finite being.

This suggestion will at first sight alarm the orthodox. Are we then to abolish all distinction of principle between reason and faith, between revelation and natural knowledge? Are we to say that the one is merely the other with a certain factor reduced to the minimum, and another enhanced to the maximum?

Let us distinguish. On the subjective side we may conceive an absolutely continuous scale. There is no *a priori* impediment why faith and reason should not be mixed in just whatever proportions are demanded by the nature of any object presented to us. But are there, in fact, an indefinite number of levels of object, fading gradually into one another as we ascend? There are not. On the objective side there are jumps and breaks: there are just so many 'levels', perhaps more than the three we have considered, but still not an indefinite number; and they are marked off from one another by the principles of order we exhibited above. The independence of revelation is guaranteed, not by the absolute singularity of our subjective response to it, but by the objective nature of what is revealed, and its relation to other levels of our knowledge.

That 'rational theology' is 'of faith' when compared with sciences of the finite, 'of reason' when compared with revealed truth, is pretty evident. Let us take its relation to what is connatural with us. Our 'nature' was defined by restriction to a certain range of finite objects. In apprehending the infinite existence as the ground of finite existence, we exceed this range and vindicate the share our intellect has in the nature of absolute intellect. In such an act there is a self-transcending tendency; and the natural mind can in fact tread round the beaten path of finite nature without ever aspiring to this apprehension. But compared with the apprehension of revelation, it is more merely human. For it apprehends God only in so far as he is revealed as a factor in the existence of those objects which are 'connatural' with us. Whereas faith apprehends him revealing aspects of himself not implicit in the mere existence of our connatural objects.

Again, if we take the manner of its procedure: as compared with the finite sciences, it is far less able to define its object; and, since that object is unique, it cannot reason about it on the basis of exact analogy. Since its object is intellectual (non-sensual) it cannot be apprehended without the aid of mental discourse: we wrestle with words in the painful work of distinguishing its uniqueness from all else, and giving some sort of account of it. It is easy to mistake this dialectical discourse for reasoning as (for example) natural science knows it. But in fact it is a directly opposite symptom: the abundance of discourse is not an evidence of abundant cross-reference and exact analogy, but of a desperate lack of these things.

None the less, it is rational even in procedure when compared with the theology of revelation. God as the creative ground of finite existences is more near to being comprehensible and describable than Trinity, Incarnation, Redemption. And, with whatever painful clumsiness and bewilderment, rational theology does proceed by way of analysing what we apprehend always in the fact of existence, and so touches the scientific universal.* But revelation

* The existence, goodness, power, etc., of the divine often strike us in connection with the existence of particular finites—a saint, a sunset, an earthquake. Here, it is triumphantly claimed, the God of rational theology shows himself by particular revelation and so the distinction between the rational and the revealed must be abandoned. The conclusion does not follow. According to rational theology, the divine attributes are implicitly revealed in finite existence. Why should I not then, here and there, jump to the apprehension of them? Similarly, I might jump to the apprehension of a geometrical truth without reasoning and in connection with a single figure which very favourably exhibited it. But it would be the universal geometrical truth none the less; to confirm it I should

is apprehended by a bare acceptance of those things which God chooses to show concerning himself through certain events, signs and words of his own selection.

5 FAITH AS SUPERNATURAL

The stated conclusion, that reason and faith are polar opposites and may be present in various degrees, follows only upon a certain view of faith, namely when the character of the mental act is formally regarded in respect of the absence or presence of certain conditions favourable to knowledge. And this is the view of faith which it is proper to propose to philosophers desirous of understanding by what act we suppose theological objects to be apprehended. But there is another view of faith important to theologians, who may wish to define it as *supernatural* apprehension, and the question might then be raised, whether according to this definition faith will still admit of degree or retain its ambiguous sway over 'rational theology'.

The simplest way to introduce the supernaturality of faith is this. We defined faith negatively, by the fading out of the favouring conditions.* But since it is in virtue of the presence of these conditions that a cognitive 'nature' of the specifically human kind is able to apprehend, in proportion to the failure of the conditions our nature falls short as efficient cause of the apprehension. What then is the supplementary efficient cause? Presumably the divine will, enabling us with a special illumination, which, not springing from our 'nature', is supernatural to us. That faith is thus a divine gift is not a mere philosophical inference, but a revealed truth.

So much is easy enough to state, but the problem arises when we ask at what point the capacities of our nature are exhausted, and supernatural aid is either necessary or appropriate. We cannot say that *in proportion* as the favouring conditions fade out, the

---

need to reason on universal grounds, and geometry would not become any more a revealed science than before.

  * *Addendum:* In connection with the supernaturality of faith: the failure of the 'favouring conditions' is compensated by a divine action which cannot be thought except analogically. (As 'inferred virtue', as a quasi-conditioning of the object, etc.) And here again we may if we like exclude *particular* grace from rational-theological thinking: for the rational creature is 'supernatural' himself to himself.

supernatural must enter, for that would be to deny all elasticity whatever to the human mind. The mind can to some extent compensate the weakening of objective favouring conditions by subjective concentration and effort; and to deny this would be in fact to deny that the human mind exceeds that of the beasts. For the easiest apprehensions of all are those that are merely animal: we became human by transcending our animal basis and this always involves some slight spirituality, some straining of the tether which ties us to the animal basis of our being. Scholastics may have been confident to define those capacities which are proper to the human reasons as such. We have not this confidence: we can see not an inch beyond the definition *animal rationalis* ['rational animal'], or rather perhaps *ratio animalis* ['animal mind']. We see man as that instance of reason in general which is tethered to a certain animal basis and starting-point, and aspires from there upwards as far as it can. The nature of the basis, and the manner of the tethering, can be to some extent defined, and so can the nature of reason (intellect) in general. But the limits set to the operation of the human reason *qua* human—the length of the tether—do not seem to be definable with any exactness. We can, of course, see limiting barriers that we could not conceivably pass. But of the barriers we do pass, which ones are passed by our own strained aspiration, and which only by supernatural aid, cannot perhaps be settled either *a priori* or by particular experience. Still, in order that we may state some sort of conclusion, the following line of argument may afford probability.

(a) As to the line of investigation open to reason without supernatural aid—it seems fitting that this should include a metaphysical refinement upon the knowledge of what is connatural with us. Connatural with us are certain finite natures or agents sensibly manifested. We can understand events in so far as we refer them to the natural operation of these agents. But now (as above stated), it is a necessary truth about the natural operation and indeed the existence of these agents, that it is grounded in the existence and the activity of God. Thus to have some apprehension of God in so far only as he is expressed in the existence and natural activity of these finites, is part of the knowledge of these finites themselves, and so belongs to us by nature. Whereas to apprehend an order of activity and purpose in the world not proceeding from, nor implied in, the natural operation of these finites, but super-added to them by God's overruling—on his assumption of the finite into himself—does not similarly belong to our nature.

(b) As to the solidity of the conclusion open to natural reason—it seems fitting that in proportion as reason stretches her animal tether and by her own force aspires after the apprehension of the more remote, the content apprehended should become thinner, more abstract, less exactly defined. And so it is in the whole metaphysical movement of the mind, culminating in 'rational theology'. The system of natural reason is a pyramid diminishing upwards and vanishing in a point: the broad base representing the sense-manifested finite order, the apex the groundedness of this order in the supreme being. Rational theology conforms to this pyramidal diminution; revealed theology does not, but gives us detailed and vivid knowledge of God.

On these grounds, then, we may conclude to the placing of rational theology in the natural, revealed theology in the supernatural, division.

In conclusion, we may restate the three schemes which we have described, and from whose mutual confusion all error in this field arises.

(*a*) There are several levels of objects—sense-phenomena, finite substance, the infinite being as such, revealed facts concerning him; and these levels are ordered by fixed relations of priority and posteriority in our knowledge of them.

(*b*) The act of intellect varies in character as it ascends up this scale, becoming gradually stripped of the confirmatory processes dependent upon the presence of 'favouring conditions'.

(*c*) The mind is capable of ascending this scale some distance by her own forces, and presumably as far as 'rational theology'—requiring thereafter the assistance of supernatural grace. But this distinction does not imply that *in fact* the mind unaided by grace will be able to arrive at an adequate rational theology, for the pure case of a natural mind may not exist. The mind that is unaided is also unredeemed and so its natural forces are to some extent weakened or depraved.

Theology and Analogy 1
The Concept of Analogy†

Analogy is the name both of a philosophical problem about the meaning of theological statements and of a particular solution offered to that problem.

1 THE PROBLEM OF ANALOGY

It is obvious that much religious language is metaphorical, figurative or parabolical. It bases itself upon some sort of analogy between divine things and creaturely things, using the latter to set forth the former, as St Paul uses the relation of members to head in an animal body to express the relation of Christians to Christ. When we use simile and metaphor outside theology, e.g. when, using music to illustrate painting, we talk of colour-*tones*, the analogy is an aid, but one with which we can dispense. We can talk about colours in non-analogical terms—about *shades*, not *tones*. To interpret an analogical statement is to substitute proper terms for analogical terms. But the special problem of theological analogy lies in the fact that theological truth cannot be stated in terms which are wholly 'proper', and from which all analogical character has been eliminated.

Admittedly some theological terms appear to be more proper than others: it is more proper to speak of God as the eternal Spirit who wills the continuation of our existence, than as the Rock of Ages on which we are founded; and, if called upon to interpret the second description, we should substitute the former for it. But the former description is not free from analogicality. God really is eternal Spirit, and really wills; but the positive meaning we assign to the words 'eternal', 'spirit', and 'will' is borrowed from finite experiences of our own. Our type of the eternal is (say)

† Reprinted from the *Twentieth Century Encyclopedia of Religious Knowledge*, 1955, under 'Analogy'.

a law of nature exemplified in all physical events throughout time; our type of spirit is our own rational consciousness; our type of will is our own act of will. When we apply such ideas to God, we throw in additions like 'supreme', 'absolute', or 'perfect'. Such additions express the belief that there is in God an eternity, spirituality, voluntariness we should find at that supreme height, if we could go so far. But we are left to judge the superlatives we cannot conceive, from the positives that we can. Unless finite, eternity, spirituality, and will bear some real analogy to aspects of God's being, what we say about him in such terms must be meaningless.

The problem of analogy is not avoided by claiming for the human spirit a direct contact with God. We are condemned to analogize in speaking of God not because God is inferred by us from other things but because, whether inferred or encountered, he transcends us. We cannot enter into God's way of being and acting: his touch upon us is wholly ineffable unless it moves us to stammer about it in creaturely terms. Nor can the problem be evaded by a pretended renunciation of the claim to objective truth. We cannot say, 'It is unnecessary to claim that what we say of God is true of God. It suffices that it is true of our *idea* of God, so long as that idea guides us into a suitable attitude towards God.' By attributing loving-kindness to God we are certainly determining the nature of our attitude to him as one of responsive love; but we cannot give responsive love to a being we do not actually believe to have loved us first.

The problem was formalized by St Thomas Aquinas thus. If we are to apply creaturely terms significantly to the Creator without degrading him to creaturely status, there must be terms applicable to creature and Creator neither *univocally* (in an identical sense) nor merely *equivocally* (in unrelated senses) but in some third way, namely *analogically* (in senses not identical, but somehow related). *How* related, then? St Thomas offers a solution.

2 THE DOCTRINE OF ANALOGY

St Thomas finds his key in the metaphysics of being. He claims to have demonstrated philosophically that being belongs to things in various degrees of fulness or of intensity, and that in God alone

F

sheer or unqualified being is to be found. Such a way of thinking was greatly assisted by the physical theories of medieval science. He could quote the theory of heat. Things are hot in various degrees, through the direct or indirect influence of flame. But flame is hot of itself: it is elemental heat. In like manner God is elemental being, while other things *are* in various degrees, and in dependence on his influence. We do not know how hot flame is, for our sensory organs are destroyed by so great a heat and cannot register it. Similarly our intellectual faculty is incapable of appreciating how full, or intense, the being of God is. Nevertheless the mere notion of sheer or elemental being is intelligible: to say that while creatures possess being partially and derivatively, God is being elementally and absolutely, is to express an intelligible relation between created and uncreated being; a relation which, in scholastic language can be called a simple proportion. And so between created and uncreated being there is an *analogy of proportion*.

According to St Thomas's Aristotelianism, sentences which, when put into their most appropriate form, have the verb 'to be' as their verb, express in some way the being of their subjects. To say that God is wise is to place wisdom in the being of God. Now the sense in which a predicate is to be understood is always relative to the sort of being its subject has. I may say that a man is wise and that a project is wise. 'To be wise' is a different thing for a man and for a project, because 'to be' is a different thing for a man and for a project. A man has the being of a finite self-subsistent individual; a project has the being of a form taken by an interior act of a man's mind. To understand that difference is to understand the difference between 'being wise' in the one case and in the other. If, then, it is right both to say that a man is wise and that God is wise, the difference between 'being wise' for God and for man will be determined by the difference between what it is for God to be, and what it is for a man to be. We can therefore say, 'As human wisdom is to man's being, so divine wisdom is to God's being', and this is called *analogy of proportionality*. When we are talking about God's wisdom we are talking about something which we do not directly or properly know, and of which we are forced to judge from our knowledge of our own. So to say that God is wise is to say that something stands to God's being as our wisdom stands to our being. It would mean nothing to say this, unless we had some understanding (however formal) of the relation or 'proportion' between our being and God's. But, according to St Thomas, we have such an understanding. We have understanding of God's being by analogy of proportion with our own, and therefore we can have understanding of his attributes and acts by analogy of proportionality.

This lucid, coherent, and relatively simple doctrine of analogy appears to be part and parcel of St Thomas's metaphysics. It is the effort of modern Thomists to extract from St Thomas a formula which shall be independent of the purely medieval elements in his system, and tenable in conjunction with a more advanced physics and logic. The success of such efforts is very variously estimated. But the doctrine of analogy can be saved only as part of a more comprehensive pattern of metaphysical doctrine.

St Thomas's doctrine was reformed and elaborated by Duns Scotus, and turned against itself by William of Occam. Occam's criticism is of more than historical interest. Accepting the doctrine that all theological conceptions are analogical, he called attention to the impossibility of reasoning validly from analogical premises. If we can at best know that there is in God's being something analogous to the excellences of our own, but differing from them by an infinite and indeterminable difference, can we ever say, 'God is wise, and therefore . . .'? For the 'therefore' must repose upon the confidence that God's wisdom is like our own in a certain respect; and how can we ever know that the difference between God's being and ours does not make his wisdom unlike ours precisely in that respect? Occam showed that rational or metaphysical theology employs analogical arguments throughout and is therefore inconclusive, and so he removed it to make way for a theology wholly dependent on divine revelation. But the Occamist cannot escape the analogical net so easily. For if all reasoning from analogical premises is utterly worthless, revealed theology itself is useless. Its statements are themselves analogical in form, and theological statements from which no inferences, practical or otherwise, can be drawn are sterile and virtually meaningless. Theological thinking, not theological statement only, must be possible; and it is possible, for we engage in it. If it is not governed by the strict rules of syllogistic form, it must be governed by other rules, or by some sort of intellectual tact; and this will be a proper subject for philosophical enquiry. Moreover, it will have to be considered whether the sort of intellectual tact which makes thinking about revealed theology possible does not in like manner make thinking about natural or metaphysical theology possible.

Thomism underwent a revival in the Counter Reformation period, and the doctrine of analogy was systematized and defended by commentators, especially by Cajetan. But the rising tide of scientific rationalism in the seventeenth century confined the scholastic philosophy to the seminaries. The temper of Descartes and his successors was particularly unfavourable to the doctrine of analogy, as being a doctrine of half-knowledge. They aimed at building on clear knowledge only and neglected the twilight regions as unprofitable. Bishop Berkeley summarized Cajetan on analogy for the benefit of an objector: but not without an ironic apology for being so unfashionable. Kant shook the hard and bare dogmatism of eighteenth-century deism and held a highly sophisticated view about our twilight knowledge of real being and especially of God; but he turned away from the mysteries and lacked that desire to contemplate divine being which is the motive for a serious consideration of analogy.

The latter part of the nineteenth century and the beginning of our own saw the spread of agnosticism about the nature of God. The contemporaneous revival of Thomism had appeared to its disciples to furnish the instrument required for dealing with the trouble of the times: analogy removes the confusions of agnosticism. But their attempts to modernize analogy have met with little acceptance outside Roman Catholicism and the circles most sympathetic to it. The doctrine has been opposed not only as logically and metaphysically obsolete but also as anti-Christian. Karl Barth and his school have denounced *analogy of being* for attributing too much to corrupted human reason; laying down a rational theology *a priori*; controlling the interpretation of revealed truth by it; and not allowing the self-revealing God to be his own interpreter. What is rejected by such a polemic is the Thomistic doctrine of analogy. But the problem of theological analogy remains,[1] and the critique exercised by modern linguistic philosophy upon the very meaningfulness of theological statements forces it upon our attention. The inescapableness of the problem appears to a believer to be the shadow cast by the transcendent mysteriousness of God.[2]

Theology and Analogy 2
Knowledge by Analogy†

St Thomas introduces the doctrine of knowledge by analogy in connection with statements about the divine being, because God appears mysterious to us and our knowledge of Him in some manner indirect. When we look around us now, the field of mystery seems so much expanded, we seem to have indirect knowledge of so many things beside the supreme Being, that it becomes a natural experiment to extend the analogical method.

The plight of modern philosophy surely clamours for it. If we cast our eye back over the last three centuries, we see one realm after another lose its straightforwardness and cover itself with mystery, so that the philosophers are no longer assured in giving a positive account of it. Modern philosophy began with two convictions: anyhow there were two things of which we had clear, distinct, and proper knowledge: our own, active conscious being within, and extended physical substance without. It was clear that man knew these two realities, not of course in all their particular detail—there he might be baffled—but in their general nature. He knew what soul was, and what body was; and to these two pieces of knowledge he could add a third—he knew the process by which he apprehended them, the knowing act. That was the starting-point. But what has the journey been like? Since Berkeley, only the rash have been confident of knowing what physical body is: since Hume and Kant, the enduring soul or self has been hunted for among the various data of consciousness, a hypothetical needle in an apparent bundle of hay. And as for the knowing act, what has become of that? It is handled with confidence only in so far as it is not the act of real knowledge: its structure is analysed, but its real veridicality is sometimes not allowed to be a question at all, and

† A lecture delivered to the Aquinas Society, London; reprinted from *The Downside Review*, 1947, under the title 'The Extension of St Thomas's Doctrine of Knowledge by Analogy to Modern Philosophical Problems'.

sometimes defined in a negative manner which is at variance with the beliefs by which men must live.

The course of modern philosophy is like the story-book Russian journey, where one after another of the sledge-team is thrown to the following wolves: knowledge of body, knowledge of soul, knowledge of knowledge glut in turn the jaws of darkness. But who is the Prince? Which is the sacred person whom we are anxious to convey safe at any sacrifice to journey's end? He is the ideal of clarity and distinctness, the principle exclusive of all mystery, of everything that is baffling and opaque.

Now it cannot be denied that such a prince has the marks of royalty about him, fit to command the allegiance of a true philosopher. If he had no rival, we should have no choice but to follow him. But he has a rival, and we have to choose. In the end we have got to make up our minds about the ideal and standard of philosophic knowledge. Either the ideal is subjective—the maintenance of the highest clarity in our own thinking: or it is objective, the fullest apprehension of what really exists, whether we can get our thinking about it perfectly clear or not. Naturally the two ideals are not completely antithetical. If our ideal is the apprehension of real being, it will do us no harm to think clearly—indeed we must think as clearly as the subject-matter allows. But in the last resort we cannot worship two gods. Either objective apprehension or subjective clarity must take precedence. If it is to be subjective clarity, then we shall make of it a sort of sieve or filter, and only what will come through it will exist for us: we shall have erected an effective barrier against the apprehension of anything, however important, which cannot be handled by our standard technique; we shall be too intellectually fastidious to know God or the soul. If, on the other hand, our first loyalty is to real apprehension, we shall bend and twist our mental techniques in whatever way is required for fitting them to the nature of things: of which the supreme example is, of course, the knowledge of God, the view of whom strains to the utmost and almost breaks the best faculties of the human kind.

One of the reasons why the Christian thinker may find himself discontented and baffled in the world of modern philosophy is that his appetite is for real being, and not for subjective integrity: and his discontent may find solace with the medieval philosophers, who did at least prefer the grasp of *what is* to the most spotless intellectual respectability. But it is idle to pretend that we can reassert today the straightforwardness of medieval epistemology. So many centuries of philosophic criticism and scientific development cannot be written off. The modern passion for intellectual clarity really has shown that other realities beside the divine are incurably mysterious: and we have got to wrestle with the mystery, and not deny it. If we want to borrow from the medievals, let us borrow what can help us. They did develop an instrument for wrestling with mystery, where they saw mystery, namely the analogical method. It is for us to apply it in fresh fields.

The traditional Thomist would have drawn a hard and sharp distinction between our knowledge of sensible finite substances and our knowledge of God. The finite substance, he would say, offers itself to us through its sensible accidents: and it is the very business of our intellect to grasp the thing of which these sensible accidents are the accidents. In many cases, no doubt, we are unable to obtain an intellectual grasp of the specific essence, but we have a genuine concept of the generic: I may not see from watching a cat just wherein cathood consists, but I have a proper knowledge of the cat as an animal. I may not penetrate the special nature of gold, but I know it properly as physical body with certain distinguishing marks. Such recognitions of the real in the sensible world are the *typical* achievements of the human intellect, its first and natural employment. It is otherwise with the knowledge of God. The divine being does actually (like the finite sensible being) come to bear on my conscious existence, and that indeed at every point, since the presence of the finite is always the effect of infinite creative power. But here the similarity ends. The lineaments of the divine essence do not present themselves in and with the immediate objects of sense-knowledge, as the forms of creaturely essence do. The creatures are not perceptible aspects of the divine being in which his nature is known, they are signs quite other than himself whereby he is indirectly signified. Therefore my knowledge of God is analogical, whereas my knowledge of finite substances is not. I apprehend finite substances for what they are, but to God's being I can only analogize from the creaturely signs. I perceive that the act of existing, always limited in the creature, must be unlimited in the supreme original; but as to what manner of act this unlimited act must be, I cannot tell, except by analogizing from

creaturely effect to creative cause. I can think about God only by
the aid of diagrams, in which the least inadequate aspects of
creaturely being are paradoxically combined to yield some representation of the Creator.

Now I am about to suggest that for a modern the balance of
this contrast has considerably altered, and that what we take to be
our apprehension of finite substances approximates far more
towards the traditional account of our apprehension of God than
strict traditionalism would have said. I hope I do not need to fore-
stall the accusation that I eliminate the impassable gulf which must
always yawn between knowledge of the Creator and knowledge of
the creature. The gulf remains. By subjecting the finite to analogical
method we do not de-finitize it. Not all objects in the knowledge of
which there is an element of indirectness are equally indirectly
known or equally transcendent to our apprehensions. The finite
substance does not transcend my knowledge *as* the infinite substance transcends it, and yet it may transcend my knowledge all the
same.

The modern mind (let me now venture to say) does find much
of what we said about the knowledge of God applicable to our
knowledge of finite being. We are most of us in much doubt about
the nature of the physical world, and how far the theories of
physicists can be taken as descriptive of what it really is: but in any
case there are few of us who think that the lineaments of physical
reality are directly signified to us by the sensible accidents. We
say of the physical, something far more like what the medieval
would say of the divine being, that it is indirectly signified to us by
the sensible signs, that we cannot give ourselves a clear and proper
account of it, but are reduced to using diagrams, in which certain
elements selected from the sensible signs are combined to yield
some sort of indirect representation—presumably an analogical
representation.

I should like to explain myself here by way of reference to a
contemporary writer who—to her great praise be it said—does
grapple with real being, without in any way masking the difficulties of the attempt. Miss Dorothy Emmet, if I do not misrepresent
her, gives the following account of our knowledge of physical
being.* The external reality acts on us, not first on our intellect or

* *The Nature of Metaphysical Thinking*, Macmillan, 1945—Ed.

sense, but on the process of our existence: we are affected by it not first in the order of knowing, but in the order of being and cause. This is the fundamental fact for all our knowledge to build upon. This real interaction of the other being with our own gives signs of itself at the conscious level in the phenomena of sense. The scientific intellect interprets the sense-phenomena as revealing not primarily the external real things, but the interaction-events between those things and our own sensitive bodies; from which it proceeds to an interpretation of further interaction-events, not between external things and our sense-organs, but between external things and other external things.

But (Miss Emmet proceeds) how can we talk about interaction-events between real things, *signified* to us by sense-signs, but not actually revealed *in* those signs? For the raw-material of our physical knowledge must surely be the data of sense and whatever is directly revealed in those data, if anything is, and if we have to try to talk about some other mysterious events of interaction, lying behind the data, but not actually revealed in and with the data, how are we to do it? We do it, she replies, by the use of analogies drawn from the sense-data. Physicists admit that they make use of mental 'dummies'; e.g. they think of the structure of the atom as a planetary system. They allow themselves to contemplate visible coloured balls rotating at a speed slow enough to be watched round a central ball or group of balls, and this they find it convenient to do, though they do not seriously believe that electrons are coloured, visible or spherical, or indeed inclosed within a simple contour of any kind. Yet by these sensible dummies they think usefully about their non-sensible realities. How can this be? If this is not knowledge by analogy, what is?

Miss Emmet reports that the physicists, taxed with this, are mostly inclined to deny that they take the dummies seriously: they would like to call them mere imaginative aids, mere mental clothes-horses on which to hang the algebraic formulae which are the real stuff of their art. It is only the algebra that signifies. But Miss Emmet will not let them get away with this. She agrees, of course, that if the physicists say the mathematical business is their stock-in-trade, no outsider is in a position to contradict them. But she claims the right, as a philosopher, to ask what the algebraical formulae *are about*. Physics may be mathematical, but it is not just mathematics: it is mathematics applied: but applied to what? To the physical world, no doubt, but what is the physical world, unless it is that which we represent analogically to ourselves by these ridiculous dummies? We may not take the dummies very seriously, but they do at least signify to us something existing in itself, spatially located, and interacting, and so distributed as to allow of the mathematical formulae being applied to it in some sort of way. It is no use saying (for example) that the mathematical formulae apply to the appearances of sense, for plainly they do not. It is all right, then, for the physicists to say that it is only in the mathematical aspect of physical interaction that they are interested, but it is vain for them to deny that they have any notion of physical interaction at all: and so the philosophers are entitled to tie the dummies round the physicists' necks and make them wear the badge.

Miss Emmet proceeds, now, to give an opinion of her own. The dummies do not (she suggests) positively signify at all the nature of the forces interrelated in physical interaction: it is simply the relations between the dummies which are analogies of the real relations. Now here a point of crucial importance arises; and I feel moved to accuse Miss Emmet of the logical fault which she finds in her mathematical physicists. It is no use, she says, their saying that their art is all mathematics, for what are the mathematics *about*? So now we will say to her: it is no use her saying that the analogical representation is of relations only: for what do the relations relate? We cannot have a complex of relations which might be relations between any terms whatsoever: some general description of the related things is implied in the mere statement of the relations. If we say 'A is to the north of B', we have not said what A is—it may be a cyclone, an elephant or a haystack; but it cannot be a moral virtue or a logical implication. Thus if we give a significant analogical description of physical interactions, we must be at least implying some general description of physical forces—presumably itself also an analogical description.

This point is pretty familiar to us from the discussion of theological analogy. Kant appears to have said that theological analogies are about the relation we bear to God and not about God. Thus, if we call him Father we mean that we are related to him as sons. Well, father is, in any case, a relative description. One is a father because one has children. But not any sort of being can significantly be made the father-term in a father-child relation of which man is the child-term; not even if the relation is analogically interpreted. Suppose we knew about God no proposition except of the following type: 'God is an X to which we are related as children to father, in whatever sense the nature of this X admits the father-relationship with us: but we do not know in the least what the nature of this X is.' If that were all we knew, we should not know anything very valuable, and it is pretty obvious that those who acknowledge God their Father begin with the conviction that he is a living spirit, after the pattern of whose similitude we have been created. But this is to proceed from analogical knowledge about our relation with God to analogical knowledge about what God is like. We may, of course, make to Kant the same *practical* concession as Miss Emmet made to the physicists. They can, if they like, concentrate their attention on the mathematical relations only, to the neglect of physical being; and in like manner, if there is a school of theologians who wish to concentrate their interest entirely on what God does for them, to the exclusion of all interest in God Himself, we may dislike their religion, but we cannot object to their logic. It is only if they go on to say that their consideration of man's relation to God presupposes no conception of what God is; or that the truth of their conception of the relation is completely independent of the truth of their conception of God—it is only if they say these things that we shall add absurdity to impiety on the list of their crimes.

To return to the physical realm, and to Miss Emmet. Let us recall that, according to her, the beginning of physical knowledge is not the interaction of the external with the external, but the interaction of the external with us. It is on this interaction, the interaction in which we are implicated, that we found our primary analogical interpretations. We afterwards extend them to the purely external realm: though even there they continue to bear the mark of their personal origin. All this only goes to strengthen the parallel between theological analogy and physical analogy. In both cases reality beyond ourselves (God, the physical substance) comes to bear upon us; in both cases we respond by analogizing: analogizing, according to Miss Emmet, upon the relation of the reality to ourselves, and not upon its nature.

Now we have complained that this will not do: that we cannot analogize upon a relation without by implication determining the nature of the terms related. Of course we might give an analogical account of the relation, while having a proper, direct, non-analogical conception of the related terms; that would be even better, but it seems plain that Miss Emmet does not suppose we are in such happy case. If we had any conception of the external reality itself, it would be an analogical conception, she thinks. So when we complain to her that she gives us an analogical account of a relation with one of its ends unhappily hanging in air, she will have to take it that we are challenging her to give an *analogical* account of the missing term, not a straight account of it. And at this point (I think) she replies: 'I can make no sense of such an account: you may tell me that I have got to give it, but I can only say that I cannot, and that I do not see it to play any actual part in our thought about the physical world, or about God.' If this is her position, then presumably she will adopt a formulation which avoids the difficulty of a relation relating one knows not what: and it seems probable that she will turn to the conception of continuity of process in which the distinction between terms and relations, apparently asserted in the analogue, disappears in the analogate.

But it is not our business to chart out imaginary journeys for Miss Emmet. Since we are going a different way ourselves, and propose to maintain analogical knowledge both of God and of physical being, it will profit us more to consider her difficulties about such alleged analogical knowledge. They are real enough, and are centred round the Thomist doctrine of 'proportionality'. She says, and rightly, that the notion of knowledge by proportionality alone is nonsense. If we know of God, for example, that existence applies to him, not in the sense in which it applies to us, but in some sense which we are powerless to fix *in any way whatsoever*, then we know just exactly nothing about him: and if we use this nothing as a scale by which to determine other analogies, telling ourselves that God's wisdom is proportional to his existence as our wisdom is to ours, we do not increase our sum of knowledge. If there is some clothes-horse of non-analogical knowledge, however sketchy, then we may hope to drape it with any number of handsome analogies, but if there is none, the draperies will simply not stand up, the analogies will tell us nothing.

This comment must be allowed to hold good. Pure analogical knowledge, in the sense of the analogy of proportionality, is pure nonsense, and St Thomas did not maintain anything of the sort, nor does Miss Emmet think that he did. He meant, and we mean, that the reflective mind, in connection with its apprehension of the finite being, has a confused conception of infinitude of being as that essence whereof the finite is a reduced and limited copy: and as that existence whereof every contingent existence is the effect. It is here that Miss Emmet cannot follow St Thomas. He saw that this apprehension was very obscure, and could only be rendered intelligible by means of analogical comment; indeed the analogical comment springs up along with the apprehension from the very start. Yet unless the apprehension were there, there would be nothing for the analogical comment to clarify.

I propose now to make a dogmatic exposition of theological and physical analogy by means of a distinction between three terms. I will speak of a supernatural object, a connatural object, and a perspicuous object.

The supernatural object is God, who utterly transcends our nature and our faculties. The connatural object is finite physical being which transcends in some degree our faculties, but does not transcend our nature, for we share the same nature. The perspicuous object is the sensible sign, which transcends neither our nature nor our faculties: and that is why I call it perspicuous, because our faculties perceive all that there is in it. A sense-datum, a patch of colour *qua* seen, a tone of sound in so far as heard, and so forth, is perspicuous by definition: it is only when we raise the question what physical being it is the sign of that we arrive at the non-perspicuous.

Now what is it that drives us to the employment of analogy? Is it the object which transcends our nature, or the object which transcends our faculties? Surely it is the object which transcends our faculties—every non-perspicuous object—not the supernatural object only. The supernatural object is certainly non-perspicuous, and supremely so: but the connatural object is also non-perspicuous, and it is surely evident that the non-perspicuous needs to be analogized from the perspicuous. For example, I believe myself to have an indubitable awareness of my own acts of voluntary decision; this is a connatural object, for it belongs to my own nature, but it is not a perspicuous object, for if it were, there would not have been endless discussion of its nature from the beginning of philosophical history, until the present day, nor would it be possible for the philosophic fool to say in his heart, There is no will. It is not a perspicuous object; and in thinking about its nature I find myself quite unable to proceed without using analogies of it drawn from the realm of perspicuous objects, i.e. the objects of sense. I may say, for example, that a voluntary decision is a choice between alternatives; and this statement carries with it the shadowy fable of a hand taking an apple and leaving a pear, or whatever the analogy may be. And yet the mental decision precisely is not the perceptible event: we know before we start thinking about mental decision that hands take apples to the neglect of pears; we are not discussing that, we are discussing the inward event which we believe sometimes to be the cause of such outward events. And yet we use the outward event analogically to help us with thinking the inward event: and I do not believe that we can do without this analogy, or some other.

Let it be agreed, then, that we have a confused awareness of the connatural object, and a still more confused awareness of the supernatural object reached by suitable reflection upon the connatural object: and that we analogize about the connatural object from the perspicuous object, and about the supernatural object from the connatural object: and that, however odd it may seem, we do by means of such analogizing make thought possible for us about our non-perspicuous objects.

We found ourselves saying above that the human mind may, in fact, concentrate its attention on the relation between our objects and ourselves, and not on the nature of those objects. For example, there might be some theologians who want to think of the relation of the soul to God, and not about God. We were inclined to feel that in theology such an exclusive direction of attention would be arbitrary and perverse, but that it might well be otherwise with physics. It may be that a concentration on measurable interactions is the proper business of physics; and that an attempt to grapple with what physical being or force is in itself would always yield meagre and uninstructive results. Here is a distinction ready to hand dividing several fields of knowledge: fields in which it is natural or profitable to direct our analogizing upon the being of real objects, and fields in which it is not, but where we are content to study the patterns of interaction. Science of most kinds appears to belong to the second class; historical and personal knowledge to the first: for it would be odd if I had to admit that I take no interest in what my friend's existence is in itself, but only in how his existence affects his environment: and it would be equally odd if I had to make the same confession about my interest in the mind of Virgil or whomever else I delight to read.

This distinction between fields of knowledge may help us to tidy up something that we have all heard of. Wilhelm Dilthey distinguished rigidly between humane studies, *Geisteswissenschaften*, in which we interpret other people's minds, and natural sciences, in which we construct hypothetical patterns of natural law. He made out his case: and anyone who, having read him (or more probably Professor H. A. Hodges's admirable exposition of him)* goes away and continues to treat *either* the method of natural science *or* the method of personal understanding as typical for all knowledge, must be impervious to argument. But the sturdy realist is left with a dissatisfied feeling. There cannot, surely, be two sorts of knowledge quite distinct: knowledge is just getting hold of the way things are. And there can hardly be two quite distinct realms of finite being open to our inspection, as though we were studying (a) physical bodies and (b) angels. For we start from sense-signs in either case, and the world which signifies itself to us through sense-signs must surely all be the same world, whether the signs speak of things or persons.

In this perplexity we may perhaps derive some comfort from the system of ideas which was propounded above. Whether we are approaching personal being by the method of the humane studies, or laws of nature by the method of the natural sciences, we are in any case approaching the connatural object by the aid of the perspicuous object. But we are turning our attention, and applying our analogical interpretation, in different directions. In the case of personal understanding we attend to what the connatural object's existence is like, in the case of natural science we attend to the action of the connatural object upon us or on another connatural object, in so far as that action is measurable. But this limitation of

---

* *The Philosophy of Wilhelm Dilthey* (1952); Dilthey is usually associated with the philosophy of *Weltanschauung*—Ed.

attention involves no limitation of belief: we do not disbelieve that
the *physical* being or force is something in itself or deny that we
have some idea of it, however shadowy; still less do we disbelieve
that the *personal* being acts on his environment by actions regular
and measurable. There would, indeed, be no possibility of confusion here but for the fact that we analogize. If we had a simple
clear and wholly direct awareness of the objects of physical and
personal study respectively, we should see that what we call the
physical realm is a tissue of relations between real forces always
taken for granted but never brought into the central focus of
attention: whereas what we call the personal realm is the revealed
existence of actual beings. This would all be clear if our view of
these two realms were direct. But since we do in fact view them
both not without analogical constructions, we are liable to be
puzzled. The physical construction seems to represent a realm of
being, a type of object, and so does the personal construction: and
so we find ourselves wondering which construction gives us the
true realm of being, or if both are true, how they are to be accommodated together in one universe.

We have been suggesting one possible fruit of the extension of
analogical method to the study of finite being. But analogical
method will not simply assist the solution of this and that philosophical puzzle: it must save philosophy itself. The modern
philosophers, having nailed the colours of clear-and-distinct thinking to the mast, have been obliged by their principle to throw
more and more of the cargo out of the ship. Now there is no going
back upon the work of the critical philosophers, and if we are to
re-apply philosophical method to the world of real being and
recover the science of metaphysics, we have got to give a credible
account of how the mind proceeds in approaching real being—the
supernatural object ultimately, but primarily the connatural
object. It is no use telling men who have devoted themselves to the
ideal of the clear-and-distinct that our thought about the connatural object is clear-and-distinct, because it is not, and they have
discovered that it is not. But if it can be agreed that this thinking
is analogical, then the champions of the clear-and-distinct can
apply their special talents to the analysis of analogical form, and
make that analysis clear-and-distinct. For though analogy may not
give us clear-and-distinct knowledge of that about which we

analogize, there is nothing to prevent our having a clear-and-distinct account of what analogizing itself is, and of its several varieties or modes. And by such an enquiry we shall justify analogical thinking, including that metaphysical thinking which is analogical, and we shall gain a clearer understanding of the nature of our knowledge of the real.

Metaphysics and Analogy†

I suppose that a man who is in any case a theologian, and who descends into the present philosophical bull-ring with the red rag of metaphysics in his hands, may be fairly suspected of spoiling for a fight. But such is not my state of mind at all. I simply desire to propose a subject for enquiry, and to enlist any help I can get in the pursuit of it. My presumption is that all decent philosophers have two causes equally at heart: to banish confused statement or inconclusive argument; and to give every significant form of discourse its due rights—no more than its due rights, but its due rights nevertheless. As to metaphysics, we are all probably agreed that there is scarcely a page of the traditional metaphysical writing but teems with bogus propositions and demonstrations demonstrating nothing. And it is certainly very important, and well worthy of a philosophic spirit, to point out this painful fact. But it is equally philosophical to ask, what remains when we have refuted the logical fallacies and corrected the confused statements. On any showing, of course, something remains. Descartes and Leibniz may have talked a deal of nonsense, but they were not such nonsensical fellows as to talk nonsense *about* nonsense; they talked their nonsense about some sense or other: but what was this *sense*? Was it something which can be adequately expressed in non-metaphysical discourse, or is there a sort of sediment of metaphysical discourse remaining, which we cannot analyse away into non-metaphysical discourse without losing some of the real content expressed in it?

I hope you will not here object that I am waving a red rag after all, for I am asserting the rights of metaphysical discourse, whereas metaphysical statements have been branded as universally nonsensical by those at whose shrines our incense burns. But if you make this objection, you will be wrangling with me over words. If

† Farrer's collection on Leibniz—see par. 3—was published 1951, and dates this accordingly.

'the metaphysical' has been defined as a certain class of nonsense, then it is not the metaphysical in that sense that I wish to consider. I have already said that we shall be concerned in any case with separating in the body of traditional metaphysics between the dross and the metal. And if those whom we revere have given the name 'metaphysical' to the dross, then I do not quarrel with them: it is not the dross that I wish to take seriously, but the gold (supposing there is any); and if you wish me to call the gold by some other name, e.g. *physametical*, I have really no objection, except that I prefer my words the right way round.

Through a train of circumstances over which I had not complete control, I found myself spending last vacation in the study of Leibniz. In the course of my study, there came to me one of those intuitive flashes which endow platitude with all the dazzle of discovery. What occurred to me was this: the later seventeenth (and early eighteenth) century philosophers were reacting all in their several ways to the nasty split which was opening between the common-sense description of the world of things and the description given by physical science, or, as they called it, natural philosophy. The cause of the split lay, of course, in the development of physical science itself. Their several reactions to the split should surely retain an interest for us, since the split is still with us. The split has, indeed, widened—for our imaginations to see visible chairs and tables as identical with the extraordinary systems the atomic physicists seem to put in their place, is even harder than for Newtonians to reconcile the sense-phenomena with collections of impenetrable *corpuscula*. Yet in another way the split has become paved over for us, and is not so clean. For to them it appeared that there was only one science of nature, mathematical physics, whereas we aren't quite so sure. Perhaps biology has its own rights, and introduces fresh principles;[1] perhaps there is a whole scale of sciences presenting different apparent descriptions at different levels, some nearer to common sense and perceptual consciousness, others more remote from it.

However that may be, the split was a simple bifurcation to the seventeenth century, a bifurcation between science and sense: and the cleanness of the issue gave a certain dramatic charm to the philosophical theories which attempted to cope with it. If you accepted the bifurcation, you might seem to have three choices open to you; and all of them found adherents. (1) You could say that the scientific description was in principle correct or even adequate, and that the description based on ordinary perception had no rights of its own: it was only valid in so far as it coincided with, or approximated to, the scientific description; and this was the position of Descartes. (2) You could take the opposite position, as Berkeley did, and say that the appearances to sense, just as they come, are the realities, and that if the scientific description appears to say something different, it must nevertheless be supposed to be merely referring in an indirect manner to the sense-appearances, or to the relation and order of their occurrence. But (3) you might refuse to take sides as between perceptual descriptions and scientific descriptions; you might refuse, that is, to identify the real nature of things with what either sort of description appeared to describe. You might say that both were conventional or approximative accounts of something whose real nature eludes them both: and this was the position of Leibniz.

Now Leibniz, as we all know, said the most extraordinary things, and I shall hardly get away with it if I try to pass him upon you as the commonsense philosopher of his age. He appears to have said that what is known to me as the sole of my boot is known to God as an actual infinity of low-grade spirits, no one of which has any direct dealings with the one next door, yet each of which reflects and epitomizes the universe. And a philosopher who says this sort of thing has certainly got a great deal to live down. The man speculated, that was his trouble. No sooner had he distinguished the nature of the realities or things-in-themselves from the accounts which perceptual commonsense and science respectively give of them, than he was off on the speculative trail, demonstrating to himself the true nature of a reality which perceptual common sense and scientific hypothesis equally failed to reveal. But the discredit attaching to the speculations should not blind us to the merit of Leibniz's general position with regard to things-in-themselves, perceptual consciousness, and scientific constructions. One cannot read his discussions of Locke or his criticisms of the Cartesians or his controversy with Clarke* without appreciating the singular maturity and freedom of his attitude in that age of

* Samuel Clarke (1675–1729); a collection of the papers which passed between them (1715–16) was published in 1717—Ed.

philosophical nostrums. Because he has withdrawn the reality of things into a magical realm of which metaphysical reason alone holds the key, he can consider perceptual consciousness and physical theory as they come and for what they are, without involving himself in the unhappy attempt to prove the claims of either to be first philosophy.

After reading a good deal of Leibniz, what I sigh for is a philosopher who will try to make sense of the thing-in-itself position which Leibniz occupied—on its merits, and without the speculations. For I find myself hankering after this position. It may turn out, of course, that it cannot be stated intelligibly at all: but viewed from a lazy distance, it appears comfortable. Confronted as I am with *common-sense* descriptions of things, and *scientific* descriptions of several sorts and at several levels, my lazy mind hankers after the evasion: we keep using different mental constructions about things, and the nature of the things no doubt to some extent justifies the various constructions, but none of the constructions informs us of what the things properly are—they somehow stand beyond. I should like to know whether this is really nonsense, or even if it is, then what *sort* of nonsense it is.

Now it might seem as though Kant were going to discuss for me just what I want to have discussed, for we all know that he took up the Leibnitian position about things-in-themselves and about the phenomenal things, whether of common sense or of science; and we all know that in so doing he vigorously renounced the Leibnitian speculation on the nature of things-in-themselves. We were, said Kant, to be content with the bare notion of the thing-in-itself as of that which stands behind all our thing-consciousness and all our interpretations of it: we were to give up the attempt to define or elucidate the thing-in-itself. So far so good; and now surely, we say to ourselves, Kant will go on to discuss the nature of this twilight sort of thinking we do about the thing-in-itself. We are disappointed: he devotes little consideration to it. It may be that Kantian scholars can put together some sort of Kantian doctrine on this subject, by putting together hints from here and there. But Kant did not, certainly, place it in the front line of his attention, and we can see well enough why he did not. He was writing a corrective to the metaphysical dogmatism of the Leibnitian school, for whom the conception of the thing-in-itself was all too positive and definite. Kant would naturally feel that negation was his business, not construction.

And even if Kant had given (or, in deference to the Kantian scholars, let us say, even if he gave) an account of thing-in-itself-thinking, any such account must be vitiated for us by Kant's metaphysical speculations. For while he renounced speculation about the thing-in-itself, he speculated about the thing-phenomenon, and that in effect was just as bad. For it led him to pronounce in a way that seems to us arbitrary about the elements in our thing-thinking which must belong to the mind's own contribution, rather than to the thing-in-itself. By means of these arbitrary speculations he denied so much of the thing-in-itself that he doubled and trebled the difficulty of thinking about it at all. For example, in the attempt to resolve logical puzzles which, surely, ought to be resolved by logical means, Kant asserted that spatiality was the contribution of our own sensitive nature to our picture of things. Now the effort to think of a thing-in-itself which is not spatial taxes us beyond all tolerable limits, for if there is one thing rather than another that I am prompted to say about the thing-in-itself, it is that it is whatever, being over there, gets described by physicists in one way and by common sense in another. Deny spatiality of it, and I give it up. To put it in a phrase: the thing-in-itself for Kant is what is left when he has finished doing his speculative amputations. But the thing-in-itself I want to consider, is the apparent subject of the sort of thinking I in fact do, when I distinguish the veritable nature of things from any nature which my various ordinary ways of talking may attribute to them.

Perhaps I ought to apologize for this perfunctory historical survey: Leibniz and Kant won't do. Why talk about Leibniz and Kant? Because I do want to show that the notion I am talking about is one which has haunted the European mind since the beginning of the great age of physics; but at the same time I want to show how it got tangled and confused with speculations from which we shall wish to dissociate ourselves. Enough, then, of that.

What is it, then, that I want to say for myself about things-in-themselves? Simply this: first, nobody believes (whatever he may say) that experience is the occurrence of phenomena, but always that it is an encounter with things, things which are going concerns in themselves, whether we are there to experience them or not.

Second, nobody nowadays believes that either sensation or any verbal construction based upon it gives us more than an approximative or conventional account of what the things, as going concerns out there, are. And so we in fact tell ourselves that the things are what we don't know. It isn't merely that there is more and more to be found out about things, besides what we know already; it is that all the thinking we do is more or less mythical.

Now I shall be told that a train of the proper sort of philosophical reflection will cure me of the problem which is worrying me, and which leads me to agonize in consequence over the mystery of the thing-in-itself. If I see how common-sense perceptive descriptions arise, and how scientific physical constructions arise, I shall see no special puzzle about the relation of the one to the other, or of either to a supposed reality of things. Moreover, I shall realize that I can only *think* about things as I can *talk* about them, and I can only talk about them in so far as they come into my experience; whether unasked by way of ordinary sensations, or under torture in response to contrived experiments. And since the things-in-themselves apparently mean things in so far as they fail to do this, to talk about them is to talk about what cannot be talked about; and if anything is a waste of time, that will be.

I shall reply to this gospel, that it is being preached to the already converted. I am not at all worried about the relation of common-sense descriptions to scientific constructions: I see that each does its own job properly and that they do not fall foul of one another. Nor do I set up the thing-in-itself as an answer to any imaginary problem, I just find that it plays a part in my thinking, wherever I reflect on the incompleteness, conventionality, etc. of what I say about things. And I suspect that the same thoughts occur in your mind as in mine, and that after your repeated and severe logical exorcisms of them, they keep turning up again.

Further, I shall say that I am not agonizing about the nature of things-in-themselves, nor am I attempting anything so frustrating as to talk about them. In so far as I talk *about* them, I shall be disclosing aspects of them which have come into my experience in the ordinary way: their mysterious and withdrawn in-itself-ness is by hypothesis what I can't talk *about*. It is, at the most, something that I might *aspire* to talk about.

Well, now, but this is surely absurd. Am I not, then, asserting that there is an X absolutely undefined? But if so, what difference is there between asserting and denying its existence? How do I know that it isn't the snort of a hippopotamus or the left great toe of an archangel or the taste of asparagus? Surely we agreed long ago that you can't assert a *that* without even the shadow of a *what* or, to use an even more antiquated language, you can't assert an *existence* pure from the least suggestion of an *essence*? No, of course you can't: so naked an assertion is not merely a logical, but a psycho-logical, impossibility. But my so-called thinking about the thing-in-itself isn't a psychological impossibility, for it happens, and impossibilities don't happen: *ab esse ad posse valet illatio* ['If something exists, it must be possible']. So how, in fact, do I think about the thing-in-itself? There is no mystery in that, surely: I do it by an analogical extrapolation. Let me explain so opaque a phrase.

I take a relation within my experience, and I make as though to extend it beyond my experience. For example, I am quite familiar with the relations between primary and secondary descriptions. I can talk about nations or masses, or I can talk about the Toms, Dicks, and Harrys who really compose them. Or again, I can see my road upon a map, or I can see my road in the landscape. But now I may say: as Toms, Dicks and Harrys to masses or nations, as landscapes to maps, so things-in-themselves to things as I can in any wise describe them. That such thinking uses analogy is obvious: that it extrapolates is equally obvious. For whereas both Toms, Dicks, Harrys and masses can be talked about, and both maps and landscapes can be studied, the nature of things-in-themselves can neither be talked about nor studied. And so I run my graph, as it were, completely off the page.

But is not such analogical extrapolation nonsense? Yes, if you like, but a virtuous and irreplaceable piece of nonsense, a sort of twilight between some meaning and none. After undergoing all the logical therapies in the world, I should still, I strongly suspect, go on asserting that things carry on their own business, and that our accounts of that business are always defective, not only in extent or detail, but in manner of description as well.[2] I shall go on think-ing that it is true that there is something more and other to things than talk can say or sense perceive. And such an assertion appears to involve the sort of nonsensical extrapolation which I have pleaded guilty to. So there it is.

Is this confession all that we have to contribute? Not quite. There are several different analogies that we are inclined to use about things-in-themselves, and by reflecting on one, we find ourselves impelled to shift over to another. For example, we begin with the sort of analogy we have been describing—as landscape to map or as straight view to distorted view, so thing-in-itself to our knowledge of it. Such analogies, we then reflect, represent the nature of the thing-in-itself as though it were a more perfect sense-phenomenon behind the sense-phenomena, and diagrammatized or distorted by them. But, we now say to ourselves, the thing-in-itself can't be well symbolized by a sense-phenomenon of any sort: for sense-phenomena always arise out of an external contact between the thing and us, they are always phenomena of it, they represent its impact on us rather than what it itself is or does. We want an analogy with a relation, one of whose terms is an ordinary sense-phenomenon and the other is something somehow more intimate and direct. Let us use the analogy, then, of my watching with my eyes the movement of my hand as I write, while at the same time I consciously live and act in the business of the writing. Here is a sort of inward event, my activity of writing, and an exterior perception of it through my watching it. Let us say that similarly there is an inward process or activity in the thing-in-itself, and also the outward phenomena of it which I pick up. But this, taken literally, is absurd, for it involves the personification of the things; it involves saying that physical process or activity is conscious life, and this I do not mean in the least to say. Leibniz rejoins us here, for this was his line of thought; he took it in deadly earnest and he drew all the consequences without flinching.

We have no desire to follow him on any such path. We drag the concealed analogies out of their crepuscular lair in order to unmask them and, if you like, explode them. And if anyone likes to say that the proper philosophical treatment of metaphysical analogies is wholly negative, I will agree with him in a sense. In so far as they pretend to give us proper information, they must be exploded; but they are to be accepted in this sense, that by means of them the bare notion of the transcendence of things over our perception of them or description of them has obtained some expression in our minds.

I have talked about the thing-in-itself. But I do not think that it is the only example of this curious sort of thinking on the part of the human mind. Kant, we remember, thought there were two other transcendents we should have to think about in the same equivocal manner, selves-in-themselves and, on rather curious grounds of his own, a supremely transcendent reality—God. I agree with Kant about both, though I do not wish to place my theology on quite the same grounds. The theologians long ago discovered that their thinking had the curious twilight analogical character I have been discussing in this paper, and that it had all in a sense to be refuted or denied; and yet it managed to express something. They supposed that this was an oddity, and peculiar to theology. I think that they were wrong, and that thought about things-in-themselves and selves has the same oddity, and the same curious combination of expressiveness and sterility.

The Physical Theology of Leibniz[†]

As a man with an idea, with a philosophical nostrum, Leibniz may be compared to Bishop Berkeley. There was never any more doubt that Leibniz was a Leibnitian than that Berkeley was a Berkeleian. But there is no comparison between the two men in the width of their range. About many things Berkeley never took the trouble to Berkeleianize. To take the most surprising instance of his neglect—he assured the world that his whole doctrine pointed to, and hung upon, theology. But what sort of a theology? He scarcely took the first steps in the formulation of it. He preferred to keep on defending and explain his *esse est percipi*.[1] With Leibniz it is wholly different; he carries his new torch into every corner, to illuminate the dark questions.

The wide applicability of pre-established harmony might come home to its inventor as a rich surprise. The reflective historian will find it less surprising, for he will suspect that the applications were in view from the start. What was Leibniz thinking of when the new principle flashed upon him? What was he *not* thinking of? He had a many-sided mind. If the origins of the principle were complex, little wonder that its applications were manifold. Every expositor of Leibniz who does not wish to be endlessly tedious must concentrate attention on one aspect of Leibniz's principle, and one source of its origin. We will here give an account of the matter which, we trust, will go most directly to the heart of it, but we will make no claims to sufficient interpretation of Leibniz's thought-processes.

Leibniz, then, like all the philosophers of the seventeenth century, was reforming scholasticism in the light of a new physical science. The science was mathematical in its form, mechanistical in its doctrine, and unanswerable in its evidence—it got results. But it was metaphysically intractable, and the doctrines of infinite

† An excerpt from 'Editor's Introduction', *Theodicy* (1951).

and finite substance which it generated furnish a gallery of meta-physical grotesques—unless we are to except Leibniz; his system is, if nothing else, a miracle of ingenuity, and there are moments when we are in danger of believing it.

It is a natural mistake for the student of seventeenth-century thought to underestimate the tenacity of scholastic Aristotelianism. Descartes, we all know, was reared in it, but then Descartes over-threw it; and he had done his work and died by the time that Leibniz was of an age to philosophize at all. We expect to see Leibniz starting on his shoulders and climbing on from there. We are dis-appointed. Leibniz himself tells us that he was raised in the scholastic teaching. His acquaintance with Descartes's opinions was second-hand, and they were retailed to him only that they might be derided. He agreed, like an amiable youth, with his perceptors.

The next phase of his development gave him a direct knowledge of Cartesian writings, and of other modern books besides, such as those of the atomist Gassendi. He was delighted with what he read, because of its fertility in the field of physics and mathe-matics; and for a short time he was an enthusiastic modern. But presently he became dissatisfied. The new systems did not go far enough, they were still scientifically inadequate. At the same time they went too far, and carried metaphysical paradox beyond the limits of human credulity.

There is no mystery about Leibniz's scientific objections to the new philosophers. If he condemned them here, it was on the basis of scientific thought and observation. Descartes's formulation of the laws of motion could, for example, be refuted by physical experiment; and if his general view of physical nature was bound up with it, then so much the worse for the Cartesian philosophy. But whence came Leibniz's more strictly metaphysical objections? Where had he learned that standard of metaphysical adequacy which showed up the inadequacy of the new metaphysicians? His own disciples might be satisfied to reply, that he learnt it from Reason herself; but the answer will not pass with us. Leibniz reasoned, indeed, but he did not reason from nowhere, nor would he have got anywhere if he had. His conception of metaphysical reason was what his early scholastic training had made it.

There are certain absurd opinions which we are sure we have

been taught, although, when put to it, we find it hard to name the teacher. Among them is something of this sort: 'Leibniz was a scholarly and sympathetic thinker. He had more sense of history than his contemporaries, and he was instinctively eclectic. He believed he could learn something from each of his great predecessors. We see him reaching back to cull a notion from Plato or from Aristotle; he even found something of use in the scholastics. In particular, he picked out the Aristotelian "entelechy" to stop a gap in the philosophy of his own age.' What this form of statement ignores is that Leibniz *was* a scholastic: a scholastic endeavouring, like Descartes before him, to revolutionize scholasticism. The word 'entelechy' was, indeed, a piece of antiquity which Leibniz revived, but the thing for which it stood was the most familiar of current scholastic conceptions. 'Entelechy' means active principle of wholeness or completion in an individual thing. Scholasticism was content to talk about it under the name of 'substantial form' or 'formal cause'. But the scholastic interpretation of the idea was hopelessly discredited by the new science, and the scholastic terms shared the discredit of scholastic doctrine. Leibniz wanted a term with a more general sound. 'There is an X', he wanted to say, 'which scholasticism has defined as substantial form, but I am going to give a new definition of it.' Entelechy was a useful name for X, the more so as it had the authority of Aristotle, the master of scholasticism.

Under the name of entelechy Leibniz was upholding the soul of scholastic doctrine, while retrenching the limbs and outward flourishes. The doctrine of substantial form which he learnt in his youth had had *something* in it; he could not settle down in the principles of Descartes or of Gassendi, because both ignored this vital *something*. Since the requirements of a new science would not allow a return to sheer scholasticism, it was necessary to find a fresh philosophy, in which entelechy and mechanism might be accommodated side by side.

If one had asked any 'modern' of the seventeenth century to name the 'ancient' doctrine he most abominated, he would most likely have replied, 'Substantial form'. Let us recall what was rejected under this name, and why.

The medieval account of physical nature had been dominated by what we may call common-sense biology. Biology, indeed, is the science of the living, and the medievals were no more inclined than we are to endow all physical bodies with life. What they did do was to take living bodies as typical, and to treat other bodies as imperfectly analogous to them. Such an approach was *a priori* reasonable enough. For we may be expected to know best the physical being closest to our own; and we, at any rate, are alive. Why not argue from the better known to the less known, from the nearer to the more remote, interpreting other things by the formula of our own being, and allowing whatever discount is necessary for their degree of unlikeness to us?[2]

Common-sense biology reasons as follows. In a living body there is a certain pattern of organized parts, a certain rhythm of successive motions, and a certain range of characteristic activities. The pattern, the sheer anatomy, is basic; but it cannot long continue to exist (outside a refrigerator) without accompanying vital rhythms in heart, respiration and digestion. Nor do these perform their parts without the intermittent support of variable but still characteristic activities: dogs not only breathe and digest, they run about, hunt their food, look for mates, bark at cats, and so on. The anatomical pattern, the vital rhythm, and the characteristic acts together express dogginess; they reveal the specific form of the dog. They *reveal* it; exactly what the specific form *consisted in* was the subject of much medieval speculation. It need not concern us here.

Taking the form of the species for granted, common-sense biology proceeds to ask how it comes to be in a given instance, say in the dog Toby. Before this dog was born or thought of, his form or species was displayed in each of his parents. And now it looks as though the form of dog had detached itself from them through the generative act, and set up anew on its own account. How does it do that? By getting hold of some materials in which to express itself. At first it takes them from the body of the mother, afterwards it collects them from a wider environment, and what the dog eats becomes the dog.

What, then, is the relation of the assimilated materials to the dog-form which assimilates them? Before assimilation, they have their own form. Before the dog eats the leg of mutton, it has the form given to it by its place in the body of a sheep. What happens to the mutton? Is it without remainder transubstantiated from

sheep into dog? It loses all its distinctively sheep-like characteristics, but there may be some more basically material characteristics which it preserves. They underlay the structure of the
mutton, and they continue to underlie the structure of the dog's
flesh which supplants it. Whatever these characteristics may be, let
us call them common material characteristics, and let us say that
they belong to or compose a common material nature.

The common material nature has its own way of existing, and
perhaps its own principles of physical action. We may suppose
that we know much or that we know little about it. This one thing
at least we know, that it is capable of becoming alternatively
either mutton or dog's flesh. It is not essential to it to be mutton,
or mutton it would always be; nor dog's flesh, or it would always
be dog's flesh. It is capable of becoming either, according as it is
captured by one or other system of formal organization. So the
voters who are to go to the polls are, by their common nature,
Englishmen: they are essentially neither Socialist curs nor Con-
servative sheep, but intrinsically capable of becoming either, if
they become captured by either system of party organization.

According to this way of thinking, there is a certain *looseness*
about the relation of the common material nature to the higher
forms of organization capable of capturing it. Considered in itself
alone, it is perhaps to be seen as governed by absolutely determined laws of its own. It is heavy—then it will fall unless ob-
structed; it is solid—then it will resist intrusions. But considered as
material for organization by higher forms, it is indeterminate. It
acts in one sort of way under the persuasion of the sheep-form, and
in another sort of way under the persuasion of the dog-form and
we cannot tell how it will act until we know which form is going
to capture it. No amount of study bestowed on the common
material nature will enable us to judge how it will behave under
the persuasion of the higher organizing form. The only way to
discover that is to examine the higher form itself.

Every form, then, will really be the object of a distinct science.
The form of the sheep and the form of the dog have much in common, but that merely happens to be so; we cannot depend upon it,
or risk inferences from sheep to dog: we must examine each in
itself. We shall really need a science of probatology about sheep,
and cynology about dogs. Again, the common material nature has

its own principles of being and action, so it will need a science of itself, which we may call hylology. Each of these sciences is mistress in her own province; but how many there are, and how puzzlingly they overlap! So long as we remain within the province of a single science, we may be able to think rigorously, everything will be 'tight'. But as soon as we consider border-issues between one province and another, farewell to exactitude: everything will be 'loose'. We can think out hylology till we are blue in the face, but we shall never discover anything about the entry of material elements into higher organizations, or how they behave when they get there. We may form perfect definitions and descriptions of the form of the dog as such, and still derive no rules for telling what elements of matter will enter into the body of a given dog or how they will be placed when they do. All we can be sure of is, that the dog-form will keep itself going in, and by means of, the material it embodies—unless the dog dies. But what happens to the matter in the body of the dog is 'accidental' to the nature of the matter; and the use of this matter, rather than of some other equally suitable, is accidental to the nature of the dog.

No account of material events can dispense with accidental relations altogether. We must at least recognize that there are accidental relations between particular things. Accident in the sense of brute fact had to be acknowledged even by the tidiest and most dogmatic atomism of the last century. That atomism must allow it to be accidental, in this sense, that the space surrounding any given atom was occupied by other atoms in a given manner. It belonged neither to the nature of space to be occupied by just those atoms in just those places, nor to the nature of the atoms to be distributed just like that over space; and so in a certain sense the environment of any atom was an accidental environment. That is, the particular arrangement of the environment was accidental. The nature of the environment was not accidental at all. It was proper to the nature of the atom to be in interaction with other atoms over a spatial field, and it never encountered in the fellow-denizens of space any other nature but its own. It was not subject to the accident of meeting strange natures, nor of becoming suddenly subject to strange or unequal laws of interaction. All interactions, being with its own kind, were reciprocal and obedient to a single set of calculable laws.

But the medieval philosophy had asserted accidental relations between distinct sorts of *natures*, the form of living dog and the form of dead matter, for example. No one could know *a priori* what effect an accidental relation would produce, and all accidental relations between different pairs of natures were different: at the most there was analogy between them. Every different nature had to be separately observed, and when you had observed them all, you could still simply write an inventory of them, you could not hope to rationalize your body of knowledge. Let us narrow the field and consider what this doctrine allows us to know about the wood of a certain kind of tree. We shall begin by observing the impressions it makes on our several senses, and we shall attribute to it a substantial form such as naturally to give rise to these impressions, without, perhaps, being so rash as to claim a knowledge of what this substantial form is. Still we do not know what its capacities of physical action and passion may be. We shall find them out by observing it in relation to different 'natures'. It turns out to be combustible by fire, resistant to water, tractable to the carpenter's tools, intractable to his digestive organs, harmless to ostriches, nourishing to wood-beetles. Each of these capacities of the wood is distinct; we cannot relate them intelligibly to one another, nor deduce them from the assumed fundamental 'woodiness'.

We can now see why 'substantial forms' were the *bêtes noires* of the seventeenth-century philosophers. It was because they turned nature into an unmanageable jungle, in which trees, bushes, and parasites of a thousand kinds wildly interlaced. There was nothing for it, if science was to proceed, but to clear the ground and replant with spruce in rows: to postulate a single uniform nature, of which there should be a single science. Now neither probatology nor cynology could hope to be universal—the world is not all sheep nor all dog; it would have to be hylology: for the world is, in its spatial aspect, all material. Let us say, then, that there is one uniform material nature of things, and that everything else consists in the arrangements of the basic material nature; as the show of towers and mountains in the sunset results simply from an arrangement of vapours. And let us suppose that the interactions of the parts of matter are all like those which we can observe in dead manipulable bodies—in mechanism, in fact. Such was the

H

postulate of the new philosophers, and it yielded them results.

It yielded them results, and that was highly gratifying. But what, meanwhile, had happened to those palpable facts of common experience from which the whole philosophy of substantial forms had taken its rise? Is the wholeness of a living thing the mere resultant of the orderly operations of its parts? Is a bee no more essentially one than a swarm is? Is the life of a living animal indistinguishable from the rhythm of a going watch, except in degree of complication and subtlety of contrivance? And if an animal's body, say my own, is simply an agglomerate of minute interacting material units, and its wholeness is merely accidental and apparent, how is my conscious mind to be adjusted to it? For my consciousness appears to identify itself with that whole vital pattern which used to be called the substantial form. We are now told that the pattern is nothing real or active, but the mere accidental resultant of distinct interacting forces: it does no work, it exercises no influence or control, it *is* nothing.[3] How then can it be the vehicle and instrument of my conscious soul? It cannot. Then is my soul homeless? Or is it to be identified with the activity and fortunes of a single atomic constituent of my body, a single cog in the animal clockwork? If so, how irrational! For the soul does not experience itself as the soul of one minute part, but as the soul of the body.

Such questions rose thick and fast in the minds of the seventeenth-century philosophers. It will cause us great surprise that Leibniz should have quickly felt that the Formal Principle of Aristotle and of the scholastic philosophy must be by hook or by crook reintroduced—not as the detested *substantial form*, but under a name by which it might hope to smell more sweet, *entelechy*.

Nothing so tellingly revealed the difficulties of the new philosophy in dealing with living bodies as the insufficiency of the solutions Descartes had proposed. He had boldly declared the unity of animal life to be purely mechanical, and denied that brutes had souls at all, or any sensation. He had to admit soul in man, but he still denied the substantial unity of the human body. It was put together like a watch, it was many things, not one: if Descartes had lived in our time, he would have been delighted to compare it to a telephone system, the nerves taking the place of the wires, and being so arranged that all currents of 'animal spirit' flowing in them converged upon a single unit, a gland at the base of the brain. In this unit, or in the convergence of all the motions upon it, the 'unity' of the body virtually consisted; and the soul was incarnate, not in the plurality of members (for how could it, being one, indwell many things?), but in the single gland.

Even so, the relation between the soul and the gland was absolutely unintelligible, as Descartes disarmingly confessed. Incarnation was all very well in the old philosophy: those who had allowed the interaction of disparate natures throughout the physical world need find no particular difficulty about the special case of it provided by incarnation. Why should not a form of conscious life so interact with what would otherwise be dead matter as to 'indwell' it? But the very principle of the new philosophy disallowed the interaction of disparate natures, because such an interaction did not allow of exact formulation, it was a 'loose' and not a 'tight' relation.

From a purely practical point of view the much derided pineal gland theory would serve. If we could be content to view Descartes as a man who wanted to make the world safe for physical science, then there would be a good deal to be said for his doctrine.[4] In the old philosophy, exact science had been frustrated by the hypothesis of loose relations all over the field of nature. Descartes had cleared them from as much of the field as science was then in a position to investigate; he allowed only one such relation to subsist, the one which experience appeared unmistakably to force upon us—that between our own mind and its bodily vehicle. He had exorcized the spirits from the rest of nature; and though there was a spirit here which could not be exorcized, the philosophic conjurer had nevertheless confined it and its unaccountable pranks within a minutely narrow magic circle: all mind could do was to turn the one tiny switch at the centre of its animal telephone system. It could create no energy—it could merely redirect the currents actually flowing.

Practically this might do, but speculatively it was most disturbing. For if the 'loose relation' had to be admitted in one instance, it was admitted in principle; and one could not get rid of the suspicion that it would turn up elsewhere, and that the banishment of it from every other field represented a convenient pragmatic postulate rather than a solid metaphysical truth. Moreover, the correlation of the unitary soul with the unitary gland might do justice to a mechanistical philosophy, but it did not do justice to the soul's own consciousness of itself. The soul's consciousness is the 'idea' or 'representation' of the life of the whole body, certainly not of the life of the pineal gland nor, as the unreflective nowadays would say, of the brain. I am not conscious in, or of, my brain except when I have a headache; consciousness is in my eyes and finger-tips and so on.[5] It is physically true, no doubt, that consciousness in and of my finger-tips is not possible without the functioning of my brain; but that is a poor reason for locating the consciousness in the brain. The filament of the electric bulb will not be incandescent apart from the functioning of the dynamo; but that is a poor reason for saying that the incandescence is in the dynamo.

Certainly the area of representation in our mind is not simply equivalent to the area of our body. But in so far as the confines of mental representation part company with the confines of the body, it is not that they may contract and fall back upon the pineal gland, but that they may expand and advance over the surrounding world. The mind does not represent its own body merely, it represents the world in so far as the world affects that body or is physically reproduced in it. The mind has no observable natural relation to the pineal gland. It has only two natural relations: to its body as a whole and to its effective environment. What Descartes had really done was to pretend that the soul was related to the pineal gland as it is in fact related to its whole body; and then that it was related to the bodily members as in fact it is related to outer environment. The members became an inner environment, known only in so far as they affected the pineal gland; just as the outer environment in its turn was to be known only in so far as it affected the members.

This doctrine of a double environment was wholly artificial. It was forced on Descartes by the requirements of mechanistical science: if the members were simply a plurality of things, they must really be parts of environment; the body which the soul indwelt must be *a* body; presumably, then, the pineal gland. An untenable compromise, surely, between admitting and denying the reality of the soul's incarnation.

What, then, was to be done? Descartes's rivals and successors attempted several solutions, which it would be too long to examine here. They dissatisfied Leibniz and they have certainly no less dissatisfied posterity. It will be enough for us here to consider what Leibniz did. He admitted, to begin with, the psychological fact. The unity of consciousness is the representation of a plurality— the plurality of the members, and through them the plurality of the world. Here, surely, was the very principle the new philosophy needed for the reconciliation of substantial unity with mechanical plurality of parts. For it is directly evident to us that consciousness focuses the plurality of environing things in a unity of representation. This is no philosophical theory, it is a simple fact. Our body, then, as a physical system is a mechanical plurality; as focused in consciousness it is a unity of 'idea'.

Very well: but we have not got far yet. For the old difficulty still remains—it is purely arbitrary, after all, that a unitary consciousness should be attached to, and represent, a mechanical collection of things which happen to interact in a sort of pattern. If there is a consciousness attached to human bodies, then why not to systems of clockwork? If the body is *represented* as unity, it must surely be because it *is* unity, as the old philosophy had held. But how can we reintroduce unity into the body without reintroducing substantial form, and destroying the mechanistical plurality which the new science demanded?

It is at this point that Leibniz produces the speculative postulate of his system. Why not reverse the relation, and make the members represent the mind as the mind represents the members? For then the unity of person represented in the mind will become something actual in the members also.

Representation appears to common sense to be a one-way sort of traffic. If my mind represents my bodily members, something happens to my mind, for it becomes a representation of such members in such a state; but nothing happens to the members by their being so represented in the mind. The mental representation obeys the bodily facts; the bodily facts do not obey the mental representation. It seems nonsense to say that my members obey my mind *because* they are mirrored in it. And yet my members do obey my mind, or at least common sense supposes so. Sometimes my mind, instead of representing the state my members are in, represents a state which it intends that they shall be in, for example, that my hand should go through the motion of writing these words. And my hand obeys; its action becomes the moving diagram of my thought, my thought is represented or expressed in the manual act. Here the relation of mind and members appears to be reversed: instead of its representing them, they represent it. With this representation it is the opposite of what it was with the other. By the members' being represented in the mind, something happened to the mind, and nothing to the members; by the mind's being represented in the members something happens to the members and nothing to the mind.

Why should not we take this seriously? Why not allow that there is two-way traffic—by one relation the mind represents the members, by another the members represent the mind? But then again, how can we take it seriously? For representation, in the required sense, is a mental act; brute matter can represent nothing, only mind can represent. And the members are brute matter. But are they? How do we know that? By brute matter we understand extended lumps of stuff, interacting with one another mechanically, as do, for example, two cogs in a piece of clockwork. But this is a large-scale view. The cogs are themselves composed of interrelated parts and those parts of others, and so on *ad infinitum*. Who knows what the ultimate constituents really are? The 'modern' philosophers, certainly, have proposed no hypothesis about them which even looks like making sense. They have supposed that the apparently inert lumps, the cogs, are composed of parts themselves equally inert, and that by subdivision we shall still reach nothing but the inert. But this supposition is in flat contradiction with what physical theory demands. We have to allow the reality of *force* in physics. Now the force which large-scale bodies display may easily be the block-effect of activity in their minute real constituents. If not, where does it come from? Let it be supposed then, that these minute real constituents are active because they are alive, because they are minds; for indeed we have no notion of activity other than the perception we have of our own. We have no notion of it except as something mental. On the hypothesis that the constituents of active body are also mental, this limitation in our conception of activity need cause us neither sorrow nor surprise.

The mind-units which make up body will not, of course, be developed and fully conscious minds like yours or mine, and it is only for want of a better word that we call them minds at all. They will be mere unselfconscious representations of their physical environment, as it might be seen from the physical point to which they belong by a human mind paying no attention at all to its own seeing. How many of these rudimentary 'minds' will there be in my body? As many as you like—as many as it is possible there should be—say an infinite number and have done with it.

We may now observe how this hypothesis introduces real formal unity without prejudicing mechanical plurality. Each of the mind-units in my body is itself and substantially distinct. But since each, in its own way and according to its own position, represents the superior and more developed mind which I call 'me', they will order themselves according to a common form. The order is real, not accidental: it is like the order of troops on a parade-ground. Each man is a distinct active unit, but each is really expressing by his action the mind of the officer in command. He is expressing no less his relation to the other men in the ranks—to obey the officer is to keep in step with them. So the metaphysical units of the body, being all minds, represent one another as well as the dominant mind: one another co-ordinately, the dominant mind sub-ordinately.

But if the metaphysically real units of the body are of the nature of mind, then *the* mind is a mind among minds, a spirit-atom among spirit-atoms. What then constitutes its superiority or dominance, and makes it a mind *par excellence*? Well, what constitutes the officer an officer? Two things: a more developed mentality and the fact of being obeyed. In military life these two factors are not always perfectly proportioned to one another, but in the order of Leibniz's universe they are. A fuller power to represent the universe is necessarily combined with dominance over an organized troop of members; for the mind knows the universe only in so far as the universe is expressed in its body. That is what the *finitude* of the mind means. Only an infinite mind appreciates the whole plurality of things in themselves; a finite mind perceives them in so far as mirrored in the physical being of an organized body of members. The more adequate the mirror, the more adequate the representation: the more highly organized the body, the more developed the mind.

The developed mind has an elaborate body; but the least

developed mind has still some body, or it would lack any mirror whatever through which to represent the world. This means, in effect, that Leibniz's system is not an unmitigated spiritual atomism. For though the spiritual atoms, or monads, are the ultimate constituents out of which nature is composed, they stand composed together from the beginning in a minimal order which cannot be broken up. Each monad, if it is to be anything at all, must be a continuing finite representation of the universe, and to be that it must have a body, that is to say, it must have other monads in a permanent relation of mutual correspondence with it. And if you said to Leibniz, 'But surely any physical body can be broken up, and this must mean the dissolution of the organic relation between its monadical constituents,' he would take refuge in the infinitesimal. The wonders revealed by that new miracle, the microscope, suggested what the intrinsic divisibility of space itself suggests—whatever organization is broken up, there will still be a minute organization within each of the fragments which remains unbroken—and so *ad infinitum*. You will never come down to loose monads, monads out of all organization. You will never disembody the monads, and so remove their representative power; you will only reduce their bodies and so impoverish their representative power. In this sense no animal dies and no animal is generated. Death is the reduction and generation the enrichment of some existing monad's body; and, by being that, is the enrichment or the reduction of the monad's mental life.

'But', our common sense protests, 'it is too great a strain on our credulity to make the real nature of things so utterly different from what sense and science make of them. If the real universe is what you say it is, why do our minds represent it to us as they do?' The philosopher's answer is, 'Because they *represent* it. According to the truth of things, each monad is simply its own mental life, its own world-view, its own thoughts and desires. To know things as they are would be simultaneously to live over, as though from within and by a miracle of sympathy, the biographies of an infinite number of distinct monads. This is absolutely impossible. Our senses represent the coexistent families of monads *in the gross*, and therefore conventionally; what is in fact the mutual representation of monads in ordered systems, is represented as the mechanical interaction of spatially extended and material parts.' This does not mean that science is overthrown. The physical world-view is in terms of the convention of representation, but it is not, for all that, illusory. It can, ideally, be made as true as it is capable of being. There is no reason whatever for confusing the 'well-grounded seemings' of the apparent physical world with the fantastic seemings of dream and hallucination.

So far the argument seems to draw whatever cogency it has from the simplicity and naturalness of the notion of representation. The nature of idea, it is assumed, is to represent plurality in a unified view. If idea did not represent, it would not be idea. And since there *is* idea (for our minds at least exist and are made up of idea) there is representation. It belongs to idea to represent, and since the whole world has now been interpreted as a system of mutually representing ideations, or ideators, it might seem that all their mutual relations are perfectly natural, a harmony of agreement which could not be other than it is. But if so, why does Leibniz keep saying that the harmony is *pre-established*, by special and infinitely elaborate divine decrees?

Leibniz himself says that the very nature of representation excludes interaction. By representing environment a mind does not do anything to environment, that is plain. But it is no less plain that environment does nothing to it, either. The act of representing is simply the act of the mind; it represents *in view of* environment, of course, but not under the causal influence of environment. Representation is a business carried on by the mind on its own account, and in virtue of its innate power to represent.

Very well; but does this consideration really drive us into theology? Is not Leibniz the victim of a familiar fallacy, that of incompletely stated alternatives? '*Either* finite beings interact *or else* they do not directly condition one another. Monads do not interact, therefore they do not directly condition one another. How then explain the actual conformity of their mutual representation, without recourse to divine fore-ordaining?' It seems sufficient to introduce a further alternative in the first line of the argument, and we are rid of the theology. Things may condition the action of a further thing, without acting upon it: it acts of itself, but it acts in view of what they are. We are tempted to conclude that Leibniz has introduced the *Deus ex machina* with the fatal facility of his age. 'Where a little further meditation on the characters in the play would furnish a natural *dénouement*, he swings divine intervention on to the scene by wires from the ceiling. It is easy for us to reconstruct for him the end of the piece without recourse to stage-machines.'

Is it? No, I fear it is not. There is really no avoiding the pre-established harmony. And so we shall discover, if we pursue our train of reflection a little further. It is natural, we were saying, that an idea should represent an environment; indeed, it *is* the representation of one. Given no environment to represent, it would be empty, a mere capacity for representation. Then every idea or ideator, taken merely in itself, *is* an empty capacity. But of what is the environment of each made up? According to the Leibnitian theory, of further ideas or ideators: of empty capacities, therefore. Then no idea will either be anything in itself, or find anything in its neighbours to represent. An unhappy predicament, like that of a literary clique in which all the members are adepts at discussing one another's ideas—only that unfortunately none of them is provided with any; or like the shaky economics of the fabled Irish village where they all lived by taking in one another's washing.

It is useless, then, to conceive representations as simply coming into existence in response to environment, and modelling themselves on environment. They must all mutually reflect environment or they would not be representations; but they must also exist as themselves and in their own right or there would be no environment for them mutually to represent. Since the world is infinitely various, each representer must have its own distinct character or nature, as our minds have: that is to say, it must represent in its own individual way: and all these endlessly various representations must be so constituted as to form a mutually reflecting harmony. Considered as a representation, each monadical existence simply reflects the universe after its own manner. But considered as something to be represented by the others, it is a self-existent mental life, or world of ideas. Now when we are considering the fact of representation, that which is to be represented comes first and the representation follows upon it. Thus in considering the Leibnitian universe, we must begin with the monads as self-existent mental lives, or worlds of ideas; their representation of one another comes second. Nothing surely, then, but omnipotent creative wisdom could have pre-established between so many distinct given mental worlds that harmony which constitutes their mutual representation.

Our common-sense pluralistic thinking escapes from the need of the pre-established harmony by distinguishing what we are from what we do. Let the world be made up of a plurality of agents in a 'loose' order, with room to manœuvre and to adjust themselves to one another. Then, by good luck or good management, through friction and disaster, by trial and error, by accident or invention, they may work out for themselves a harmony of *action*. There is no need for divine preordaining here. But on Leibniz's view what the monads do is to represent, and what they are is representation; there is no ultimate distinction between what they are and what they do: all that they do belongs to what they are. The whole system of action in each monad, which fits with such infinite complexity the system of action in each other monad, is precisely the existence of that monad, and apart from it the monad is not. The monads do not *achieve* a harmony, they *are* a harmony, and therefore they are pre-established in harmony.

Leibniz denied that he invoked God to intervene in nature, or that there was anything arbitrary or artificial about his physical theology. He was simply analysing nature and finding it to be a system of mutual representation; he was analysing mutual representation and finding it to be of its nature intrinsically pre-established, and therefore God-dependent. He was not adding anything to mutual representation, he was just showing what it necessarily contained or implied. At least he was doing nothing worse than recognized scholastic practice. Scholastic Aristotelianism explained all natural causality as response to stimulus, and then had to postulate a stimulus which stimulated without being stimulated, and this was God. Apart from this supreme and first stimulus nothing would in fact be moving. The Aristotelians claimed simply to be analysing the nature of physical motion as they perceived it, and to find the necessity of perpetually applied divine stimulation implicit in it. No violence was thereby done to the system of physical motion nor was anything brought in from without to patch it up; it was simply found to be of its own nature God-dependent.

It seems as though the reproachful description '*Deus ex machina*' should be reserved for more arbitrary expedients than Aristotle's or Leibniz's, say for the occasionalist theory. Occasionalism appeared to introduce God that he might make physical matter do what it had no natural tendency to do, namely to obey the volitions of finite mind. Ideas, on the other hand, have a natural tendency to represent one another, for to be an idea is to be a representation; God is not introduced by Leibniz to make them correspond, he is introduced to work a system in which they shall correspond. This may not be *Deus-ex-machina philosophy*, but it is *physical theology*;[6] that is to say, it treats divine action as one factor among the factors which together constitute the working of the natural system. And this appears to be perhaps unscientific, certainly blasphemous: God's action cannot be a factor among factors; the Creator works through and in all creaturely action equally; we can never say 'This is the creature, and that is God' of distinguishable causalities in the natural world. The creature is, in its creaturely action, self-sufficient: but because a creature, insufficient to itself throughout, and sustained by its Creator both in existence and in action.

The only acceptable argument for theism is that which corresponds to the religious consciousness, and builds upon the insufficiency of finite existence throughout, because it is finite. All arguments to God's existence from a particular gap in our account of the world of finites are to be rejected. They do not indicate God, they indicate the failure of our power to analyse the world-order. When Leibniz discovered that his system of mutual representations needed to be pre-established, he ought to have seen that he had come up a cul-de-sac and backed out; he ought not to have said, 'With the help of God I will leap over the wall.'

If we condemn Leibniz for writing physical theology, we condemn not him but his age. No contemporary practice was any better, and much of it a good deal worse, as Leibniz liked somewhat complacently to point out. And because he comes to theology through physical theology, that does not mean that all his theology was physical theology and as such to be written off. On the contrary, Leibniz is led to wrestle with many problems which beset any philosophical theism of the Christian type. This is particularly so in the *Theodicy*, as its many citations of theologians suggest. His discussions never lack ingenuity, and the system of creation and providence in which they result has much of that luminous serenity which colours the best works of the Age of Reason.

Every theistic philosopher is bound, with whatever cautions, to conceive God by the analogy of the human mind.[7] When Leibniz declares the harmony of monads to be pre-established by God, he is invoking the image of intelligent human pre-arrangement. Nor is he content simply to leave it at that: he endeavours as well as he may to conceive the sort of act by which God pre-arranges; and this involves the detailed adaptation for theological purposes of Leibnitian doctrine about the human mind.

The human mind, as we have seen, is the mind predominant in a certain system of 'minds', namely in those which constitute the members of the human body. If we call it predominant, we mean that its system of ideas is more developed than theirs, so that there are more points in which each of them conforms to it than in which it conforms to any one of them. The conception of a divine pre-establishing mind will be analogous. It will be the conception of a mind *absolutely* dominant, to whose ideas, that is to say, the whole system simply corresponds, without any reciprocating correspondence on his side. In a certain sense this is to make God the 'Mind of the World'; and yet the associations of the phrase are misleading. It suggests that the world is an organism or body in which the divine mind is incarnate, and on which he relies for his representations. But that is nonsense; the world is not *a* body, nor is it organic to God. Absolute dominance involves absolute transcendence:[8] if everything in the world without remainder simply obeys the divine thoughts, that is only another way of saying that the world is the creature of God; the whole system is pre-established by him who is absolute Being and perfectly independent of the world.

Of createdness, or pre-establishedness, there is no more to be said: we can think of it as nothing but the pure or absolute case of subjection to dominant mind. It is no use asking further *how* God's thoughts are obeyed in the existence and action of things.[9] What we can and must enquire into further, is the nature of the divine thoughts which are thus obeyed. They must be understood to be volitions or decrees. There are indeed two ways in which things obey the divine thought, and correspondingly two sorts of divine thoughts that they obey. In so far as created things conform to the mere universal principles of reason, they obey a reasonableness which is an inherent characteristic of the divine mind itself. If God wills the existence of any creature, that creature's existence must observe the limits prescribed by eternal reason: it cannot, for example, both have and lack a certain characteristic in the same sense and at the same time; nor can it contain two parts and two parts which are not also countable as one part and three parts. Finite things, if they exist at all, must thus conform to the reasonableness of the divine nature, but what the divine reasonableness thus prescribes is highly general: we can deduce from it only certain laws which any finite things must obey, we can never deduce from it which finite things they are to be, nor indeed that there are to be any. Finite things are particular and individual: each of them might have been other than it is or, to speak more properly, instead of any one of them there might have existed something else; it was, according to the mere principles of eternal reason, equally possible. But if so, the whole universe, being made up of things each of which might be otherwise, might as a whole be otherwise. Therefore the divine thoughts which it obeys by existing have the nature of *choices or decrees.*

What material does the finite mind supply for an analogical picture of the infinite mind making choices or decrees? If we use such language of God, we are using language which has its first and natural application to ourselves. We all of us choose, and those of us who are in authority make decrees. What is to choose? It involves a real freedom in the mind. A finite mind, let us remember, is nothing but a self-operating succession of perceptions, ideas, or representations. With regard to some of our ideas we have no freedom, those, for example, which represent to us our body. We think of them as constituting our given substance. They are sheer data for us, and so are those reflections of our environment which they mediate to us. They make up a closely packed and confused mass; they persevere in their being with an obstinate innate force, the spiritual counterpart of the force which we have to recognize in things as physically interpreted. Being real spiritual force, it is quasi-voluntary, and indeed do we not love our own existence and, in a sense, will it in all its necessary circumstances? But if we can be said to will to be ourselves and to enact with native force what our body and its environment makes us, we are merely willing to conform to the conditions of our existence; we are making no choice.

When, however, we think freely or perform deliberate acts, there
is not only force but choice in our activity. Choice between what?
Between alternative possibilities arising out of our situation. And
choice in virtue of what? In virtue of the appeal exercised by one
alternative as seemingly better.

Can we adapt our scheme of choice to the description of God's
creative decrees? We will take the second point in it first: our
choice is in virtue of the appeal of the seeming best. Surely the
only corrective necessary in applying this to God is the omission of
the word 'seeming'. His choice is in virtue of the appeal of the
simply best. The other point causes more trouble. We choose
between possibilities which arise for us out of our situation in the
system of the existing world. But as the world does not exist before
God's creative choices, he is in no world-situation, and no alternative possibilities can arise out of it, between which he should
have to choose. But if God does not choose between intrinsic
possibilities of some kind, his choice becomes something absolutely
meaningless to us—it is not a choice at all, it is an arbitrary and
unintelligible *fiat*.

Leibniz's solution is this: what are mere possibilities of thought
for us are possibilities of action for God. For a human subject,
possibilities of action are limited to what arises out of his actual
situation, but possibilities for thought are not so limited. I can
conceive a world different in many respects from this world, in
which, for example, vegetables should be gifted with thought and
speech; but I can do nothing towards bringing it about. My
imaginary world is practically impossible but speculatively possible, in the sense that it contradicts no single principle of necessary and immutable reason. I, indeed, can explore only a very little
way into the region of sheer speculative possibility; God does not
explore it, he simply possesses it all: the whole region of the possible is but a part of the content of his infinite mind. So among all
possible creatures he chooses the best and creates it.

But the whole realm of the possible is an actual infinity of ideas.
Out of the consideration of an infinity of ideas, how can God
arrive at a choice? Why not? His mind is not, of course, discursive;
he does not successively turn over the leaves of an infinite book of
sample worlds, for then he would never come to the end of it.
Embracing infinite possibility in the single act of his mind, he

settles his will with intuitive immediacy upon the best. The inferior, the monstrous, the absurd is not a wilderness through which he painfully threads his way, it is that from which he immediately turns; his wisdom is his elimination of it.

But in so applying the scheme of choice to God's act, have we not invalidated its application to our own? For if God has chosen the whole form and fabric of the world, he has chosen everything in it, including the choices we shall make. And if our choices have already been chosen for us by God, it would seem to follow that they are not real open choices on our part at all, but are pre-determined. And if they are pre-determined, it would seem that they are not really even choices, for a determined choice is not a choice. But if we do not ourselves exercise real choice in any degree, then we have no clue to what any choice would be: and if so, we have no power of conceiving divine choice, either; and so the whole argument cuts its own throat.

There are two possible lines of escape from this predicament. One is to define human choice in such a sense that it allows of pre-determination without ceasing to be choice; and this is Leibniz's method, and it can be studied at length in the *Theodicy*. He certainly makes the very best he can of it, and it hardly seems that any of those contemporaries whose views he criticizes was in a position to answer him. The alternative method is to make the most of the negative element involved in all theology. After all, we do not positively or adequately understand the nature of infinite creative will. Perhaps it is precisely the transcendent glory of divine freedom to be able to work infallibly through free instruments. But so mystical a paradox is not the sort of thing we can expect to appeal to a late-seventeenth-century philosopher.

One criticism of Leibniz's argument we cannot refrain from making. He allows himself too easy a triumph when he says that the only alternative to a choice determined by a prevailing in-clination towards one proposal is a choice of mere caprice. There is a sort of choice Leibniz never so much as considers and which appears at least to fall quite outside his categories, and that is the sort of choice exercised in artistic creativity. In such choice we freely feel after the shaping of a scheme, we do not arbitrate simply between shaped and given possible schemes. And perhaps some such element enters into all our choices, since our life is to some extent freely designed by ourselves. If so, our minds are even more akin to the divine mind than Leibniz realized. For the sort of choice we are now referring to seems to be an intuitive turning away from an infinite, or at least indefinite, range of less attractive possibility. And such is the nature of the divine creative choice. The consequence of such a line of speculation would be, that the divine mind designs more through us, and less simply for us, than Leibniz allowed: the 'harmony' into which we enter would be no longer simply 'pre-established'. Leibniz, in fact, could have nothing to do with such a suggestion, and he would have found it easy to be ironical about it if his contemporaries had proposed it.

A Moral Argument
for the Existence of God†

1

The old method of philosophizing about theology was the endeavour to prove. This meant, to prove theological conclusions from
non-theological premises; otherwise the argument would have
seemed circular. Admittedly there were topics of doctrine which
did not allow of philosophical proof, but only of historical evidence; divine revelation, for example. To reveal himself or not
was a free choice lying in God's will; that he had revealed himself
was a certainty resting on testimony alone. Yet even in this field
there was something for the philosopher to attempt. He could
hope to establish *a priori* and from non-theological premises the
possibility, even the naturalness, of revelation; could hope to
show that God was such, and man was such, that it was more
credible God would reveal himself to man, than that he would
not.

Such a method of proceeding is now out of fashion, not so
much because theology cannot be philosophically demonstrated
as because nothing can; not, that is, in the implied sense of
'demonstrated'. Every science, art, or manner of speaking is now
supposed to find its own justification in its own use. Philosophical
analysis tries to show how any sort of talk goes, and what it does.
This does not mean that no accustomed province of discourse has
anything to fear from philosophical examination. Its pretensions
may, on the contrary, be severely curtailed; if, for example, it
emerges that theology is an art of talking oneself out of anxiety
by the entertainment of unreal supposition.

In such a philosophical climate the difference of status noted
above between the demonstrable and the indemonstrable parts of
theology, between 'rational' and 'revealed' doctrines, largely disappears. The God about whom, and to whom, believers speak is

† Reprinted from *Faith and Logic* (1957) under the title 'A Starting-Point for
the Philosophical Examination of Theological Belief'.

the self-revealing God. The 'God of pure reason' is scarcely encountered outside philosophical argument and it is harder to see what function, if any, talk about him performs. Let us, then, take typical sentences about the self-revealing God, or about the dealings we have with him in consequence of his having revealed himself. Here, if anywhere, is religious language in real use. Let philosophy proceed to see what the use is and how the language works.

No proposal, you might think, could be more straightforward. But there is an unlucky complication. How does the philosopher proceed? He takes specimen sentences from the language he investigates, he isolates them, he subjects them to analysis. If his procedure is to be fruitful, two conditions must be fulfilled. First, the sentences selected must be understood at the ordinary, pre-philosophical level before they are analysed; and second, they must be analysed adequately. What philosophers like to do is to make sure that no difficulty will arise over the fulfilment of the first condition by picking specimen sentences which everyone understands at first sight. Then they can proceed without more ado to the analysis which is, after all, their proper philosophical task. But it is the peculiar difficulty of philosophizing about theology that it contains no sentences about which such immediate and agreed understanding is forthcoming.

Because the primary subject of theological statements is according to unbelievers preposterous, and according to believers 'transcendent', the statements about him cannot be anything but parables borrowed from the world of our more direct acquaint-ance. And since he is by supposition very different from those things or persons from which the parabolic material is borrowed, no parable of itself expresses him truly, and every parable needs to be balanced by a different parable with a contrasting bias. The art of balancing parables is acquired in use by believers, without their being conscious of it. That they use such an art becomes evident as soon as we attempt to fix upon them all the apparent logical consequences from any single parable. They will then begin to pick and choose, admitting some consequences and refusing others: and if we ask them why, they will draw in further parables supporting what they allow, and hostile to what they reject. 'God became "flesh" '—'He is, then, subject to change?'—

'By no means: He did not change himself, it was the "flesh" he changed, by acting uniquely in it'—'You would wish, then, to withdraw the statement that he became flesh?'—'No, I would not: it expresses as nothing else can his complete self-identification with his incarnate action.' And so forth.

It is plain, then, that we cannot take a single sentence in this area of speech and proceed forthwith to its logical analysis. For the sentence will be a parable, and to establish its mere religious sense is to recover the context of very strangely contrasted parables in which it stands, together with the art of balancing parables. This is a long and complicated task. And it is a task for believers. It is impossible to study the art except from within the serious personal use of it; for the believer has the art, and to him one use of parable is truth and another nonsense or heresy; to the un-believer it is all nonsense, he lacks the criterion of use. It is possible for the unbeliever to acquire a sympathy which enables him to see himself believing; but there are specially strong and notorious obstacles in the way of his doing so. It is difficult for him to study the supposed apprehension of an activity most vigorous and present (that of God) in terms which to him are empty and absurd. And even if he has the intellectual sympathy, will he have the patience? It seems that the tendency of the unbelieving philo-sopher is to seek a short way with the believer. And it is only reasonable that a man should either let alone what he is inwardly convinced is rubbish, or else look for a quick means to rid the world of it.

But some philosophers, anyhow, are believers; so why should they not go quietly on with the work? Why should we always have our heads turned over our shoulders, watching to see how our unbelieving colleagues are taking it? Well, certainly believers can philosophize to themselves about their own belief. But philo-sophy is a debate, or a complex of debates, actually proceeding in the world; and no one who contracts out seems quite to be philosophizing. Besides, the believing philosopher who remains within the world at all cannot escape from intellectual sympathy with unbelief. Unbelief may write belief off, but belief feels the force of unbelief and wrestles with it.

If, then, we are to keep in the ring, what ground shall we take? There is another side to theological talking, beside the nice art of balancing parables; there is the referring of the parables to that to which they apply. Here lies the hope of a more promising start. The parables themselves appear to unbelievers to be all up in the air; but that to which they are applied may be, by common consent, solid ground. 'That to which the parables are applied' is, indeed, an ambiguous phrase. In one sense the parables are applied to God, and to his action. But in another sense the whole parabolic discourse about God and his action is applied to 'life'; in 'life' divine action finds an effect which it concerns us to acknowledge or to deny. And life, anyhow, is lived. No one disputes that.

We cannot, obviously, set out to discuss anything so vague as 'life', but only some aspect of it to which religious language applies. But is there any one such aspect? Belief defines God as universal cause and will not allow his action to be excluded from anything. No; but belief is speaking here with a somewhat theoretical voice. If challenged, the believer must be prepared conscientiously to read the parables of belief into almost anything that comes before his attention. His doing so is no mere apologetic dodge; it is part of the exercise of his faith, that it should set itself to embrace all things. Nevertheless there remains a difference between those things *into* which we have to read divine activity, and those things *off* which we simply do read it. We could scarcely claim the status of believers if we had to read divine activity *into* everything and read it *off* nothing; if, for example, duty sounded in our ears no echo of the voice of God.[1]

From a strictly formal point of view there may be no ultimate difference between 'reading into' and 'reading off'. To interpret without conscious effort is still to interpret; the intellectual form does not change its logical nature because it is used without fuss. Yet practically the difference is real enough. While we are reading the interpretation into the thing, the thing merely admits of the interpretation. But when the interpretation is read off the thing, it is for us part and parcel of the thing, not to be stripped away without maiming or falsifying the object. Now some sorts of interpretation do not begin to have their full characteristic use or effect until they are 'read off'. For whereas the value of scientific hypotheses is independent of our actually seeing things as concrete instances of our theorems, the value of personal interpretations (for example) is not. We interpret people so as to react to them appropriately, and the reaction is scarcely forthcoming until we see them in terms of the interpretation. Psychological theory is the test case. We think it will help us to understand our friends, but we find that the more we psychologize them the less we can live with them; for we cannot see our neighbours as embodied psychological theorems, or not without falling into a sort of notional lunacy.*

It is scarcely necessary to draw out the theological application. Religious belief has its use in evoking our responses, and this it does when it is 'read off', not when it is 'read into', our life. What we have to consider, then, is some aspect of our life, or some class of situations, *off* which ordinary believers read the action of God. We have already thrown out the suggestion that our moral life, with its characteristic situations, carries such a significance. But we do not propose to content ourselves with so jejune an observation. Moral activity or experience is a complex and many-sided thing, and we will endeavour to show in which of its aspects its religious meaning is found to lie.

2

The philosopher who approaches religion through moral thinking finds his feet on the beaten track to a mare's nest. For philosophy likes to concern itself with the logical analysis of formulated discourse in common use, and especially of argument. Now men talk and argue a great deal about morality, but scarcely about that aspect of it on which religion comes principally to bear.

The foundations of morality are platitudinous valuations; the subjects of moral discussion are contested priorities. People who discuss the platitudes are intolerable—who try, for example, to make an issue of the question, whether it is good that we should care for other men or for ourselves alone; or whether instinctive appetite should ever be controlled. But we can fairly discuss the priority to be given to the objects of this and that appetite or interest; we can discuss the priority of the claim made upon us by humanity in general or by particular loyalty; and within the area

* This is not to deny that psychological theory assists us to form personal interpretations. What is so corrosive is the application of the theory 'neat'.

of loyalty, the claim of this person or group, and of that. Moral rules, like moral discussions, aim at the settlement of priorities; and the difference between one civilized 'way of life' and another, so far as it is a moral difference, lies in the priorities it assigns.

Moral thinking, then, is taken to be the discussion, assertion, or working out of moral priorities; and religion is taken to be the assertion and veneration of some absolute authority. Bring the two into direct relation, and it is obvious what conclusion results. God's will must be the ultimate authority for priorities. In the end, we hear it said, there is no earthly appeal in moral argument, and no earthly authority for moral rules, beyond the whole mental attitude and way of life proper to the culture we accept. Since (hitherto at least) the several cultures of mankind have taken a tinge from the religion prevalent in each, it may be true in some measure that the moral differences between cultures are differences of religion. And the fact that religion is ultimately belief—that its evidence is somehow intrinsic—seems to square with the fact that the moral 'options' of a culture are in the last resort simply those which the men of that culture cannot help thinking it right to uphold. Is not this ultimate option religious belief? Or is not religious belief a special way of feeling, backing, or formulating this ultimate option?

Following such a line of thought we come to see religion as that whereby men's attitudes to life differ. But such a way of regarding religion is at best extrinsic and casts no light on the nature of religion, still less of its object. It would be like describing the aesthetic sense as that in virtue of which Englishmen, Indians and Chinese differ in their attitude to volcanoes and fruit blossom. The aesthetic sense is not primarily a cause of division and mutual incomprehension; it is a common way of reacting to things, having a specific character which distinguishes it from other, non-aesthetic, ways of reacting. When we first become aware of differences in the standard of taste from nation to nation our feeling is one of surprise. We do not dream of saying 'Of course; for isn't "aesthetic sensibility" just a class of attitudinal oppositions?' It takes us time and thought to see how a common thing, good taste, can admit the varieties it exhibits without forfeiting its whole virtue.

It is true, no doubt, that several religious cultures appeal each to their God (or to God as each conceives him) in support of their way of life. But none of them would dream of saying that the purpose of divine direction is to create interesting moral differences between cultures; or (alternatively) to save nations the perplexity of choosing between open options, by laying down local and arbitrary by-laws. Cultures differ not through understanding the will of God but through taking partial views of it. The priorities, so far as they differ, are all too human, and result from divergent appreciations of the fundamental values between which priorities are assigned. The 'authority' is in the values themselves, which 'demand' to be graded one way rather than another. The direct impact of the divine will is to be found, if anywhere, in the platitudinous region of basic valuation.

Valuation is of two sorts, if both of them ought to be called valuation: (1) We value human beings, and any other beings we can regard in the same way—angels if we can know them, dogs if we can love them. But for the purposes of the present discussion we will leave the dogs and angels out. (2) Because we value human beings, we value what we take to be desirable features in human life, or things contributory to the realization of such features.

The second sort of valuation differs from the first in being disputable. We try to have a 'correct' valuation of the several features or constituents of human life, and we disagree. Valuation of this sort requires good judgement. But in the valuation of persons there is no 'correct' and no 'incorrect', nor any exercise of judgement: only sensitiveness, depth, sincerity, or the reverse of these. And since valuation suggests the valuer, going round and sticking his labels of comparative price on one thing after another, the very phrase 'valuation of persons' is detestable. We respond to, care about, love, or, in the ancient sense, worship our neighbour. Unless, of course, we ignore, neglect, hate, dishonour him; but these are not alternative expressions of moral judgement; they are crimes. It is not an error of moral judgement to care about a blackguardly cousin, but only to mistake what spoils him for what it spoils in him. We may, indeed, commend him to the hangman. But that is not the effect of valuation (1). It is due to the intervention of valuation (2). We are viewing him not in himself as a person, but as a feature in the moral landscape of others. A violent clash between the two sorts of valuation results: we must love him as a cousin, and hang him as a nuisance. But we cannot do both. Hence the moral agony of destructive punishment—not to mention military slaughter.

Even though in such instances the two sorts of valuation may compete for the guidance of our action, they are on different logical levels and any direct comparison between them is, in the logical sense, nonsensical. 'Which is healthier, beer or cider?' But not 'Which is healthier, beer or Henry?' 'Which is more valuable, Bulganin's plan or Malenkov's?' But not 'Which is more valuable, Bulganin's plan or Comrade Ivanovich?' unless we are regarding Ivanovich's personal qualities (for which Bulganin's plan affords no scope) as being of service to the Russians; and similarly Henry might be more healthy than beer, as a means of keeping Mary in good spirits.

It would be convenient if we could find a single word for the value we place on the human being. The difficulty is that all our words are used antithetically. Take 'regard' for example. 'I have a regard for Henry, but none for John'. It is true that my uncle may retort, 'Then you ought to be ashamed of yourself', but in that case I shall feel that he has unfairly changed the meaning of the word 'regard', in order to preach at me. I did not mean that I have a policy of disregarding John; I meant that, in the sense in which no one can help having personal preferences, my regard goes to Henry. There is a sense, no doubt, in which it is a crime not to regard John, or any other person with whom I have to do; and the force of my uncle's sophistry lies in the closeness to one another of the two senses of 'regard'. My first line of defence will be to distinguish them sharply: 'I ought to regard John' means 'I ought to allow him his rights'; 'I have a regard for Henry' means 'I pay him friendly attention'. But as soon as I have said this, I see that it will not do. It is a good quarrelling position, the masculine pose. It throws on my disputant the ridicule of being soft; but it does not convince my heart. The regard I ought to pay to John is hard to distinguish from the regard I do pay to Henry. I ought to open myself to John, to appreciate him, to consider him, to put myself in the way of feeling the pull of his humanity, and to be willing to act in accordance with my resulting sense of the man. Maybe I do not have to go so far with John as with Henry; and certainly it comes more natural with Henry than with John. But something of the same sort is called for in both cases. My regarding of Henry is itself not effortless; if I do not take trouble about it when Henry is provoking, I shall lose his friendship.

There is, then, a sense of regard in which regard is universally due, and such regard is the heart of virtue. Ethical men regard their friends and are fair to their neighbours; good men regard their neighbours and love their friends. For want of a better word, we will call the first sort of valuation which we distinguished above 'regard', reserving 'valuation' itself for the second sort. We will say that persons are regarded, while everything else is valued in relation to them.

If all men are to be regarded, it should be possible to say something about men in general, in virtue of which they are all the proper objects of regard. If we say 'Because they are men', we may seem to make regard coterminous with the race-consciousness of a species. But in that case we should feel it tautological to say 'Man is a proper object of our regard', and absurd to suggest that we could even establish communication with creatures of another species who would be fit objects of our regard. And we do not find either the second idea absurd, or the first tautological.

We might agree about certain limits to the range of our regard —we cannot *regard* anything that is not sentient, and does not develop some degree of rational activity: always understanding that 'activity' may be talking or thinking as well as doing, and that 'rational' is a conventional term distinguishing the characteristically human level of action from the brutish.

'Rational agent' may be a true description of the proper object of regard, but it is not a complete description. I may say that it is with the insurance agent that I do business; it is irrelevant that he is Mr Jones and that he loves his children or plays the piano. It is not similarly the rational agent that I regard, but Tom, Dick, or Harry; and in regarding any one of them I abstract from nothing that makes the man. Beauty cannot move my senses, this lovely picture may. Rational agency cannot waken my regard, Henry may.

Henry may, and what is more, he *should*, move my regard, in the sense that I *ought* so to consider him and respond to him, as to give him every chance of moving it, and that there is something amiss if he fails to move it. And by what is he to move it? By all that he is. And what is he? Whatever is expressed in the action of his life, good, bad, or indifferent is Henry, and Henry is the object of my regard. It appears, then, that forms of action which considered abstractly are disvalued, become when considered in the agent of them the object of positive regard; and this appears psychologically impossible. For if something is disvalued, we are against it; and if it is regarded, we are for it. Can we be for, and against, the same thing at the same time? Well—to complete the cliché—not, anyhow, 'in the same respect'. When we are valuing or disvaluing forms of action, we are holding them away from the agent, we are considering them as alternative suits of clothes his conduct might put on, to his credit or his discredit. But once he has clothed himself in one of them, if it is a bad one, we may say, 'Poor Henry! He's done it again!' To regret a man's error or even his crime for his own sake is a way of being for him, not against him. We do not at once both disvalue, and regard, the form of the unhappy act. We simply disvalue it; but we *regard* the man expressing himself in it, because he expresses himself in other ways at other times; he is a luminary of whom we regret the present eclipse.

But the more unfortunate choices Henry makes, the harder it is to be all for his 'normal' self, to let ourselves go in the simple warmth of regard for him. Sympathy is the magic word; and yet if we sympathize with a man for failing to pursue a good which he does not value in the least, it is difficult to see what we are sympathizing with: not with the man who is, but with some shadow of a man who should be. And realities, not desirabilities, are the objects of regard. I am to love my neighbour, and not my idea of my neighbour.

The misfit between the absolute regardableness of men, and the relative disvalue of their lives, gives rise to all sorts of strains and impurities in our regard for them. We abdicate all judgement and worship what we should condemn, or we let detached censure freeze regard; or, the most gross and common fault of all, we do not sufficiently see men for what they are in themselves, to regard them, because their lines of action make no easy or harmonious contact with our own.

We are talking now in a somewhat pedantic and general way about what everyone knows to be the chief difficulties of personal life. Every sort of practical 'philosophy', or what does duty for one, grapples with these troubles, and in so doing shows its serious practicality. It is obvious that Christianity claims moral efficacy in claiming to do the same job uniquely well. It commands us to carry regard for our neighbours to the point of loving them as we love ourselves; and it teaches us how to do this by directing us first so to worship God that we love him with all our mind.

The worship of God is most directly brought to support the regarding of man through prayer. Speaking psychologically, and leaving aside all religious mysteries, we can say that prayer places the neighbour we pray for in relation with the action of God, and that it views this action in two lights. On the one hand the action of God is creation; through all the processes of events contributory to the formation of our neighbour, God has shaped and is shaping an unique creature, and is to be reverenced in his handiwork, in the very man as he is. On the other hand, God's action is redemption. Patient of the man's imperfections, God forgives but does not tolerate. For, by a costly and incessant action bearing on the man's free will, he persuades him towards his everlasting good.

Our sole present concern with these sentences of doctrine is to observe their effect on regard for our fellow man. The regard we owe him is unqualified, because it is owed to God through him. And yet he is no mere channel through which regard is paid to God, for God is regarded by regard for what he regards, and what he regards is the man. The worth of the man is determined by his place in God's purposes; and it is not a worth which in any way hides or palliates his imperfections. For it is measured by the infinite cost at which God is willing to redeem him from them. His worth lies, however, in nothing else than in what he actually is, for this is the subject of divine redemption, this very man whom I know: not, indeed, as God knows him; but in so far as I have any capacity for knowing my fellow-creatures at all, what I know is what God redeems.

This is the man whom, with God, I am bound to regard, and prayer itself is an exercise of such regard, which, Christians claim, does not terminate in itself. For though no one lives as he prays, no one who genuinely prays lives as though he did not.

Our business is not with religious commonplace but with its philosophical criticism, and we have in mind a criticism which finds a clue to the meaning of discourse in the uses of it. Now if the whole use of the discourse we have been illustrating, that is to say, of prayer, is denied, then there will be nothing to discuss. But if, for the sake of argument, it is acknowledged, what is the first question to arise? The philosopher wishes to restrict the meaning of language within the bounds of its real use. He will ask, therefore, whether the sober and human task of talking ourselves into due regard for our neighbours can require the use of statements which seriously mean that God, a spirit dwarfing us and them and all our world into insignificance, is the actual maker, producer, and redeemer of men? The terms of the task are, to see how we may so describe men as to regard them worthily; and the means arrived at are, that we place them in an admittedly parabolical frame of description, calling them the objects of divine making and redemption. Surely, then, the real objects of our contemplation are the same at the completion of the task as they were in the first statement of it. All that has been added is a parabolic convention in which to describe them. We have no business with metaphysical assertion; we have all that we require if we set ourselves to feel for our neighbours *as though* they were the creatures, etc., of an infinite living goodness.

Nothing can be more instructive than an examination of this suggestion, and we will take it up in the terms in which it is stated, even though it is necessary, before we do so, to enter a protest. The suggestion makes all theology ridiculous by the implied assumption that religion is *essentially* the discharge of finite obligations by invoking an infinite metaphysical credit. But no one who believes any religion will agree to this for a moment. The inadequacies of our finite equipment for our finite tasks are some slight signs and tokens of our relation to God, but that relation is far more important for its own sake than for its supplementation of human defects. The evidence of God is not essentially that in him we can see our neighbours straight, but that in so seeing our neighbours, we are drawn into relation with him.

The detached critic of belief wields a Morton's fork, and we can do little in our own defence while we leave this instrument in his hands. 'Either,' he says, 'your evidence of God is his special impact on you, or else it is the way things are. If it is his special impact on you, it is something you may acknowledge, but no one else can. If it is the way things are, we should all be able to acknowledge it. But the way things are is the subject of empirical description, or the field of particular action; and though there are many mysterious factors in the natural scene, it is scarcely worth considering whether any one of them can be shown to be infinite, supernatural, and absolute.' Like most sophistical dilemmas, this one is sufficiently exposed by being openly stated. There is no need to choose between an evidence by impact and an evidence lying in the way things are. The impact is through the way things are. The unbelieving mind acknowledges the way things are, but not the divine impact. We try to explain how our view of the way things are is illuminated by our acknowledgement of the divine impact. Our present argument is a case in point.

So much for the protest. We return to the question whether the function of religious language in establishing a proper regard for our neighbour involves a serious intention to assert God's existence. The first point to consider is the relation in general between existential assertion and an attitude of regard. And about this we must say that the paying of regard involves an existential assertion of a special kind. Students of philosophy are most familiar with existential assertions about physical objects, and have, perhaps, learnt to abandon as meaningless or at least unfruitful the question what any physical thing or process 'essentially is'. It is enough to assert that the constituents of our physical environment make themselves felt in the way they environ us. Whatever we have to reckon with on the level of physical action is physically real. But if we are going to *regard* anything we must be convinced not only that it is there, but that it really possesses in itself, and not merely in our sense of it, those characteristics in virtue of which we regard it. The test case is that in which we risk our lives out of regard for another; we certainly should not do so for the most exalted of notions, or for the most useful and enjoyable feature of our environment. The first step to regarding our neighbour as ourself is to see that he is as real as ourself, and that his reality has the same sort of actual structure and quality as our own.

To turn, now, to the theological question. What was the praying mind seen to do? It steadied and reinforced regard for man by relating it to regard for God; or, to put it another way, acknowledged that what makes the unqualified claim on our regard is not simply our neighbour, but our neighbour and God in a special sort of relation with one another. If God is not an object of our regard, or, to speak less artificially, of our worship, the whole action of our prayer is paralysed. But if God is regarded, then he is taken as real, just as seriously as our neighbour is. You may hold that prayer is the highest wisdom or the flimsiest folly, but in any case the assertion of God's existence is integral to it.

Yet even though God's existence is accepted by the praying mind as something beside the existence of the friend for whom prayer is being made, it is not in some fabulous world beside the human that God is recognized or honoured, but in the friend. We distinguish the action of God from the mere conduct and character of our friend, but that does not mean that God's action is expressed to us in terms of something different from the man or his ways. God the creator of the man is seen and regarded in the man, even if the man has rebelled against his creator. Creation is, of course, creation, an unique and uniquely divine act about the nature of which we might philosophize a great deal. But creation is met and acknowledged in its only effect and only possible phenomenon, the creature. Similarly, redemptive love: it is itself, and real in God, but not to be encountered by us except in the case of the man whom it forgives, whom it persuades, and whom it calls. The forgiveness, the persuasion and the calling are acknowledged in the man's actual defects and graces, and in the paths of possible good which open from his actual character or situation.

3

We began this chapter with a distinction between the parables of religious belief, and those fields of common experience *off* which (and not merely *into* which) the parables are read. It seemed that the proper business of a philosophical critique was to examine the parables, and see how they were used; but it appeared that, if we plunged straight into such a critique we might find ourselves all up in the air. And so we decided to start with a description of a commonly acknowledged province of thinking, and show how it receives that immediate religious interpretation which we call 'reading off'. And this we have attempted to do. Even if we have succeeded, we have not reached any end, but only a beginning. We have come round to the parables, though by a more circuitous route; and the parables have still to stand their philosophical trial. For the divinity which we find as it were embedded in the believer's account of his neighbour is already parabolic. What is 'creation'? What is 'redemption'? My neighbour may be the case, but of what is he the case? Creation is a parable from human invention or manufacture; redemption is a tissue of figures from various types of deliverance and restoration met with in human life. Even the divine love which animates both redemption and creation is a parable from human kindness.

Philosophers tend to be less interested in arguments than in the form and force of arguments. We have sketched out an argument: let us now consider what sort of an argument it is. It seems tempting to compare the procedure we have suggested with a classic example. In the *Critique of Pure Reason* Kant raised the ghosts of theological parable; in his moral writings he let them drink the blood of life. First, that is to say, he showed how and out of what materials the parable of creative providence arises, and how purely parabolic, that is to say, how dubious, its logic is. Only afterwards he set out to show that, whatever its logic may be, it is treated as real in our personal or moral life, because the action of moral persons is so directed as to count God in as a real power. As part of a total picture of the world, held away from us and contemplated, the Kantian theological ideas are utterly unconvincing, they are the veriest ghosts of thought. They receive reality when they condition our moral action. Kant's 'world' is the merest diagram; whereas moral action is for him the exercise of real existence and concerns itself with real existences. Kant takes the cosmological diagram first, with its ghostly theological extensions. We propose the opposite order, and begin with the moral life; we give the ghosts the blood first, surmising that, until they have drunk it, they will not speak to us.

But, however tempting the Kantian analogy is, we must not allow it to mislead us. We are not ourselves talking Kantianism; not even Kantianism in reverse. We could not accept as it stands any part of Kant's doctrine, either where it concerns the logic of theological parable or where it concerns the way in which God enters into moral life. Nor can we argue with Kant's assurance. He claimed to give an account of moral principle in which all honest men capable of philosophy must recognize the very form of their consciences. And on the basis of this account he claimed to show them that a duty was incumbent upon them which they could not undertake with any intelligent hope of fulfilling it unless they counted on the action of God. He regarded his argument as a demonstration at both stages, not as a persuasion. He did not persuade us in favour of certain moral principles; he proved that these principles were morality and that morality was these. Nor did he persuade us to see the obligation to justice in the setting of Providential Government; he proved that the very intention to discharge the obligation implied a belief in the Providence.

So at least Kant claimed. We do not claim for our argument any such rigour. It is a persuasion, though, of course, a persuasion of a very special kind. We persuade men of the importance of so contemplating their fellows that they may regard them. We persuade them that regard should acknowledge no limits but those set by the conditions of our life. We persuade them that this regard should be at once so pure and so entire as to find its frustration in the imperfections of men. We persuade them that the frustration is due to an incomplete definition of the object of regard—that what claims our regard is not simply our neighbour, but God in our neighbour and our neighbour in God. Here are four stages of persuasion, and at any stage the persuasion can fail. We shall probably have to be content, like Gideon, to reduce our following step by step as we advance. Most of our fellow-tribesmen will take the first step with us; they will go with us in admitting a duty to cultivate regard for their neighbours. It's a persuasion of which they are already persuaded. But the next step may well halve our following, the third halve it again, and the fourth yet again.

Those who draw their swords for the Lord are aware that they must face the Gideon predicament. If the canon is laid down that nothing is to be accepted for philosophical consideration but what is at least virtually contained in the flattest common sense and that the *homme moyen sensuel* is to be the measure of all things, the Christian argument has nothing to say. We know, surely, that the acknowledgement of God involves a sharpening and

K

stirring of the conscience, an acceptance of unqualified claims. This acceptance may be forced upon us in more ways than one: through our being thrown into situations which bring the weight of such claims to bear on us; through the example of others; through verbal persuasion.

Acquiescence in the Gideon predicament may suggest an ultimate reliance on the exquisite discernment of a spiritual élite, who have cultivated their sentiments to a pitch of unreal refinement. Such a suggestion insinuates artificiality and saps the force of the persuasive argument. No doubt people can make a cult of moral refinement and reflect curiously on the purity of their personal attitudes, especially if they have no more pressing business on hand. But their doing so may appear an odd basis for serious metaphysical belief.

We have several things to say about this suspicion, and here is the first. Although our persuasive argument, as it advances, may lose adherents, it begins not from any point of special exquisiteness but from the broad platitudes of the moral mind. Nor, in advancing, does it leave the main road for any finicking bypaths; it merely takes a platitudinous persuasion in deadly earnest and follows it as far as it leads. The principle of utter devotion or unlimited regard is acceptable to the most work-a-day people. When Gideon's army has become small enough to reach its objective, he finds himself still surrounded by common faces, indistinguishable from those which turned away.

Now to the second point. The sort of enthusiasm which leads the three hundred to follow Gideon is not anything induced by his militant demagogy, nor is it anything peculiar to the emotional constitution of the three hundred. On every side we see men for whom it is a necessity to acknowledge an absolute claim and to spend themselves in answering it. If they are not shouting for the Lord and Gideon, they will be crying 'One race, one realm, one leader' or whatever is the enthusiasm of the time. Gideon has no need to create devotion, he need only capture and direct it. It is not, of course, evident without examination that the capacity for devotion to an object of limitless regard belongs to the moral perceptiveness of man. It might be an endemic psychological disease; and if it is not a disease itself, it is unquestionably liable to dangerous diseases. Maybe it could be wholly eliminated by conditioning or psychological manipulation; and so, perhaps, could many of what we take to be features of the human spirit. Surgical interference with the brain might ensure an even more effective riddance. But whether such a modification of the human being would ennoble or debase him is what we should have to judge, and could not evade judging; let everyone consider what he thinks.

Devotion, though constantly deceived, and bestowing its worship on preposterous objects, must suppose them to call for what it bestows on them; for otherwise it loses the nature of devotion. And this consideration brings us to the third point we have to make about the seriousness of our persuasive argument. It is not a persuasion towards adopting a policy or taking up an attitude, although it involves doing both. No, primarily it is the persuasion to acknowledge a claim. Now it may be that there is something pedantic and gratuitous about refining too much upon moral self-culture whether individual or corporate; and that persuasions about this, pushed beyond a point, become fantastic and impertinent. But if what our neighbours are, whether in themselves or as the objects of divine care, claims our devotion, then it seems we can scarcely go too far in advancing a persuasion which has the effect of bringing us to acknowledge both the claim and the reality which makes the claim. We are in no danger of being over-nice in clearing our eyes so that they may see.

The metaphor of sight, though a very violent figure in this connection, is useful by way of corrective to a far more disastrous linguistic violence. Logic establishes that no 'is' implies an 'ought', no factual assertion allows the inference of an imperative. There is nothing of which the claim upon our attention or action can be deduced from the descriptions we give ourselves of what it is like. The only sort of sentence from which such a claim could be deduced would be a precept commanding us to bestow attention or action of a certain sort upon a class of objects inclusive of the thing before us. But such a precept appears itself to rest on something more fundamental: the decision that such behaviour is the appropriate reaction to such an object. And so we are led on to say that our duties to our neighbour are what *we decide* to be due. The 'we' is editorial; it stands for that enlightened body of opinion which we represent. *We have decided* that drowning strangers are to be rescued, not laughed at. Lucky for them; they might have got into deep water among the Hottentots, who have made the opposite decision.

Such a way of talking is, to say the least, misleading. In making our 'decision' we are not expressing our royal pleasure as joint sovereigns of a moral universe. The action is not due because we decide it shall be. What we decide, or come to a common mind about, is that it is due. Heaven help the Hottentots; but if we go Hottentot, heaven will not help us. We decide that the action is due; and even this is not a decision simply about the action. We do not decide that the rescue as such is an obligatory performance: as we get the dog to regard it as due that he should fish out of the pond the stick we have thrown. What we come to a mind about is that our fellow-man is such that we should assist him in danger, whether he happens to enjoy the advantage of our acquaintance or not. And so it is natural to say that we *see* something about him, namely that his humanity claims our succour.

It is a logical truth that the claim made on us by the drowning man cannot be deduced from any genuinely descriptive statements we may make either about him or about ourselves; but that is not to deny that the claim arises out of his nature and ours. All the logical negative excludes is that it arises from descriptive statement by way of logical implication. It arises, nevertheless; it is not to be deduced, but acknowledged in the way in which basic non-conventional claims are acknowledged. And if we say that we have *decided* such a claim, we mean that we have come to an acknowledgement of it, after whatever contemplation or consideration we may use for getting into a position to be capable of such acknowledgement.

To return, now, to our persuasive argument. If we exercise persuasion on moral Hottentots we are not just spoiling the natives; we are putting them in the way of acknowledging real claims which will else go unregarded. It is a pity, for example, that the strangers in their rivers should drown. But how do we know that they are wrong and we are right? Why shouldn't the Hottentots start working among us? Let them, and let's see who can open the others' eyes to more, the Hottentots or we.

The recognition of our neighbours' claim upon us arises out of our knowledge of them; but is it, in addition, itself a sort of knowledge about them? Perhaps this is a question of words. It does not add to our other knowledge of them, our factual knowledge, that is. 'Claimingness' in the moral sense is not an addition to such a list of characteristics as those of being heavy, yellow-haired, malleable, easily led, and consolable with *aqua vitae*. And yet I do not find I wish to deny that the exercise of a claim upon me by my neighbour's existence is in any sense a fact about him, or to say that whatever fact there is lies simply in response on my part.

It even appears to me that there is a significant analogy between moral knowledge and physical knowledge. My knowledge of the physical properties of things is all, in the end, reducible to my discovery of the ways in which they limit and condition my bodily being and action: to such facts as that I can walk across the floor and not through the wall. I *cannot* walk through the wall, I *must not* override my neighbour. I *cannot* escape the gravitational pull, I *must not* evade the claim of kindred. If the 'active properties' of bodies are any sort of facts about them, why are not the 'claimingnesses' of persons some sort of facts about them?

If such a way of speaking is at all justified, and if the Christian's way of taking his moral life is the right one, then a fact about God is a part of his daily experience. For the personal claim which meets him on every hand is exerted not simply by men, but by God. So the Christian may think; but he must not suppose that such a fact about God can conceivably stand alone. A God who was simply 'the X with the absolute claim' could exert no claim at all. The 'claimingness' of anything is always consequent upon what we take that thing to be. And, as we said in the body of our argument, the God who makes claims upon us through our fellows is taken to be their maker and redeemer. The consideration of moral experience uncovers a point at which the faith of Christians can most easily be seen to bear upon their lives. It is no substitute for examining the faith.

Philosophical Theology
The Analysis of Faith

God and Verification 1
The Nature of God as Personal Act†

The Christian religion is entirely concerned with the worship and service of God, the Being or Spirit who is not less actual, or seriously taken, than finite spirits, but far more so. No analysis or account which evacuates the seriousness of statements about his acts of knowing, willing, loving, etc., is of the least use to us, or to be considered otherwise than as an explosion of our faith.

When we say that God *is*, we mean primarily that he exercises his existence, not that a body of phenomena of any kind presents him to our knowledge. The same is true of our statements about other persons. It may be true (if you and Ryle like) that what other persons do does not add up to much beyond what we can perceive them to do: that (so to speak) their action describes a diagram in space which is the diagram made by the phenomena of their action. Even so, to say that the events perceptibly occur, and to say that the person is exercising his 'life', is to say different things.

When we say that God exercises personal acts, we mean primarily just that. No doubt we must also mean that something does the duty of perceptible phenomena in making some of his personal acts apprehensible to us, or why should we be talking about them? But let us for the moment abstract from the 'evidences' and consider the personal acts.

The problem of conceiving God as personal act has not altered materially (that I am aware of) since the thirteenth century. We conceive his active existence as an infinitely higher *analogon* to our own—that is to say, we do not conceive it in its proper form at all;[1] and if we could, then by everyone's admission God would not be God. It is possible for any believing logician, with any box of logical tools which are adequate for talking about persons and acts, to refine upon and describe the mind's process in shooting

† Written for a philosophical conference at Windsor, 1951, in the form of a letter to its convener, Miss Dorothy Emmet.

her analogical arrows at that transcendent mark. The result of such logical descriptions will at the best be something which believers accept because it describes their groping after the transcendent, and unbelievers reject because what is groped after transcends the groping.

The problems which are new to our age are not concerned with the venerable puzzle of 'analogy of being', in so far as an attitude of disbelief towards the transcendent as such prevails. Our special problems are concerned with the 'phenomena' by which that supreme Act which is God 'appears' to us. It used to be said that the 'phenomena' of God's act were just everything, for all finite, secondary causes referred us to a Cause infinite and 'first' and so forth. And doubtless to a believing mind *caeli enarrant*, etc. [the beginning of Psalm 19—'The heavens declare the glory of God']. But we shall probably wish to draw a distinction between the field of sheer belief and the field of evidence. Undoubtedly the mind, convinced of God by whatever evidence, extends her faith to a belief that God's hand is in all things: as we extend our perceptions of the intelligent purpose in certain of X's actions to a general supposition of intelligent policy where we cannot make it out. It may be, indeed, that there is some faint 'evidence' in the whole field of finite things, but if it does not stand by itself, it is unwise to begin with it.

If we look at the ancient method of finding God in the whole field, i.e. the universe, we can see that it was done by universal anthropomorphy, the universe was the macrocosm of our microcosm. Man is, in truth, taken as the clue to the whole, and it is probably stupid to suppose that we can escape from this and still think theologically. Nevertheless, man is not the clue in the ancient manner, we cannot be as naïve as that. But if we cannot say that ourself (or our neighbour) is by far the most informative instance to us of a 'creature', from which the 'creaturehood' of all other things must be conjectured or interpreted, then we are unlikely to persist in religious belief. Here, then, is the field of evidence, or of greatest evidence.

A faith in providence is based on the belief that God wields all agents or active persons from within, and not (as it were) by the external compulsion of superior force: they 'obey' him. What this 'obedience' is cannot be understood in them, but (if at all) in ourselves. The primary religious fact is the coincidence of the Infinite Person and the finite person in the enactment of the finite person's 'obedient' acts,[2] for they are not only 'obedient' but 'enabled' or inspired'. This primary fact gives rise to the so-called 'problem' of grace and free will, and (at its extreme) of God and Man in Christ. Here are antinomies which are not really problems of religion but the statement of what religious existence is. If we are not tough enough to assert that the act of religious obedience is our privileged access to the knowledge of God, we shall be beaten out of the field. And when it is said to us, 'But surely this is all metaphor? You can't be so un-Occamist as to accept a *maximum* hypothesis to account for these trivial and limited facts?' we shall not be shaken. And, as evidence that non-believers have some smothered perception of what they reject, we shall point to the persistence of those 'limiting' questions, that demand for the authority behind all authorities, and the 'Cause' behind all causes or reasons.[3]

Once it is seen that the infinite being condescends to act in and as his creature, it becomes possible to look for his self-disclosures or *revelations*; and that, we know, is where Christianity starts.

Lastly, to turn back to our philosophical situation: if we are serious in our desire to philosophize our theology, we must attempt to describe the realm which, let us say, Gabriel Marcel describes;[4] and, when we have got a good deal of description, try to introduce some order and economy, and advance to a reflection on logical form. But if our philosophical equipment deals only with the logic of the sciences; of ethical reasoning *in abstracto*; of language as such, and of statements about a self which chatters to itself and others, profits from experience, keeps studied rules and exercises acquired skills: then I do not think we have any special cause to complain that there is a wide gulf between our philosophic practice and our religious faith. We are not suffering from too much logic, but from too little contemplation.

God and Verification 2
On Verifying the Divine Providence†

I want to begin by recurring to the problem about old Mr Jones's rheumatism and the benevolence of God. If God is omnipotent and allows it, is not his benevolence being interpreted in a Pickwickian, indeed a nugatory sense? And is not the principle of the Pickwickianism or nugification this, that faith sets up a determination that nothing shall count against the benevolence of God?

When the problem is put to us like this, we feel immediately that we are being drawn on to false ground, but we do not immediately perceive what the falsity of our situation is, or how to remedy it. My first reaction is to apply a routine distinction. Is the problem being put as one belonging to natural, or to revealed, theology? The distinction between natural and revealed theology may not be what it has been cracked up to be,[1] but it is at the worst a traditional way of indicating different arguments and the problem of old Mr Jones's rheumatism looks very different in the two contexts.

The context in natural theology would be something like this. The appreciation of the 'contingency' of things leads us on to a belief in a simple or absolute 'Cause'. (I apologize for 'contingency' and 'cause'. These are traditional terms. We know how to put a complexion on them, but this is not the moment.) Well, the simple and absolute being is conceived by us as a spiritual being, and a purely good being: and therefore as a charitable or benevolent being. But if so, what about Mr Jones's rheumatism? On the one side, it is an aggravated example of contingency, and so part of the 'evidence' (so to speak) for God. 'Change and decay in all around I see', and especially in Mr Jones. But on the other side it is a difficulty in the way of conceiving how the divine benevolence takes effect. It is a difficulty, but a difficulty by which, in the context of this argument, we have no need whatever to be daunted.

† Written sometime between 1951 and 1954.

The assertion of God's benevolence, in this argument, does not arise from an attempt to describe the way in which God appears to conduct the world, but from a description of the sort of being who transcends the world's contingency and general messiness. The problem, how the goodness of this transcendent being is compatible with the world's coming out as messy as it does, or how his benevolence takes effect on or in such a world, undoubtedly remains. But so far as our chosen argument goes, we have a perfect right to decline any attempt at a solution. Perhaps the angels know what the solution is, but we haven't the data. The argument from contingency is an argument from one aspect of things abstracted, namely their contingency. And it is possible to say that we are capable of having some grasp of the relation of this abstracted aspect of things to God's perfection, but incapable of grasping the relation of particular occurrences to God's providence. So we assert God's formal perfection, including his benevolence, but we are agnostic about the bearings of this on Mr Jones's rheumatism as a case of apparently unmerited and apparently useless suffering.

So much for the question in 'natural theology'. But, as Flew and Nowell-Smith would be quick to point out, men do not live by natural theology: they are not content to say that God must be kind, they claim to show, or at least conceive, how his kindness takes effect; and there's the trouble. Very good. But now we come into the realm of revealed theology or, to speak more particularly, of the Christian religion. And in the Christian religion we do not, in practice, encounter the difficulty these philosophers set before us. The plausibility of their argument turns, in fact, on a confusion between the way of thinking which belongs to natural theology, and that which belongs to revealed theology. They cull from Christianity the claim of faith to encounter God's goodness in detail, but they turn it away from the particular range of redemptive activity in which Christianity declares the goodness of God to be reliably visible, and make of it a flat-rate generalization about good things and bad things, skylarks and earthquakes, happy marriages and fits of the gout. The Christian, having encountered the goodness of God where it can reliably be encountered—in the realm of grace—of course *believes* that God is justified in all his works, without being able to see in detail how. But there is no difficulty of a logical kind arising from such an act of belief. It is sufficiently analogous to the case of our judging of a man's actions into which we have no insight, from those actions of his into which we have some insight.

So far I have made a sort of rude *prooemium* out of a dogmatic handling of the distinction between natural and revealed theology. But I am not going to follow that line out any further. It seems more profitable to do what was suggested last time, and consider how a man comes to believe the Christian faith, and what things appear to probabilify that faith to him, and what appear to put obstacles in his way. Then we shall see how far the goodness of God is open to verification/falsification, and how it happens.

The story I shall tell will be a true story. But I shall corrupt it in two ways. I shall make the convert more explicitly intelligent than he was and I shall make him a little more typical than he was —straighten out the kinks of idiosyncrasy. What is worse, I shall mix the stages of my exposition. I shall not tell the story first and moralize afterwards. I shall moralize all over the place and as the fit takes me.

The convert, whom it will be convenient to call Paul, had not been reared in Christianity, but he was acquainted in a careless and external way with the pattern of Christian thinking. Christian thinking is a way of thinking which is normally handed on from parent to child: a way of conceiving of God and of relating everything to him through Christ; an art of interpretation as well as a body of dogma. This sort of thinking is learnt as so many other ways of thinking are learnt, a favourite theme with Gilbert Ryle. But if it is persisted in, and becomes the form or clothing of a lively faith, it is because it is found in some way to be fruitful, to bring out the full savour and profoundest sense of existence. The reasons why the convert *adopts* our way of thinking will not be different from the reasons why we *persist* in it. But since the adoption of a creed is more dramatic than the persistence in a creed, it will bring out the reasons for upholding that creed more evidently.

The young Paul happened to be sent by his ungodly family to a day school of which the headmaster, whom we will call Stephen, was a convinced Christian, and the Christian way of thinking was undoubtedly commended to him by this master's example. Here was a serious and worthy man who pinned his life to the Christian faith. We may call this an external predisposing cause, apart from which Paul would scarcely have begun to take seriously a religion he had been taught to deride. A second external predisposing cause was Paul's unhappiness. His father had died, his life was not sweet to him. Dissatisfaction or duress is certainly not a positive ground for belief in Christianity; whether in the case of the young Paul unhappy at school, or in the case of the prisoner in the concentration-camp. Such a condition is a negative external pre-disposing cause, in so far as it makes the quest for the true human good a living issue. If you are easily satisfied with life as it is, all the less motive for looking further. So we will call Paul's unhappiness a negative external predisposing cause, and Stephen's example a positive external predisposing cause.

But there were also *intrinsic* predisposing factors, as Ananias, Paul's college chaplain, became aware when Paul came up to the University of Damascus. By an intrinsic predisposing factor, I mean an actual though obscure direction of the young man's mind towards belief: let us call it crypto-theism or indeterminate spirituality. Scenes of natural beauty, the infinite variety and fertility of nature, appeared to him to express something beyond themselves; and the moral conscience wore the appearance of an absolute demand. Ananias remembers working away for some time at these points, pressing nature and conscience on the young man in the hope that they might become theophanic, God-manifesting. Ananias was not (let us hope) conducting a bogus philosophical argument to prove that no account of any moral conscience, or any natural beauty, can be given without dragging in theology. That would be the mishandling of an abstract question, whereas what Ananias did was to turn attention upon a concrete experience with the hope of opening up a deeper penetration into it.

All this belonged to the realm of what used to be called natural theology: Paul was discovering, that is, that natural facts, moral judgement and visual landscape (let us say) were actually ex-perienced by him as a showing of God. When I say that they were actually so experienced by him, I mean that a theistic description of them appeared to do them more justice than any other; and that ready-armed with such a description, he could get more out of these sources of experience.

So far we have dealt with predispositions towards faith. But faith begins when Paul is ready to consider whether the God of conscience and nature has not personally revealed himself in Christ and entered into supernatural dealings with us, through things which are not parts of natural experience at all: prayer and grace and a revealed Will and a mystical body.

What can we say about the causes of faith itself? The young Paul reads and discusses the New Testament, and the first cause of faith is the mere force of the divine Word as communication. Here is something arresting, profound, realistic, backed by unmistakable conviction, beyond human wit to invent, and so on. The mere force of communication, what (slightly to pervert Cartesian terms) we may call its objective reality, is a perfectly sound initial ground for belief; in spite of the existence of propaganda, oratory, and false enthusiasm. I am always giving human witnesses initial credence on such grounds. 'If we received the witness of men, the witness of God is greater, and this is the witness of God, which he has witnessed concerning his Son.' But (and here we may cast a crumb to Nowell-Smith and Flew) not everything in the New Testament contributes to the impress of its objective reality on the young Paul's mind: indeed, many things weaken it. The testimony is impaired by what seems to him the excessive credulity of the witnesses about physical miracle, and their occasionally unedifying irascibility, and the inferiority (in some points) of their code of manners to ours. If the young Paul comes to accept explanations of these difficulties, it is not because the difficulties have no force, or fail to tell against belief, but because they are overborne by the positive factors. I should wish, as a theologian, to say much about the esential supernaturality of the divine Word and of the Holy Spirit enlightening the hearer's mind to apprehend it;[2] but though it may be that the mind unaided by God would not appreciate the force of divine communication, the force of communication is still something about which philosophers can discourse. And in the case of divine communication it inevitably plays a more important part than in the case of human communication. If we accept human communication as forcible, it in fact convinces us of two things: (a) that an actual person is addressing us, (b) that what he says is important. We readily accept (a) and get straight on to (b). But in the case of divine communication, to be convinced of (a) is just as crucial as to be convinced of (b) indeed, the two matters of conviction are inseparable and virtually identical. *If* God is really addressing me, (a) then what he says is important, (b) for God is no trifler. And conversely, *if* the communication which is the Gospel is important, (b) then it comes from the mouth of God, (a) for otherwise it is an imposture or a phantasy, and so not important (in the sense taken).

However much we accept the immediate force of communication, we do not escape from verification. We may not, indeed, seek for verification, but we may have verification thrust upon us. If someone describes to me the road in front of me, I may believe him like an oracle, but the actual road travelled will either confirm or refute my oracular mentor. And such appears to be the situation of the convert: when Bunyan dreamt of Christian, Evangelist and the King's highway, he fell into a symbolism which is virtually inescapable. The Word which the young Paul believed created expectations which could not fail to strike against the facts of existence.

Let me pause and reflect upon the Word of God and the range of immediate expectation to which it gives rise. Now the Word of God, as the girl Damaris complains in my story for the children, is a terrible jumble of logical types, and the beginning of wisdom for logicians is to recognize this. Every Word of God is, or tends to be assertory, operative, imperative and promissory all at once. 'Ye are my sons and daughters, saith the Lord.' First, this is a statement of actual relation, and so assertory; second, it is a divine recognition of that relation, and so operative: it is a υἱοθεσία ['adoption as a son, Rom. 8.15]; third, it is an injunction to filial obedience, and so imperative; and fourth, it is an assurance of paternal benevolence, and so promissory. I said elsewhere in my story for the children that the logic of religious language was a subject for the advanced class, and if that is so, it is partly because of the subtlety of the relations between the four senses I have intimated, and others may be as well. But that, as the Philosopher liked to say, would be more germane to a different enquiry, ἑτέρας σκέψεως οἰκειότερον [cf. *Nicomachean Ethics*, 1155b 7]. What concerns us here is to enquire in which of the four senses the revealed Word is most evidently verifiable; and we must answer, in the promissory sense. The assertions are, on the face of them, about invisible facts, not verifiable here and now; the operative sense confers right or

L

status, of which the reality lies in the *intentio operantis* and is not forthwith verifiable; the imperative sense is not to be verified but to be obeyed. Part of the promissory sense refers to the world to come, and is not verifiable here and now, but part of it refers to our present life and is in some sense verifiable. Only the promissory sense is verifiable, but that does not mean that the other three senses are left totally devoid of practical verification, because the relation between the four senses is such, that the verification of the one confirms the other.

All this, without any explicit logical analysis, is understood practically by the young Paul, and the verification of the divine promise becomes the vital battleground of faith. What does he suppose to be divinely promised to him? Certainly not (this is for Nowell-Smith and Flew) that he will be exempt from pain, sorrow, worldly disappointment or premature death. None of these things, therefore, would of themselves be falsifications of the promises. But if the attempt to worship and to pray were predominantly and in every sense experienced as frustration; if penitence brought no renewal of grace whereby to fulfil the divine commands; if, in fact, the way on which he had set his feet turned out to be simply unwalkable, and 'I will not fail thee nor forsake thee' were wholly falsified in the life of grace, then the young Paul would cease at length to believe.

In fact, he meets with plenty of discouragements and so there are improbabilifying factors here also to gladden the hearts of Nowell-Smith and young Flew. Learning to pray and to co-operate with grace is not easy. And this, not old Mr Jones's rheumatism, is the real *locus*, the *Sitz im Leben*, of that empirical battle of faith of which Quinton, in his paper to the Aquinas Society, gave so cruel and so telling a caricature: only that he misapplied it to stupid commonplaces like God's benevolence and divine protection from bumps in the night.*

The truth which lies so open to caricature is this. The divine promises are not verified in the exact sense in which they are first understood. For every further experience of 'walking with God'

---

* An unpublished paper, 'Statements about God', which its author now describes (in a letter, 7 April 1972) as 'a pretty brashly positivistic knockabout turn'. (Although Farrer actually wrote 'Socratic Club', it is Mr Quinton's recollection that it was delivered to the Aquinas Society.)—Ed.

(if I may allow myself so scriptural an expression) is an experience to which previous experience offers no more than analogy. We do not know what it is until we are there. Jesus Christ fulfilled the messianic promises, but not in the form in which they were stated or in the form in which they had been understood. He was seen after the event to have fulfilled them analogically. This was inevitable, because he could be known by acquaintance only. So it is with all the promises of God. The analogical relation of Jesus Christ to the promises was revealed when he was crucified by the literal sense of them: that is, for not being the messiah of literal expectation. And the revelation of the true Christ in the heart is not achieved without a certain crucifixion, an agony of discovering the purity and supernaturality of the spiritual good; that it consists not in sensible consolations, etc.

How this will be caricatured by the unsympathetic is obvious. To them the promise as originally understood, i.e. with its analogical statements taken literally, means something and is logically respectable. But the mysterious reinterpretation of it in spiritual use is unintelligible and logically infamous. For πνευματικὰ . . . πνευματικῶς ἀνακρίνεται: spiritual things are spiritually discerned, and the unspiritual (in the relevant sense) haven't a clue. So they say that the original full-blooded content of the promises is evasively emptied out by the believers when it is falsified by the facts of experience, and a bogus spiritual content substituted, so guarded with negative conditions that the fulfilment of the promise can no longer ever be verified or falsified. It is perfectly clear why unbelievers say this, and why believers cannot refute them; again, from the believers' point of view, it is perfectly clear why the unbelievers' assault has no effect.

The last thing I wish to suggest is that the young Paul supposes the ways of God to be appreciable in privileged and invisible spiritual events only. On the contrary, everything that happens has a bearing on the ways of God with him and with mankind: fits of illness and so on among the rest. God works all things together for good for those that love him, but it is in the agape and the working out of the predestination of the saints that this is understood. It cannot be understood profanely. But it must be understood inclusively, and if the young Paul reads the old Paul he will be sufficiently warned that all sorts of apparently negative factors, tribulation, persecutions, nakedness, swords, may have to be counted in, before it can firmly be declared, ἐν τούτοις πᾶσιν ὑπερνικῶμεν ['in all these things we are more than conquerors'— Rom. 8.37].

A final remark about verification: to accept any empirical verification in religious experience is to lay oneself open to the charge of accepting the absurd simplisms of the nineteenth-century philosophy of religious experience, of which the extreme form represented theology as a system of probable hypotheses barely covering the religious experiences people have had. But to assert such a doctrine is equivalent to saying that the whole four-fold sense of religious language is open to direct empirical verification. That is, in our view, absurd. Only a small part of the promissory sense is practically verifiable. Whereunto is this matter like? Like a father who has promised to take his child to the zoo. The child has never been to the zoo. But the first part of the promise, i.e. to take the child on the train to Regent's Park, is already in the course of execution. It is only when the last part of the promise is executed that the principal implied assertions will be fully verifiable: i.e. that there is a paradise in Regent's Park containing lions and eagles. Meanwhile not only are the lions and eagles unverifiable, their very nature can only be conjectured from cats and sparrows, and from imperfect scribblings and descriptions. But how misleading philosophical parables are! For the child is not in the zoo until it arrives there, and when it arrives there, it sees the wonderful creatures of God in the fair light of day. Whereas the Christian is already in the mystical body of Christ (such is his faith) even though the most part of what the Word of God says about that mystical body will only become manifest, clear and verifiable at the end of the pilgrimage.

Signification†

This paper was supposed to have been about signification, what it is. But I am incurably metaphysical and I have failed to isolate the topic of signification. Instead of that, I have built up a grandiose structure about the *genesis* of signification and the classes of things first signified. I am not altogether clear what this account I am going to give is an account of. Am I going to give a foreshortened history, but still a history, of how signification in fact arose in evolutionary development? Or is my account non-historical, a mere exposition of the pattern of our present consciousness, the *always basic* appearing in my myth as the *temporally prior*? I fear I do not know: it will be like John Locke deducing civil society from the state of nature. Now John Locke is a great example, but he is also a bad example.

Before there was anything we can call thinking, or even meaning, there was action upon imagination. Mere imagination on which no action was to be based, would be a luxury unconceivable at a low level of animal development: τί γὰρ χρήσιμον ἂν ἐίη?* An animal which acted upon imagination might be said to attach a significance to that imagination; e.g. if, on the memory-image of peanuts found here, he stopped and digged. This would be to give

† A paper read to the Metaphysicals, which explains both its style and the rather abrupt ending. Its date is important. Being written on the reverse side of discarded drafts of *A Rebirth of Images* (see Farrer's preface, p. 5–10), it establishes Farrer's treatment of language as quite early. It is interesting to note that Wittgenstein's *Philosophical Investigations*, to which it bears some analogy, was not published until 1953.

* 'What use would it be?'—a reference to the Aristotelian principle that nature does nothing without reason. See *de Generatione Animalium* 744a 36, b16; *De Caelo* 291a 24, b13; *de Partibus Animalium* 686a 22; and esp. *De Anima* 432b 21 where Aristotle maintains that faculties can be understood only by their functions and activities (II. 3, 4), and discusses the relation of imagination to action (III. 9–12)—Ed.

the imagination the significance 'something edible here'. Yet in fact nothing would be expressed or signified, as we understand signification. To dig for food is not to symbolize the idea of the edible, but to dig for it. That pigs cannot talk is not an accident, for even if they could, they would have nothing to say.

To act upon imagination is to attach significance to our imagining, but not to express it. Nevertheless, action upon imagination is the seed out of which *speech* will grow. Before we can see how it grows, we must observe another way in which significance was attached, before it was expressed. Pig A digs for the peanuts; Pig B sees him at it, and joins in the hunt. Thereby she attaches to Pig A's behaviour the significance 'digging for peanuts', or at least the significance 'on to a good thing'. It is out of such attach-ment of significance that the *understanding* of speech will grow, although, at this stage, nothing is yet understood. The pig is un-intellectual: she does not interpret to herself the behaviour of her colleague; she digs for peanuts.

Speech is a social phenomenon, and arises when Pig A, having fallen in love with Pig B, desires to bring her in on a good thing. This he does by symbolic sound or gesture. If he makes a fuss about the digging, with intent to attract attention to what he is doing, and guffles noisily, to attract attention to what he is eating, he has perhaps crossed the Rubicon and begun to talk. We may now say that he *intends* a meaning, that the symbolic acts or noises *signify* that meaning, and that Pig B (with luck) *understands* that meaning.

The beginning of thinking, i.e. of expressing a meaning to one-self, is talking, i.e. the expressing of it to someone else. In express-ing (with intention) for another's benefit, we first *thought*, i.e. constructed an expression of our own meaning, and so entered into possession of that meaning. Yet we had no idea that we were doing this. Our purpose was to *communicate* a meaning which, indeed, we did not possess as meaning, but did possess as our active existence. I do not *know* that I am digging for peanuts, but I *am* digging for peanuts. I set out to tell you what I am doing, and in the process come to know what I am doing. But of this subjective by-product to communication, I am scarcely aware. The implicit (digging with intention) has merely been raised into explicitness (knowing that I dig), and this is not the sort of change that a pig will observe. For you, on the other hand, a real and startling change has come about. You did not know that here were peanuts, or that I was digging for them. Now you know. What an illumination!

It follows that talk is first said to signify the meaning of a talker to one who understands him. It is only at a stage of unnatural and philosophic refinement that talk is seen to signify our own meaning to ourselves; or that we talk to ourselves, to find out what we mean, or to construct a meaning for ourselves.

There are two aspects to the primitive speech-situation: there is the noteworthy environmental factor; and there is the intended response. These will naturally find expression in nouns and verbs respectively: e.g. Peanuts, and Dig. The verb requires at this stage neither person, mood, nor tense; and the noun neither predicate nor copula. 'Peanuts: dig' is all we need to say; or 'Bull: run'; or whatever it be.

Nouns may soon associate adjectives with themselves: e.g. 'Mad bull', 'Ripe peanuts'. The use of them is taken to be statement. The statement is not primarily significant because we know how to verify it, but because we propose to act upon it. E.g. I do know how to verify a *fugiendum* [literally, 'a thing to be fled from'] or rather, I have a lively fear that it will verify itself, namely as malevolent and horned: my aim is, so to act, that no verification may take place. The first sort of verification is tentative use, or contact: all right with peanuts and hedgehogs, no good with bulls. Next comes surveying from fresh positions adopted for the purpose; last, artificially arranged tests, e.g. *aqua regia*.*

Noun-thinking (what have we here?) and verb-thinking (what are we doing about it?) fuse. If the two pigs are both sick of peanuts, they may understand one another's *malaise* and communicate

---

* The reference is presumably to Locke, *An Essay Concerning Human Understanding* (II. 23. 10.; cf. Hume, *Treatise*, I. 1. 6.), where solubility in *aqua regia* is mentioned as a test for gold—Ed.

their intentions about remedies. But if the two pigs are sick of one another, they understand one another's malady, indeed, and aggravate their own thereby: but the result is not communication. The subject of pigly *Einfühlung* ['sympathetic understanding, empathy'] becomes an environmental factor to be coped with. The thinking is *verb* thinking ('Proposing to tusk me, the swine'), but yet it is about a *noun* (a distinguished environmental factor about which something must be done). Not other pigs only, but bulls, then even rain and wind, may come to be thought of as active, i.e. thought of in verb-thinking. (The verb 'to be' is not, of course, a verb within the meaning of the act.)

There were three pigs who became philosophers; and thus they reasoned. The first pig said: We have arrived at a remarkable power, the power of knowing. And how do we know? Through expressed sentences. We know, then, what the sentences signify. And what do the sentences signify? A meaning. And in what can a meaning be found? In sentences. What then is the object of knowledge? It is that which perfect sentences would express. There is, for example, the sentence describing what it is to be a pig, and if this sentence could be made perfect, it would express sheer pighood, or the pig-in-itself. Knowledge is of what is: in so far as known, 'what is' may be called *a meaning*; in so far as subsistent, it may be called *an essence*. This pig philosophized from the nature of talk: we will call him a panlogist. He had broad shoulders, and the pigs called his system broad-shoulder-ism: the Greek pigs had a name for it.*

The second pig reasoned thus: The meanings of sentences are certainly conditioned by the system of language, but we do not talk about meanings, in talking, we *mean*; and the part of our meaning which intends reality is the part which means things, and finds first expression in nouns and adjectives. There is something *there*, to which we take up an attitude. As to the attitude we take, that is the province of verb-talk. But verb-talk is not properly to be applied to things. They are not taking up attitudes, or cannot be known to be, for how do we get inside their skins? All we know about them is, that they throw recognizable

---

* A pun on the name Plato—πλατων—meaning 'broad-shouldered'—Ed.

phenomena in series, and that we can get more of their pattern by looking for it, or testing for it. The language we use about things is shot through and through with verb-talk, more's the pity: but verb-talk is forever unverifiable. We can never know what things are up to, or whether they are up to anything. All we can know is a series of actual effects. Verb-talk about things should be reduced to the verbs which are no true verbs, express no *doing*: To begin, to cease, to be there, to change place, to change in quality. So we shall purify language, in such a way that it can be tested by perceptible effects, or by other pieces of language, one or the other. And we shall be able to make the sense of all terms and all sentences so clear and well-agreed, that the significance of a sentence will be independent of any intuitive or sympathetic estimate of the speaker's intention. To make quite sure of this, we will make it a rule in our philosophic debates, that the speakers shall always misunderstand one another as far as the verbal formulae used allow them to do! This pig philosophized from the *facts* envisaged in the language-situation, and we will call him a factualist.

The third pig reasoned as follows: It is very foolish to eliminate the sympathetic understanding of personal intention, for it was out of such understanding that language grew. If we had not understood behaviour as behaviour, we should never have understood formalized behaviour, specialized for the purpose of communication, i.e. language.[1] How far formalization goes, how far the personal, intuitive, or poetical type of understanding is called into play, is not a matter of principle, nor is there any reason to suppose that speech communicates factual truth in proportion as it is formalized, or in proportion as it is verifiable. In fact, our first understanding is of action; out of that everything grows. Verb-talk alone, talk about *doing*, is understanding in the proper sense: for here we understand other *beings*, e.g. pigs, even bulls. Whereas the so-called understanding of facts is no understanding of the facts, but only of the applicability of formulae to the facts. It is the business of a philosophical pig to understand not formulae, but realities. Only action can be understood. It is up to us, then, to trace out action in all its forms, and its most distant analogies: for the faintest analogy to action is at least a faint analogy to understanding; but when we have let go the very ghost of action, we understand nothing at all. This pig philosophized from the acts communicated in the language-situation, and we will call him an actualist.

Panlogism, factualism, actualism. Panlogism is obviously false, as a metaphysical doctrine. But what about the other two?

Commemorative Address on Berkeley†

You have done me an honour which I don't know how to express, in asking me to address you on the occasion of Bishop Berkeley's birthday. I could not be worse qualified for the job. You have among you here Berkeley scholars and specialists, with whom I should be ashamed to discuss the Bishop's works: my ignorance would soon be shown up. You can't even say that, coming from the British Isles, I can praise Berkeley to you in the tones of his own speech. Nothing could be further from the truth. It's we, not you, who have corrupted the language; and if George Berkeley were to walk in amongst us now, complete with wig and bands, it would be your rich and masculine tones he'd understand, not our thin-voiced twittering. If the culture, speech and mood of Berkeley's day survives anywhere, surely it's in New England, and not in the old.

I can only think of one qualification I might have, and it's this. George Berkeley is a literary ghost—a row of old books on a shelf. And if my name is anything to any few of you, it'll be in the same way—it's a name on the spines of a few books in the library—the difference is, you've had a look at Berkeley, you haven't had a look at me. Still, that's all I am, a phantom of the library; and it may seem appropriate, if one paper-and-ink ghost takes on the job of praising another. Now you have seen me actually come alive, perhaps you'll be looking nervously at the door, to see if Berkeley won't come in, too. The other year I was lecturing at Edinburgh, and in came an old professor (alas, he has died since) whom they introduced as Norman Kemp Smith. My goodness! Norman Kemp Smith's *Critique of Pure Reason*

† A paper read at the Berkeley Divinity School, associated with Yale University, 1961.

was an old book, with the covers dropping off, when I was a boy. My stomach turned right over. What next! Leibniz and Spinoza might just as well be entering arm-in-arm.

George Berkeley, it need scarcely be said, has the advantage over me from every point of view, and especially in the matter of birthdays. My birthdays still belong to a limited series, running uncomfortably close towards the end; and though there is something heart-warming in the way my friends remember my birthday, and in the way they still seem pleased I was born, I can't be all that light-hearted about it myself. I wonder where all those golden days and hours have fled, and how on earth, in the years that remain, I'm going to fit in those good works, which were prepared for me, that I should walk in them. But George Berkeley's birthday no longer gives place for any such doubts or regrets. He has reached a point of wisdom, from which he is able to look out on the panorama of events through the very eyes of God. That deceptive independence, which he complained of as all too ready to mislead us, has finally vanished from his vision of created things. Infinite Spirit, the one great Cause of all, shines through every part of his handiwork; and the Bishop's active mind sees those good purposes, which heavenly wisdom both designed and accomplished through his birth and life. And as for the imperfections of his days (for Berkeley, after all, was human), he sees how his faults and failings have given opportunities for the action of atoning mercy, and called forth the power which alone is able to bring good out of evil. So if we are pleased with Berkeley's birthday, we need have no doubt that he is pleased with it, too. He will be neither embarrassed nor saddened by the chorus of congratulations.

And what a chorus it is! How many parties, how many professions Berkeley has had the happiness to please! Who does not praise him? The Church loves him for his missionary zeal, and the teaching profession for his enlightened educational schemes. And as for the philosophers, there is not a school or a sect of them that is not delighted with the man. Philosophers are not distinguished from one another by being pro- or anti-Berkeley: they are all pro. But you know immediately what their allegiance is, by setting them to praise him, and hearing what it is they praise him for. Do they praise him for the stress he laid on the importance of words in our management of ideas? Then no doubt they are our up-to-the-minute linguistic philosophers. Is it his insistence on bringing our general descriptions of things down to the test of sense-evidence? Is it this that pleases them: this, and his denial of absolute validity to generalization itself? Then you know what sort of philosophers they are: they are positivists, or radical empiricists. But here is quite a different looking set of Berkeley-lovers, more starry-eyed in their admiration, and whose beards, it has to be owned, have grown both white and long—what they admire is the Bishop's courage, in maintaining that nothing has any reality, except in the mind or *for* the mind. These are the idealists; perhaps they would rather call themselves Hegelians than Berkeleians, but they know all the same that Berkeley is the first patriarch of their sect, the Abraham, as it were, of their idealist Israel. One notices that they are somewhat embarrassed by the ragged camp-followers of their host, whose paeans in the good Bishop's honour have a wild, fanatic, and discreditable ring. There, for example, is Mary Baker Eddy, so sure that matter isn't real; she will cure all bodily ills by thinking them away. Silly woman, say the true Berkeleians, rounding upon her: you will cure cancers, will you, by true thought? Berkeley knew better: he recommended tar-water.

Mrs Eddy's claim to Berkeleianism can be quenched with tar-water, but her predicament is not unique. All the Bishop's followers can be convicted of heresy, if we pick the right text from his works to confute them with. The linguisticists have to admit that the Bishop wanted to get behind words; the positivists must swallow the painful truth, that their champion believed in pure spirits, and, still worse, in God. Not one of us is orthodox; every sort of Berkeleianism is highly selective. But that is only to say that Berkeley is a great teacher: not a teacher who dominates his pupils, or forces them into his own mould, but a teacher who stimulates them with an endless suggestiveness, and sows seeds in many soils, all of which sprout and grow with an inexhaustible vitality.

Well, now I must add my mite of praise to the great sum of Berkeley's honour: I must tell you what I think most valuable among his doctrines, and most fertile of truth for us. And I will begin to say what I have to say, by comparing Berkeley with his predecessor, Descartes. Descartes has got enormous credit for his supposed discovery, that there is no fact of which a man can be so immediately certain, as he can of his own personal existence. Descartes made a great noise about this. I do not think the proposition justifies the fuss he made about it, or even that it is particularly true. There are several facts just as certain to me as my own mental existence: for example, that I have something here to stand upon, and something here to breathe. It's when we come to the nature of what supports my feet, and the nature of what I inhale into my lungs—that's when it begins to be difficult. This is the point where we really want help from a philosopher, and this is where Berkeley comes to the rescue. It is not the fact of my own existence, he says, but the nature of my own existence which is specially evident to me. I am inside myself; I'm not inside anything else. I know what it is like to live and think and feel and act, because I've got the recipe for doing it. Let's say that I have a unique access to my own way of being, because it's a way of acting, and I know how it's done. By contrast, the world outside me presents itself through a lot of dumb impenetrable signs. My eyes show me how things look to me, not what it's like, being them; and the same goes for my ears, and my other senses.

Now Berkeley said, the greatest mistake we can make is to think that things are as dumb as they look. The scientists of his time took exactly that view: real things were just lumps of stuff, neutral models of what we experience through touch and sight. Nonsense, says Berkeley. Just sitting there, the way matter was supposed to do, isn't any sort of way of existing, at all. The real forces or causes behind the phenomena are either nothing, or they are as active as we ourselves are. They must be real going concerns, carrying on business, so to speak, under their own names:[1] we cannot understand what it is like to be them by any other clue than by our own knowledge of what it is like for us to be ourselves.

Now this, as I see it, is Berkeley's great discovery: that our acquaintance with our own active existence is our key to the understanding of any existence whatsoever. Let's call this Berkeley's key to the mysteries of existence. It's the only key there is, I've no doubt of that. But when I turn to consider the way in which Berkeley used the key, I have to admit that he fumbled it. It's a master-key opening all doors; but he only managed to get it into two types of keyholes. What sort of being can we, in fact, understand by the clue of our own? None, said Berkeley—none but a being as personal as ours. Behind, and through, the screen of the phenomena I can discern the presence of other active spirits, other human minds, for they talk to me, not only by actual words, but by their whole conduct and action. But only a few patches in the whole wide picture of my environment speak to me with a human voice. What does the whole phenomenon of sub-human or lipless nature speak to me of? It speaks to me of God, says Berkeley: that is all; all the apparent furniture of earth and sky is nothing but a divine visual language, through which God speaks to us with the mind of a physical providence.

So then, according to Berkeley, there are only two doors which his key will unlock. My own existence and action are a clue to the sympathetic knowledge of other minds, and the infinite mind, God: nothing else. Not merely am I unable to unlock any other doors: there aren't any others to unlock. Nothing exists and acts behind the screen of phenomena, except other finite spirits, and the one Infinite Spirit.

Now I say that Berkeley's key is the right key, but that he did not know how to use it. His conclusion, as has always been recognized, is contrary to common sense. I know other men by sympathy, yes: but, in a steadily dwindling degree. I know animals by sympathy, too. As the animal becomes more and more remote from me, I know less and less what it is like to be such a creature. Still more, when I go below the animal, to the vegetable and physical levels: I do not know what it is like to be a cabbage, still less a packet of atomic force. Yet I do know that such beings act— they *do* things—and it is from the experience of my own action, that I know the base meaning of the word to *do*.

Here am I, like a typical intellectual, settling down to the congenial occupation of criticism, and pulling Berkeley to bits, instead of praising him. I must get a grip on myself, and switch it off. I return, then, to the proper business of the day, which was, that I should state the most valuable truths which Berkeley taught us. I've mentioned one, and I'll only mention one other.

Berkeley thought that what he called materialism stood in the way of man's acknowledging his creator. Berkeley did not quarrel with physical science. The diagrams of physical event which the scientists drew might be fascinatingly true descriptions of the patterns composing the phenomena. The world really goes like that. It was another thing, though, if the scientists began supposing that there were physical realities which were the mere counter-parts of such patterns, and nothing more. For God is not a mech-anic, and the world is not a machine. God is the father and the lover of his creatures: each of them is a reflection of his glory, and a partaker in the infinite energy of his life. God's world is a world of *creatures*, each exerting its own active existence, and praising its creator thereby. God's world is not a world of manipulable material, just there for us to push around. And if we get to looking at the world as if it were, we shall never see it as the offspring or handiwork of God.

I'm not putting this a bit well. May I start in another place? In the season of Lent, the English Church recites the *Benedicite omnia opera* in place of the *Te Deum*. Have you the same custom over here? A very nice pupil of mine, a Virginian, gave me an American Prayer book, so I shouldn't get lost in your divine service. It makes several points clear to me, especially the im-portance of always saying *those who* in place of *them that*; but it doesn't help me about the use of the *Benedicite*. Anyhow, if you ever do get around to reciting it, you find yourself calling on all God's creatures to bless him, to praise and magnify him for ever. Angels and stars, sun and moon, lightnings and clouds, seas and fountains, growing plants and flying birds, all are invoked to join the mighty anthem. It's poetry, of course; and poetry does not have the same sort of sense that cold prose carries, but it must make some sort of sense, all the same. 'O my love's like a red red rose, that's newly sprung in June.' Well, the lady can't have been like that literally of course—and yet, if it was the right lady, the poem could be just right; but not if it was the wrong one—if, for example, she was like a brown, brown chrysanthemum that's badly overblown in November.

Well now, the world of flat materialism, which Berkeley wanted to get rid of, was, and is, a world to which the *Benedicite omnia opera* simply couldn't be addressed. If such a world were true, it would be a world for atheists—but, said Berkeley, it isn't true, thank God, it's a great arrogant lie. No created thing can exist, unless it shares, at whatever remove of distance, that active being we exert ourselves, and which we derive from our great exemplar, God.

I'm still not at all content with the way I'm putting this point, and I'm going to have one more try before I stop. Anyone who reads Holy Scripture must be struck from time to time with the fact that man is treated as the supremely typical creature of God. God loves all his creatures, and they all depend on him: but what that dependence and that love are, we experience most directly in our own case. A Christian metaphysic must be man-centred; not in the childish sense that we have to suppose God created everything for our special convenience, as though the world were a Fifth-Avenue apartment, and we were the apartment-dwellers. No, not that: the man-centredness of a Christian metaphysic is simply that we have to accept our own dependence on God as some sort of clue to the way all things depend on him. Now what Berkeley showed was that such a belief is no mere superstition; it is philosophically justified. Since our own exercise of our existence is our key to all creatures' exercise of such existence as belongs to them, it is fair enough that our dependence on God should be taken as somehow typical of the way all creatures depend on their creator.

That is all I propose to say about the vital truths of Berkeley's philosophy; and I apologize to the philosophers among you for expounding the obvious, and to the non-philosophers for over-straining their attention. But no one can leave it at that, or let the subject of Berkeley's merits go, without a word about the grace of his writing. And here, at least, is something which equally concerns us all, whatever our subject of study may be. Berkeley wrote about severely technical questions, and he wrote about them like an angel; one can sigh with sheer pleasure at the clarity of his images, and the cadence of his words. We ourselves live in an age which has allowed living speech and academic writing to drift far apart. No one composing a thesis thinks he can be doing it properly, unless he writes like Hegel with a hangover. The effect is disastrous, not simply on the reader's temper, but on the writer's mind. The more we talk like ourselves, or even like human beings, the better we shall know what we are talking about. Believe me, if something can't be referred to except by a fabricated concept under a German label, the chances are it doesn't exist anyhow. Or if it

M

does, why keep it at arm's length in a cage of technical jargon, instead of incorporating it into your living thought?

I like to think that Berkeley College upholds the standards of Berkeleian style; and how I wish—if so—that you would send over a party to colonize Keble College, and drive the deadly pest of jargon out of our borders. Your College and mine are alike in this: each bears the name of an English ecclesiastic, who had nothing directly to do with either foundation. Your man was an unquestioned genius; ours much less so, but perhaps something more of a saint. And, of course, like so many things in the old country, our man is very much more recent than yours. He was a sort of poet—alas, not a very good one; your man is a far more robust and healthful influence on the use of that most divine among our instruments, human speech.

Freedom and Theology†

Gabriel Marcel delivering academic lectures in Great Britain is indeed a spectacle. It reminds me of the kingfisher I once saw perched on a dead elder tree between the gas works and the canal. A visitant from another world, a lonely phenomenon, but as a reminder of the many-sidedness of things by no means to be ignored. We shall be on the wrong track, certainly, if we approach Marcel's Gifford Lectures with the expectation of finding philosophy in them as practised by our own professionals. But then surely philosophy isn't a game to be played according to association rules, and it would be stupid to declare Marcel offside. A common rule or method among philosophers is indeed valuable if it unites them in a fertile enterprise, but it is the fertility that matters, not the rule; and if Marcel's method is also fertile, who is to order him off the field? And if he isn't what is now called a philosopher, we will appoint a sub-committee to invent a formula for whatever he is, and meanwhile we ourselves will get on with seeing how he goes to work and what he has to say.

It may be that professional usage will deny Marcel the name of philosopher, but popular usage will certainly not. The philosopher is popularly taken to be a man who reflects deeply on the mysteries of human existence, a somewhat sober first cousin, perhaps to the more serious sort of poet. If so, Marcel comes straight into view, for he is a poet, anyhow in the ancient sense, an imaginative writer: to be precise, he is a dramatist. The ordinary man feels himself prompted to philosophical reflection by good imaginative writing, especially perhaps by drama. For the situations of drama are the predicaments of life stripped of irrelevance, and the characters of drama are real people endowed with an unusual power of expression. We read or hear what they say, and we exclaim: 'Yes,

† A B.B.C. broadcast review of Gabriel Marcel's Gifford Lectures on *The Mystery of Being*, 11 and 12 December 1951.

that's life!' and then we begin to ruminate, or in the popular sense, to philosophize; we draw out the implications of the dramatist's remark, and throw it into the form of a general principle.

This is essentially what Marcel does, except that he is himself the dramatist. He both creates the primary expression and also reflects philosophically upon it. Let us trace the stages by which the philosophical truth grows. First of all there is the human race (of which Marcel is, of course, a member), living and talking. Second, there is Gabriel Marcel the dramatist, so dramatizing human existence as to bring out the saviour of it in characteristic expressions. Third, there is Gabriel Marcel the philosopher, taking these expressions, generalizing their scope, plucking them to pieces, turning them over and over, interpreting them, re-phrasing them. Fourth, there is Gabriel Marcel the Gifford Lecturer, obliged by the somewhat portentous role Lord Gifford lays upon his lecturers, to systematize a lifelong accumulation of piecemeal philosophical reflections into a body of doctrine.

It is in the third of these capacities that Marcel is really strong. Other men, of course, have lived and talked as well as he, and other men have written dramas no worse than his; but the art of philosophizing upon dramatic intuition who has practised as he has done? In the power to make us taste and feel our human existence, to lay out and analyse the structure of our living without letting go the vividness and pathos of it, whom shall we compare with him? Bergson had the gift, but his range was narrower: he had neither the sense for nuances nor the depth of moral penetration. Marcel's most characteristic work of this kind is, perhaps, to be found in his metaphysical journals, where, in his day-to-day jottings, we can see him wrestling with his intuitions, crumbling his images and fixing his ideas. There is fresh work of this kind in the two volumes of Gifford Lectures—he is never altogether content with his old pieces of existential description, he clarifies and supplements them. Yet it is not fresh work of that kind which gives the Gifford Lectures their special importance. It is what I have called the fourth stage in the development of the philo-sophical material—its systematization.

Now let me say right out—it is not that the systematization is very well done; it is that it gets done at all. Marcel is not strong at systematic exposition. He sets before us (as in his former writings)

several shots or views of philosophic truth, which he labours
to make vivid and penetrating; but the transition from one to
another is often more hinted than stated, and we are poorly
supplied by him with comprehensive panoramas. Nevertheless,
he has ranged his matter in some sort of a progression, as the
stages of a man's philosophical thought thinking itself out; and
when the argument gets lost in the text, it can be recovered from
the précis provided with the table of contents—a précis which
seems to be actually inspired, for it sometimes tells us what cannot
be found in the text at all. There is a tip I will give to the reader
of Marcel's Gifford Lectures: keep your eye on the précis.

But to return to the main point. These Gifford Lectures
present the various parts of Marcel's thought in massive balance.
and there is no lack of unity in the thought itself. The exposition
of the system may leave something to be desired, but the system is
there, and the reader may please his own vanity by writing his
own account of the structure afterwards on a few sheets of paper:
a valuable piece of expression-work in any case, after reading
philosophic matter. Nor can we say that the weakness of systematic
unity is due to a defect in Marcel's mind; it would be truer to say
that it is due to his peculiar virtues. A good systematic exposition
tends to be like a firmly-drawn diagram, and to attain unity and
clarity at the expense of detailed truth. Whereas it is the truth of
detail to which Marcel clings, because his special gift is to make us
see personal and spiritual realities; he is never happy unless he is
revealing something to us. And so he is unwilling to let go the
direct objects of vision in order to give general reviews and panor-
amic diagrams. To return to the comparison between Marcel and
Bergson; a competent third-year student may write Bergson's
system for him more accurately than Bergson wrote it, but who can
illuminate the world as Bergson illuminated it? Tidy minds are
three-a-penny, but seeing minds are rarer than fine gold. Bergson
or Marcel may not present us with a philosophy, but they turn us
into philosophers. When we have read Marcel we seize pen and
paper: 'Let us see', we exclaim, 'what this comes to.' Our ideas
flow spontaneously and we think they are our own; we look at
what we have written, and find that we have moved all the time
within the orbit of Marcel's mind.

I am still afraid, though, that our students of philosophy are going to brush Marcel aside as an undisciplined, naïve, pre-critical philosopher, simply because his work does not lie in the same plane with the Vienna-Cambridge logical axis which is our present orthodoxy; that they will say, 'This is how people philosophized before Wittgenstein,' or, more indulgently, 'We used to think this sort of thing was philosophic truth, but now we see that it is neither true nor false, it is just poetry, the imaginative expression of an attitude; and we should enjoy it more if the poetry were not spoilt by a parade of bogus philosophic argument.' I will now try to meet this sort of objection, and I will begin my defence from a phrase which I was putting into the mouth of the opponent: 'Like poetry, merely the expression of an attitude.' For that's just the battleground. Must the expression of attitude be left to the poet, or can we advance along that line from poetry to serious philosophy, as Marcel claims to do? Poetry may express attitude, but can there be a critical study of attitude from which objective certainties can be drawn?

Let us consider attitude. Attitude is always attitude *to* something. Serious minds do not attitudinize *in vacuo*, they take up an attitude towards—well, towards what? Towards their own situation, and more especially towards the other persons who enter into that situation. Now the serious man, the decent man, thinks that his attitude towards the personal realities of his situation ought to be an *appropriate* attitude. If I could feel and think and act in the way that is *called for* by the personal realities with which I have to do, then, when I come to die, I might die without shame, remorse, or retrospective regret. What, as a serious person, I want is not to keep a code of rules or to perform noble tasks, though these things too may have their place. What I fundamentally want is to respond to realities lying partly in my own being, partly in other men's. And if we speak of 'attitude' in this connection, we do not mean a static pose, but the permanent spirit of active responses.

My response, my attitude, is my effective judgement upon the realities to which I respond. If I treat a person with contempt or impatience, I judge, to all intents and purposes, that there is nothing there that greatly matters; and so forth. Now if the whole worth of our existence turns upon the suitability of our responses, then we must take seriously our beliefs about that to which we respond. We cannot respond suitably to that of whose being we are perfectly ignorant. 'Being', I say—If in this world I am to love what is worthy of love, and hate what is worthy of hate, I must know something of what my objects *are*; it will not do to know simply how they affect me.

Our valuations of personal being are doubtless a different thing from what that being actually is, but unless they are founded on what it is, and in some way correspond to what it is, then we err in the whole focus of our lives, and might as well never have been born. If after my death I pass into a world of clear knowledge, and the angels come to me and say: 'Look, this is what the persons were in themselves whom you handled thus and thus in life,' and I look, and perceive that my handling of these persons was an ignoring of what they really were, I shall be heartbroken. But if, in the same invisible future, the angels say to me: 'Look, this is the real nature of that physical energy whose configurations and effects you had to do with in life'; and if I look and perceive that all my life long I ignored the real nature of that energy, I shall remain completely unmoved. In our science, in our whole manipulation of physical things, we never even raise the question, what the reality we are up against intrinsically is; and nothing would turn on our answering the question, even allowing that we could meaningfully ask it. To talk about a deep or subtle or sympathetic understanding of physical being is just rubbish. But to talk so of understanding *personal* being is not rubbish.

Put it another way. Where is truth to be found? An empiricist may reply: 'In particular and hard fact, in the realm in which we can arrange the crucial experiment and determine a law; or the realm in which we can sift testimony and determine a historical event.' To that Marcel replies: 'But surely truth is about what something really is, about what it is to be that something.' And in establishing a truth of fact, whether in the form of a scientific law or in the form of a particular occurrence, I do not probe into the being of anything. In the scientific sphere I may, indeed, have virtual certitude; and if certitude is your mark of truth, there then is truth. But if depth of penetration is truth, then we must look elsewhere for it; and in a realm where certitude, or anyhow indisputability, is unattainable: the moral realm, the realm of those personal realities upon whose being we are forced to pass judgement, by the necessity of acting worthily or unworthily of them; in fact, the realm of that to which attitudes are taken up.

Thus for Marcel the question about the truth of being arises only in that baffling province in which our apprehensions are conditioned by our attitudes and vice versa. Baffling indeed, and far from the possibility of certitude, but not for that reason to be abandoned to the poets. What would that amount to?—to saying that we cannot use our critical faculties at all in the field where it most deeply concerns us to think truly. We might indeed be driven to so painful a conclusion, but we should not accept it unless we were driven to it.

Marcel thinks that a rational exploration of this mysterious realm is possible. By what method? By no formal method laid down beforehand. We must simply reflect upon what we suppose ourselves to be acquainted with. We must take our most important acts and attitudes, we must try to say what their character or structure is, and what, beyond themselves, is involved with them. For example, in the ninth lecture of his second series Marcel calls on us to consider the so-called virtue of hope. We think we know what it is, we think hope is the opposite of fear. He makes us see that it is not so—on reflection we do not really think so. Hopefulness is the opposite of an attitude which expects nothing of life, the opposite of listlessness rather than of alarm. But then again hope is not reasonable foresight of good to come. Men are not praised as hopeful because they have rational grounds for expecting the best; still less because they have an irrational bias towards expecting good things when bad things are more reasonably to be expected. Hope is an attitude with which we meet bad things themselves. Yet it is no mere stoicism or defiant cheerfulness. The man who resolves to sing under difficulties is not hoping for anything, he is merely singing. Hope involves some real confidence in a good to come, or a good which cannot be defeated. Yet hope (not being rash prediction) does not pin her faith to the success of any single expectation. In what sort of a world, then, is hope a virtue? In what sort of a world can hope be better than the fostering of a convenient but pathetic illusion? Is there any guarantee that the good we hope for can be hoped for with reason?

I have given you a mere fragment of Marcel's descriptive method. His attempts to grapple with the mysteries of existence have something in common with the old Socratic-Platonic approach, the enquiry (for example) into the Greek virtues. Descriptions are offered, are found to be both figurative and imperfect, are exposed and broken up, and other descriptions tried. No description is perfect, and all, perhaps, are figurative. But in criticizing and breaking one description after another we become more and more aware of what it is that is obliging us to break our descriptions; I mean, the shape of the reality we are trying to describe; for example, in the case taken above, that mysterious spirit of hope which is intertwined with life itself and almost inseparable from it. When at length he tires of breaking down descriptions and acquiesces in the use of some one formulation, Marcel has become so well aware of the reality described that he no longer fears to be misled by his formula; he is able to allow the necessary discount for its one-sidedness or its figurativeness.

It will be seen that Marcel's thought is anything rather than naïve or uncritical. If the particular philosophical wisdom of today is a caution against the deceptions of language, then Marcel has that sort of wisdom in abundance. He never trusts the form of words, but practically breaks it against the things. Nor does he postulate dubious entities or erect metaphysical constructions. What he talks about is always our life and what our life is up against. His object is to reveal depths where we have been content with shallows, to make us reflect upon what we have taken for granted, and to break the idols of the imagination.

It will be profitable to pause here and point out a striking difference between the philosophy of Marcel and that of some of our best known philosophers. It is their practice, if not their precept, to select as specimens for philosophic dissection the most commonplace examples of moral or personal reflection, as though by dissecting them they would get to the heart of the matter. The principle behind their practice is presumably Descartes's celebrated maxim, that we should begin by understanding the simple if we want the key to the understanding of the complex. But it is surely one thing to say that the complex is to be understood through the simple, and another thing to say that the trivial holds the secret of the profound. Mass-produced or careless reflection on the realities of moral being is worthless material for the philosopher, if the philosopher is concerned to penetrate to any depth.

It may be that Marcel is more concerned with profound reflection than with logical dissection, and that not all his logical dissections are logical enough. I do not care if you say that he is so much the less of a philosopher, as long as you agree that he is providing indispensable raw material for philosophy, and that he is starting in the right place. In the right place, anyhow, for a Gifford Lecturer, since it is not in the trivialities of human existence that the divine is to be found. The philosopher who will not probe the depths, or who thinks there are no depths to probe, is not going to arrive at the place where theological questions arise.

And where, in fact, do they arise for Marcel? Where does he find God? His moral analysis leads him to the absolute rejection of Sartre's view,[1] the view that our human freedom consists in our being saddled with the appalling and ridiculous task of creating our own existence. On the contrary, our freedom is always response to what already is; it is the active fulfilment of what some given reality demands. It is in the analysis of this given and demanding reality that Marcel finds God under the form of creative will. We experience our own being, and other men's being; and the relation by which our being is tied to theirs is given to us and laid upon us by a will having sovereign goodness and sovereign right. I will not attempt to set forth such argument here. But I will call upon my hearers to agree with me that if there is to be any theology this is where it lies.[2] If God is anywhere to be found, it is here, in the way in which our own being and that of our fellow-man is assigned to us as the rule of our acts and the object of our loving regard.

Transcendence
and 'Radical Theology'†

Religious faith might still be the force it always has been among mankind, if it could only shed an overload of 'transcendence'. It has become plain, however, that the anti-transcendence men are in some disagreement among themselves. At a casual glance, you might take the difference for a matter of degree—some of our radical theologians will swallow a bit more transcendence than others, much as one diner will take more mustard with his beef than another.

Well, but is 'transcendence' really the sort of thing you can have more or less of? It is time we considered what 'transcendence' means; so let's do a bit of verbal definition.

I propose to you one main distinction. 'Transcendence' is used in theology—in *theology*, mind you—in two senses which are utterly different. According to sense one, 'God transcends' means 'God is something over and above other things'. To assert God's transcendence in this sense is just a pompous and unnecessary way of saying that you believe in God; and, equally, to deny his transcendence is to renounce belief in him. According to sense two, 'God transcends' means 'God outsoars us'. To cry up his transcendence is to give a one-sided emphasis to your account of the relation between God and his creatures; to cry down transcendence is to throw the emphasis in the other direction. Sense one does not admit of degrees, for either you assert God, or you don't. Sense two admits of degrees, for you can give a more or less one-sided account of the relation of things to God. Take the two senses, and beat them up together, and you will have a high old philosophical muddle.

I will now take the two senses one by one, and in more detail.

† Last in a series of B.B.C. broadcasts on 'Secular Christianity', 8 August 1967.

In sense one, to say that God transcends things or persons is just to say that he is himself, and that he isn't any of those things or persons, whether taken one by one, or taken all together. To make the point clear, I will adopt what many people would regard as a very un-transcendent view of the divine being: a view I by no means hold—but never mind; for the sake of argument, let's suppose it. Let's suppose that the things in this world of ours constitute the whole field of God's activity and the whole sphere of his being. Let's allow him no other action but what issues in things being the way they are and doing the things they do. Let him find his whole employment, so to speak, in making nature natural[1]—which will of course include making man human. Then his field of action is our field—the field we share with all created things. None the less—and this is the point I wish to make—his living in that field, or focusing of that field, is his living or his focusing; it is none of ours. To take the obvious comparison: you and I may both enjoy the same piece of music, and can (if you like to think so) enjoy it in exactly the same way. The field and form of our awareness are identical; yet mine is inalienably mine, and yours yours: the experience finds a different actual existence in you and in me. So too with God and any of his creatures. His living of our world must be his, and not ours, even if it is our world and no other that he focuses. For otherwise, is it not obvious that talk about God can add nothing to a story about the world and its constituents? If you mean by 'God' just things being things and men being men, then why not be content to talk about men and about things? What is added to the picture by talking about God at all? What can the name of God still serve for but a piece of slang, an appreciative noise? During our Bach Festival I see scribbled on Oxford walls 'Bach is God'. But we know perfectly well that it means no more than 'Bach is tops'. Bach fans are talking about Bach, not about God. If we really wanted to say that the Bach-person is one with the God-person, we should have to presume a God-person existent in his own right, whose fusion with the Bach-person was seriously, though mysteriously, asserted. In order to flow together with the Bach-person, God would have first to transcend—to be over and above—the Bach-person as such; and, presumably, over and above all other persons and creatures as well.

To sum up: in sense one of 'transcendence', to say that God transcends natural beings is just to say he is himself, however much he overlaps them; while to deny that God transcends is to confess that his name stands for nothing real, but only for an emotional gilding on the cosmic ginger-bread. So 'God is transcendent' comes to the same thing as 'God is'. 'Transcendent' is a platitudinous addition, which may just as well be dropped off.

So much for sense one. Or no—wait a bit—there's an objection I think I must consider before proceeding to sense two, for it isn't a mere debating-point, it has much practical importance. The objection is this: Granted that, to be anything real, God must transcend you and me and every particular creature, he still need not transcend the universe as a whole. Or as some would prefer to say, natural reality as such. Why can't the assertions we make about God be assertions about the substance of reality or about the character and tendency of the universe as a whole?

I say the objection is important, because people who wish to compromise between believing in God and not believing in him can time and again be found seeking refuge in the suggestion it embodies. Perhaps there is no such being (they think) as the traditional—or, as they may like to say, the mythical—God-figure; but why should not that figure be a poetical peg on which to hang statements about Reality, or about the Universe as a whole? Well, I'll tell you why not—because there's no such thing as Reality, there are just all the things that are real; the question is, whether God is one of those, or not. And as for the Universe as a whole—the Universe isn't a whole; the question is, whether there is a God to give it the wholeness it lacks by projecting it in the single focus of his mind. I do not think we need spend time in exploding Reality with a big R—not at the present phase of philosophical development. 'Good old Auntie Reality!' burst out an undergraduate reviewer of *Honest to God*, a book for which in general he had considerable respect; but Reality—that was a drop too much for the young man, and I myself feel disinclined to be solemn over such a moth-eaten Aunt Sally at Philosophers' Fair. What does need to be said, and said again, is that there's no such being as the Universe. The universe isn't *an* organism or *a* system or *a* process: it's an unimaginable free-for-all of innumerable bits of organism, system, process; or, if you'll allow me an antiquated piece of slang, it's not a thing, it's just one damned thing after another.[2] If natural science has told us anything, natural science has told us that much. The universe is one only in the sense that its multifarious constituents condition one another, positively or negatively, in the great web of space-time relations.[3] We can make statements about the universe, as we can make statements about the contents of the British Museum. We can make general or statistical statements about the way things go; we can make diagrammatic statements about the patterns into which they fall. We cannot make statements about a common substance or ground of things, nor about a general purpose or trend in things, for there's nothing to constitute the common substance and there's nothing to have the purpose or to do the trending. There's only one way to pin God-type statements on the universe, and that is to pin the universe to a real God: a God who has unity and entity in himself; who (to use our present language) transcends the universe, and so is in a position to draw its multiplicities into the focus of a unity they themselves lack.

To have done, then, with the objection we raised: Reality or 'the Universe' does not provide a half-way house between belief and disbelief in theology. We must either assert or else deny that God transcends every creature—not only this creature or that creature, but all creatures collectively. If he doesn't transcend in this first sense, the sense we have so far considered—then the issues connected with transcendence in the second sense simply don't arise. For a God who is no more than the world cannot stand in any relation to the world, about which we could inquire *how* transcendent that relation is. So, to get on with the story, we will assume sense one transcendence, i.e. we will assume belief in God, and try to ask *how far* he transcends, or outsoars, his creatures.

Surely, though, as a question asked in sober philosophy, our new question is absurd. How high does the divine stature tower above ours? How much more masterly is his grip on the universe of things than ours? How much? One can only answer, as much as one can stretch to think, and then some! For us to cut God down to size, or to keep his monarchy within our paper-constitutions, is surely a ridiculous enterprise.

What, then, are people really talking about, when they are

inflating or deflating the divine transcendence? They are talking bugbears. They say: 'If we let God be God, he will crowd us out of the picture. If he is the Creator, then we are mere wax in his hands. If he is the fixer of values, we are the slaves of his decisions. If he is a general providence, we are not to provide for ourselves. If he is infinitely above our nature, we can approach him only by denying what we are, and turning our backs on life.' Those are a few of the bugbears; one could easily lengthen the list. Bugbears are the children of distrust; distrust, in this case, of whom? Either of God or, presumably, of mankind. We should be distrusting God, if we thought him not big enough to stand out of his own light or to bestow on his creatures the degree of independence which would make their existence most worth having. We should be distrusting mankind, if we thought them incapable of contemplating God's greatness, without sinking under the weight into repression and infantility. As to distrust of God, that is not, perhaps, very rational; but distrust of mankind in this connection can find all too much historical justification. Has not theology served to keep a multitude in tutelage, to excuse laziness, and to cloak despair? The corruptions of religion must be taken along with the corruptions of all things human. But unless we will despair of man, why should we specially despair of his religion?

Of the radical theologians whose views I have encountered the most intriguing to my mind is the author of *Gospel of Christian Atheism*,[4] Dr Thomas Altizer. As a serious account of existence, or as a scheme of philosophical theology, his work cannot stand for a moment; you might call it an essay in the preposterous. Yet in his wild, Germanic way Altizer puts his finger on the spot. The bugbears of transcendence, he says, have been done away by God himself. He did it on Calvary two millennia ago. Not that, by dying, he ceased to be in *every* sense—like the buried god in Hiawatha who sprouted up as corn, he lives again as the very humanity of us all.

There is no need solemnly to argue for or against such a tale as this. You are in no danger of believing in a God who made and animated the universe until one fine Friday he threw up the job, got himself hanged, and turned into the soul of one race of creatures on one tiny planet. But you might perhaps be willing to consider that the Crucifixion is more typical of God's whole relation to his creatures than Christians have commonly dared to suppose. Our traditional thought, as Altizer complains, has seen the universe as a Byzantine theocracy with God for emperor. Inside the framework of that august design, room has been found for a singular detail, the act of redemption: the monarch goes into the street as a beggar and gets killed in reconciling his disaffected subjects to his government.

Ought we not rather to think that the great monarch annihilates himself thoroughly and altogether wherever he moves out into creation, only entering into his creatures' existence under the very form of their own action and being?

I know that in speaking like this I am still under the Altizerian spell; I am talking a sort of metaphysical rant. The act of condescension by which God serves his creatures in making them make themselves[5] is no self-annihilation on God's part, it is simply the appropriate use of his power: it is the only way to make such a world as this is.

In spite of the title he gives his book, Dr Altizer is no atheist. How can a man be an atheist, whose theme is that man has been saved from a crushing transcendence by the singular act of God himself! I close the book, I slowly recover from the incantatory spate of abstract nouns, I push aside the outrageous load of wilful exaggeration, and I try to assess what the author really means. He cannot mean, surely, that God got hanged one Friday about the year 30, and that was that. He must mean that the Crucifixion was a decisive, a revealing point in a continuous action of God, who is constantly dying to himself that he may be reborn in the life and action of his creatures. The reason why we are not crushed by God's transcendence is not that he died for good and all two thousand years ago but that all his entry into the world passes through this filter of what Altizer chooses to call his death or self-annihilation. To talk so is to use very forced and violent language; its merit is that it is passionately expressive of God's will to set his creatures free, and only to act for them by acting in them.

Altizer still attracts me, in spite of all the trouble he gives me in finding how to discount his passionate irrationality. Why is it? I think it is because of his method for dealing with the bugbears of transcendence. He does not look for comfort in any attempt to cut God down to size; he does not try to even up the balance between a creator and his creatures. The remedy for him lies in what the creator has done. It is not a question of how much or how little he transcends us; it is a question of how he has been pleased to relate his creatures to himself, and himself to them. The more transcendent he is, the more infinite in his resources, the more self-founded in his eternity, the better placed will he be for making sense of his creation: for exercising that abnegation of external control, that transformation of his action into the creaturely mode, which Altizer miscalls 'the death of God'.

Altizer's solution is that since God has hanged himself out of our way, we can get on cheerfully with being human, and forget the divine majesty. If we can't really believe so simple a story, we shall have to look for a slightly less simplistic solution; we must hope to be reconciled to the divine majesty by accepting the way God deals with his creatures, and the liberty with which he makes them free. And that is, indeed, an old story—it hasn't the gloss of novelty upon it which Altizer's doctrine wears. But then we can't expect mint-fresh novelties every morning on the subject of realities which are themselves presumably unchanging.

The Prior Actuality of God†

I have taken as my title 'The Prior Actuality of God', and that's a
fine round phrase, is it not? What I want to discuss is the retreat
from theological absolutism, and how far that retreat should go.
We are all in retreat from absolutism—and when I say 'Absolutism' I do not mean the pantheistic absolutism of Hegel's disciples,
I mean the high-and-dry philosophy of godhead inherited by
scholasticism from Aristotle and Plotinus. According to these
philosophers, and according to their Christian disciples, the
Supreme Being is absolute in the sense that it is wholly what it is
apart from relation to, or dependence upon, anything beside itself.
The difficulties created by the dogma are notorious; and they are
as much religious as philosophical.

The religious difficulty is perhaps the easier to illustrate. A
Christian presumably believes there is joy in the divine heart over
a sinner's repentance; God obtains his desire when he recreates a
wayward creation to truth and happiness. But God's act of
recreating or forgiving is dependent on his creature's voluntary
consent; and so it appears that a satisfaction forming part of that
joy which is the life of God is relative to his creature's actions—
for it is concerned with it; and dependent upon the creature's
actions—for the creature might withhold it.

The point may be generalized. Not only God's acts of forgiveness, but his whole purpose for mankind is concerned with what
man can be brought freely to do, and dependent upon such cooperation or consent as they are willing to offer. Indeed we may
make a still more sweeping generalization, a generalization which
will carry us beyond the sphere of religion into the field of nature.
If the march of God's purpose through history must wait for the
foot-dragging and malingering of human multitudes, is it not

† A lecture delivered at Louisiana State University, Baton Rouge, and at
Southern Methodist University in the Autumn of 1966.

equally evident that God's purpose in natural evolution is a slow persuasion of brute elements which waits for and works through their inborn capacities? If there is any divine purpose anywhere in the world, it is a purpose relative to the action of the world's constituents, and dependent upon the forthcomingness of that action.

The recognition of such seeming truths as these has caused modern theologians to retreat from the absolutist position. But how far are we to retreat? Our evidence is that God *can* concern himself with the actions of his creatures in such a way as to make his action relative to theirs. But *must* he so relate himself? To put it otherwise—Has God no other action than what is relative to a creation he makes, governs or saves? And here I come round to the blessed phrase I took for my title: 'The Prior Actuality of God'. Not, of course, that anyone who wishes to assert the existence of God at all will deny his prior actuality in every sense. What I wish to do is to distinguish two accounts that may be given of it, a minimizing account and a maximizing account. And I propose to evade the great technical difficulty of the subject by employing transparent allegories.

The minimizing allegory is this. Suppose a playwright who, in consequence of some fantastic magical curse, can have no other active existence than what consists in producing plays. Suppose also that he is condemned to produce them by no other method than that of getting his actors on the stage and leading them to extemporize their characters and to weave up the plot as they go along: a lead he gives them through hints and suggestions unobtrusively thrown out to them. Even so, the playwright's action may be said to have prior actuality in respect of the creation of his plays, for everything springs out of his initiative; apart from which the actors would not be actors nor their parts parts nor the plot a plot. Nevertheless, he has no actuality, no existence as a playwright (and but as a playwright, our absurd hypothesis allows him no active existence whatever) prior to his work upon the actors and their responses to him. Such is my minimizing allegory. I do not insult my readers' intelligence by translating it line by line into theology.

And now for the maximizing story, which is not to be so maximal as to constitute a return to the scholastic absolutism; we have agreed to go with the trend in discarding that. No, all we need for the maximum we are prepared to defend is a restatement of the minimizing allegory without the witch's curse. The playwright is not condemned to confine his active existence within the production of plays. Quite apart from, and prior to, his activity as producer-playwright, he has a personal life of his own. Indeed, if the playwright had not lived outside his plays, he would have nothing to put into them. It is the content of the life he has lived offstage that moves him to make the dramatic representation. There is no need for him to make it, he could live his life and be himself without making it. In fact he chooses to make it, and it is very intelligible that he should so choose. In so far as he puts himself into the play-business, he relativizes his actions to the being and the performance of his actors, just as in the other story, no more and no less. But his *prior actuality* in respect of the play is not simply his initiative in creating it but his life exterior to it; a life out of which flows his creation of it.

You will easily recognize through the thin veil of my second allegory the substance of traditional theology. One merit of the allegorical presentation is that it brings out the substantial independence of that theology from the special forms of scholastic Aristotelianism. The doctrine of a life of God in God, above and before all worlds, can be thought, and by Christians commonly is thought, in purely personal terms; it is the fellowship of Blessed Trinity. The Trinity is the substance of personal being and the pattern of personal relation; and it is this substance, this pattern, which God is pleased to reproduce, to represent and to extend in his creation. Ask the orthodox Christian why he supposes these things to be so, and he will tell you they are to him the immediate objects of his faith and the direct form of his salvation. If he can be said to know anything *qua* Christian it is his adoption into divine sonship. There could be no adoptive sonship were there no Sonship-By-Nature, and Sonship-By-Nature is within the Trinity. The Son-By-Nature makes us sons-by-adoption through taking our condition and associating us with himself. So he lifts us into fellowship with God, shares with us the Society which is the divine beatitude, and causes us to hang on the skirts of the divine eternity, to drink immortal joy forever.

This is the language of religion, and I say nothing here about its evidential justification. I merely point out that whatever you think of it, it is no good your telling us that it is an unassimilated leave-over of Aristotelian pedantry. No use your telling us so, and still less use your telling Aristotle so; I only wish you had the opportunity to try. No doubt the doctrine was, like everything else, Aristotelized by the Aristotelian scholastics. But the rejection of the scholastic absolutism does not logically entail or even tend to suggest the propriety of abandoning the Catholic religion and adoping a minimal view of the divine priority instead.

For the present I am merely exhibiting the coherence of a confessional position, so I will follow an example which I note in the work of a somewhat different school when they are thumping the confessional drum. When your Reformed theologian wants to beg the most enormous question, he cites a Latin tag from Luther or from Calvin. Then he can fairly hope to get away with murder; so bell-like is the spurious ring of self-evidence in the classic phrase. We can all play the game—only listen to this: *nulla impotentia ponenda est in deo.* 'No inability, no restriction of power, is to be posited in God.' You might think, indeed, that this is the very text and formula of that old metaphysical absolutism which we have agreed to drop from our theology. But I say: No, the fault of the scholastic absolutism lay in its violation of this principle—it was, in a sense, not absolute enough. It placed a restriction on the power of God, for what did it say? It said in effect that God *could not* create a world with such a degree or sort of self-being as to provide the object for an action on his part genuinely relative to it; or that he *could not* relativize his action in relation to it.

We must not, of course, pretend that the applicability of the formula *nulla impotentia . . .* to any suggested case can be settled on mere verbal form. Verbally, we seem to withhold power from God in denying that he can either create square circles or commit injustice. But it would be no positive power to do either—the one is a rational surd or self-contradiction, the other a moral surd, a self-frustration; it is like the ability to make blunders in arith-metic. Not all cases are so clear as this. For example, is the power to punish everlastingly *potentia* or *impotentia*? Christians might disagree. But no Christian can (presumably) doubt that it was a real exercise of the power to act in the most effective way, and in the crucial case, when Christ subjected himself to the hands of sinners and died for our salvation on the cross. The instance is most telling for those of us who believe the incarnation in an orthodox sense, and see in the person who so subjected himself, very God made man. But anyone who claims the Christian name will grant that if any event happening in our world was an act of God, the passion of Christ was; and that should be enough to make him accept the thesis. Had God been withheld by the protocol of divine nature from so acting, it could have been an *impotentia in Deo*, and one most destructive to our hope of salvation.

But did not scholastic theologians then believe the saving death of the Son of God? Of course, but they tied themselves in knots to reconcile their Aristotelized theology with their Christian belief. Why did they not simplify their task by throwing out their Aristotelism? Professor Charles Hartshorne attributes their error to a passion for hyperbole—the desire to make God so utterly utter as to render all sense about him unutterable. That is not my reading of the history. Metaphysical hyperbole has always played its part in the rhetoric of devotion. But there were two motives pulling the same way which were less heady and less extravagant. One was a theory of causes, the other a doctrine of purity: both were Greek. The theory of causes was that Becoming depended on Being, so that the First Cause must be a being, just being itself, without reciprocity of action by anything else upon it such as to make it ever become in any particular other than, by its own nature, it was. To tell the medieval thinker to scrap this doctrine was to bid him tear up the only science of nature he could work with: so, of course, he wouldn't. The doctrine of purity was that the higher or nobler a being was, the more untouched it was by anything outside or below itself. Before this was Greek philosophy, it was pagan religion. The finale of Euripides's *Hippolytus* is a striking example. The blameless votary of Artemis lies dying, and the kind goddess stands by him to comfort him, up to the point where she says: 'And now I must leave you. You are going to die, and it would not do for a deathless deity to be in at a death.' But *nulla impotentia ponenda est in Deo*—Christ not only goes to the death of Lazarus, he goes to his own.

Since I am basing my exposition on the irrational foundation of a

Latin tag, let me have some more of it before I stop. What is the bearing of my precious formula on the minimizing and the maximizing accounts respectively of God's prior actuality? Let us recall that the maximizing account embraces all that the minimizing account contains, and an infinitude besides. It declares that God not merely initiates the process of the world, not merely acts in it, upon it and relatively to it, but above and before all worlds achieves the perfection of divine being in society by the generation of the Son and infusion of the Spirit. Now if it is intrinsically possible God should so fulfil beatitude on the level of deity itself, and if it is worth doing, then on the principle *nulla impotentia in Deo* how shall we deny that he has always done so? To limit God's action to the sphere of his inferior creation would be *ponere impotentiam in Deo* ['to posit restriction in God'], and that with a vengeance.

What then? Do the upholders of the minimizing view deny the force of our Latin maxim? Do they agree that the effect of their doctrine is *ponere quandam impotentiam in Deo*? ['to posit some restriction in God']. They do not. They say that the very notion of a life of God in God and apart from all creatures is nonsense, so that to deny to God the realization of such a life is to deny him nothing. The life of the Three in One is on all fours with the square circle.

This negative thesis may be argued on several grounds. First and most directly, it can be maintained that the action of such a divine life is contradictory of itself, like the square circle. But the contention is inconclusive. On the one hand, the comparison with 'square circle' is a manifest exaggeration; on the other, believers in the maximal view are themselves happy to admit that our minds are bound to fall over themselves to some extent, in aspiring to approach so transcendent an object of thought: and just how much confusion or paradox should be tolerated or indeed expected there, is a point scarcely possible to fix *a priori*. So the attack shifts its ground, and contends that the action is, anyhow, *vacuous*: it conveys no positive meaning to the mind. But then we run against the confidence of faith. So far from being vacuous, the idea clothes and shapes the life which the Catholic Christian understands himself to live. He is a son-by-adoption through incorporation with the Son-By-Nature: he looks for an ever closer association with infinite and eternal godhead, when, it may be, the physical creation has dropped clear away.

I suspect, however, that the real ground of the negative thesis, or rather, of man's favour towards it, finds expression in a less direct argument: an argument which it might be difficult to find fully drawn out or openly stated. It would run somewhat as follows. In theology, as in all sciences—but especially in theology —it is vital that we should reason from what is closer to us, and more immediately known, to things less familiar and more remote; not vice versa. Now if we know God at all, it is in the world, as the God of the world and as the God of us. If we do not know God as concerning himself with the world and with us, we do not know him at all, and there is no theology to be talked. Nothing in theology can be more certain than God's concern with the natural creatures or with our spiritual well-being. Such is the first step of the argument. The second is this. If God concerns himself with his creatures they must be of value or of importance to him; according to our religion, he actually loves us. We should not, then, allow ourselves the luxury of any transcendental hypothesis which makes the importance of his creatures to their creator less intelligible. But the belief that God is blessed in himself above all worlds does have this unhappy effect; for if he is so blessed why should he bother with us? If we retained a place in his interest, it must be negligible in comparison of the whole. The conclusion drawn is not, of course, that God abstains from being fully himself, so that he may have time for us. It is that the interest he takes in us shows his creatures to be the vital concerns of his action and 'being God' to be essentially 'being the God of a world'. It must be, then, that the transcendent life sketched by the dogma of the Trinity represents no real possibility, however speciously it may be made to sound in our ears.

There, then, is the argument; and what are we to say of it? I shall say that it rises on a thought of God so mean as to remove the ground of all spiritual religion. God's love for us does not follow from his natural need of us but from his being the living truth: whatever there is to be cared for, he cares for it with all the caring it will take, for that is the truth, or rectitude, of attitude and of action. *Nulla impotentia ponenda est in Deo*; God does not run short of love for us because he infinitely loves the Son of his love.

What Christian could think such blasphemy? We see the measure of God's love in the infinity of the good he confers on us and in the extremity of the means he employs to ensure our receiving it; and both are enhanced beyond all expression by the high doctrine of God's prior actuality. The benefit—everlasting fellowship with a life inexhaustibly sufficient; the means—a person infinite in bliss to take our life for his, and die our death. To say that such a doctrine obscures what Christians understand by the love of God, is surely fantastic.

So far I have been talking religion, not philosophy. For it has been my purpose to show that the high doctrine of God's prior actuality is no gratuitous philosophical encumbrance loaded on to a religion which can do just as well without it. On the contrary—it is the defining form of our traditional faith and if you throw it over you have a different religion—a different understanding of God's love for us, of our present existence in relation to him, and of our ultimate hopes. Enough of that. I will turn now to some reflections on the philosophical standing of our thesis about prior actuality.

A philosopher—even a philosopher prepared to discuss the possibility of a divine existence—will not be willing to take the articles of any creed as evidence. He may attach evidential value to the broad fact of religion; he may probe the phenomenology of religious acts. After that, his business will be to give the most reasonable account he can of the total background to the phenomena. He will be talking about the world as given in present experience, and about remoter causes or conditions only in so far as they make themselves felt in this present and experienced world. If theology comes before him it will come in the guise of an explanatory factor entering into his account of presented existences. So Whitehead found it necessary (did he not?) to acknowledge or to postulate a Principle of Concretion[1]—St Thomas would have said, of Composition—to account for or to determine the particular combinations of supposedly atomic characteristics which world-process successively exhibits. Whitehead, as he was well aware, was talking about the same function as appears in theology under the name of God's creative choice. Only it might seem more cautious, more philosophical, to speak of a principle of concretion. All we venture to state is that something, never mind what, acts as such a principle; or even, more cautiously still, that world-events fall out in accordance with such a principle, or in illustration of it. So what theology regards as a divine effect may be described almost as though it were a cosmic phenomenon. The operation of the concretive principle becomes *aliquid mundi*, as St Thomas might have said—a something attaching to the universe.

The decision to talk in this way is, on the face of it, purely procedural. The philosopher has not reached any valid conclusion, to the effect that the working of his principle is just the way the world goes. He simply leaves the question open as to what the real ground of the principle's operation may be. If he is writing a speculative cosmology, no more and no less, he may well choose to push his inquiries no further. He has taken the world for his field, and he may not want to go outside it. There's plenty to talk about, without going outside the universe. Whitehead, indeed (if we are to stick to the example we have taken) did go further. He saw the principle of concretion to be an empty form, which could not be conceived to operate otherwise than by exercise of creative choice. What was in its effect a principle of concretion was in its act the exercise of a divine mind. Very well; but might not the divine mind itself be described as *aliquid mundi*, that is, as the Mind of the World,[2] as a living purpose concerned with the direction and fulfilment of cosmic process?

Once again, we shall want to know whether such a way of talking represents a limitation of procedure or a metaphysical decision. It might only represent a limitation of procedure. One might still be talking about the world of our more direct knowledge, only with a slightly wider scope than before. One might go so far as to speak of the world as requiring for its explanation a creatively choosing Mind, *acting as* the mind of the world and persuading cosmic process along its path. If one means no more than this, one leaves open the question whether the mind so acting acts thus by nature, being just that sort of mind; or whether it acts thus by condescension, being already possessed in itself of perfect existence and *therefore* capable of freely initiating and leading the cosmic process. Alternatively one may use such language to express a metaphysical decision—that God is the creative Mind of cosmic process, *and he is nothing more*; he is the mind of the world-process in some way analogous to the way in which my consciousness is mind to my process of bodily life. And such, I suppose, is the position of some who profess a process theology. Such, perhaps, was the position of Whitehead. Or wasn't it?

About this sort of position I must content myself with making a single observation: that it appears to express, or to be animated by, a compromise between positivism and metaphysics. The metaphysician in us pushes so far as to insist that 'the principle of concretion' is at root the operation of an actual mentality of some mysterious or cosmic sort. The positivist in us reminds us to keep talking about events in the world, and the way they go; if we must mention a divine mind, it must be as a purpose exhaustively displayed in finite occurrences. The compromise is an uneasy one. Give positivism its head, and it will lead us to withdraw any sort of assertion of God's enjoying a life personal to himself—it will rephrase our statement as a piece of transparent mythology: the world-kaleidoscope shifts *as though* a principle of creative choice made the necessary options to determine the combinations realized. Give our metaphysical bent its head, and it will engage us with a cluster of the most daunting questions, such as these: If there is a universally creative mentality, what conception can we frame of it? If several ways of conceiving it are possible, which of them most fully satisfies the thirst for ultimate and total explanation which is the soul of metaphysical inquiry? Appalling questions, these; but if we admit the validity of the metaphysical quest, must we not wrestle with them? Whereas if we deny its validity, must we not surrender to the positivist argument and reduce our theology to an insipid myth about the way the world goes?

Into such altitudes of argument we will not advance; but we will scrape for a moment the lower edge of theological territory, where the divine life or action touches the world. Can we rationally suppose that God's life essentially is a creative and sympathetic living of the world-process as it proceeds? Plato, when he was feeling that way, might see God as a mind or soul living the revolution of the heaven. But then 'the heaven' to Plato was one perfect physical animal and its motions constituted one perfectly regulated and immortal animal life. Fair enough—but we cannot reinstate the Platonic cosmology. The universe we know isn't *a* system, still less *an* organism; it's a free-for-all of a million million

million bits of system, interacting as they can and largely with irrelevance to one another, according to a few elementary rules of the game controlling the nature of their mutual collisions and mutual exploitations.

Such is the so-called process of the universe. Regarded as the sole field for the activity of supreme mind it suffers from two disabilities. The first is that in overwhelming proportion it is, as Aristotle would say, ὀυδεν σεμνον—nothing much to write home about: the patches of sentence, let alone reason, are infinitely few and far between, in that restless swirl of palpitating dust. But it suffers from a more shattering disability: non-existence. The world-process is not; there's no such thing: it neither exists nor occurs nor proceeds. The universe has no history, no time-sequence, no direction. All histories, time-sequences, continuities of trend, all entities, systems, what you will—all activities, in fact, attach to the several and multitudinous constituents of which the universe is made up. 'The universe' is a name for their inter-action and mutual conditioning—for the rule according to which all entities constitute a field of force conditioning the action of any given entity. Conceived as a total coexistence of things or of events, the universe has no unity outside the mind which focuses it, and which represents it in the picture of a diagram; so the human astronomer may diagrammatize the galaxies. Supremely, no doubt, the universe is one in the focus of the divine mind; but this admission has little tendency to make the divine mind the mind *of* the universe. My capacity (such as it is) for thinking the world results from the way one bit of the world has gone, in throwing up a nervous system instrumental to such a feat. God's capacity for thinking the world cannot be supposed to result from the way the world goes—there is no super-organism of the world to provide an instrument for divine thinking. On the contrary, to entertain the idea of God is to invert the relation. God is not an act of thought resulting from the world-order; God is the act of thought from which whatever of world-order there is, results. So then, if we can't believe in God, we can't; but if we do, we shall believe in his prior actuality, as a spiritual life sufficient to itself.

I must fear that my raid into philosophical territory has been too hasty to achieve any conquest; and by way of conclusion I will return to theological ground. I step on to that ground, and look about me—and what do I find? I find a lot of biblical theologians standing on their heads in the effort to think eschatologically. The Apostles thought the world was about to come to an end and we really can't support them, because, after all, it didn't; neither do we, in our day, think it is going to at all soon, if ever. Yet somehow we feel bound to adopt the eschatological attitude. Allow me, then, to exhibit my own little contortion by way of carrying out so compulsory an exercise of the theological paradeground. What we want to do (is it not!) is to find a way of being far more truly eschatological than the Apostles: they, poor men, were merely doing it mythically but we will do it existentially. Very well then; here goes.

Let me say that an old cosmological error shared by the Egyptians, the Chaldeans and the Greeks had made of the earth and the heavenly bodies an everlasting tireless self-animated machine, whose parts never required replacement. To get rid of this monstrosity there was nothing for it but a grand almighty smash. So thought the Apostles, and no doubt it was very eschatological of them; but nothing compared with the eschatologism you and I can boast.

> *Dies irae, dies illa*
> *Solvet saeclum in favilla**

Their universe was one day to be smashed—ours is smashing itself the whole time. Their world would presently end, ours is always ending; for all its real constituents are processes whose phases perish as they pass. God has no need to destroy his creatures, he is constantly losing them. The divine life is the rock of being, which alone stands fast in the whirlpool of transience; and from that rock are stretched the hands of mercy, to rescue from the maelstrom spirits made in the divine image, and to give them fellowship with what solely endures.

Beginnings and endings tie up together. The God whose prior actuality is sufficiently entire to be the genuine first cause and creative origin of a world that need never have been, is equally the

---

* 'The day of wrath, that dreadful day, will dissolve the world in ashes.' Opening lines of a poem by Thomas of Celano and used as part of the Mass for the Dead—Ed.

God whose independence of being is sufficient for him to draw us out of a perishing world and attach us to his own eternity. Beginnings and endings—yes, and middles too; for the God who is what he is above and apart from the world is the God who can significantly be said to intervene in the midst of the world and to enter it by a true incarnation.

And now I am going to prophesy. Faith in eternal life is going to be the touchstone. A thoroughgoing theology of process is only going to believe immortal hope if it appears on scientific grounds that the world-process favours the perpetual survival of discarnate minds; and it is very unlikely that anything of the sort will prevail as scientific opinion. That is where the bluff is going to be called. Whereas if we believe in a God who saves to the uttermost we shall believe in a God who is not *aliquid mundi* but is *ens per se* ['self-existent being'].

Now it is a retort so easy to make, that any modernist theologian can make it in his sleep, without so much as turning over in bed— that it is a very selfish thing to make the survival of our precious souls a test question for faith. And, adds Professor Hartshorne, it doesn't matter anyhow because God has an excellent memory; he will get just as much satisfaction out of thinking what splendid souls we were in our lifetime as he would out of divinizing us eternally by association with his godhead. But will he? On the showing of the process-theology itself, the glory and the love of God are displayed solely in what he does with or for his creatures; and if he does not eternize nor divinize those he has deigned to lift into fellowship with himself, then the less God he. That we cannot become assured of God's goodness without becoming the recipients of his bounty is, no doubt, a very unfortunate circumstance and was felt to be so, if I remember rightly, by Milton's Satan. He found the debt of eternal gratitude intolerable; and he took suitable measures to be rid of it.

I had it in mind to compose a calm and philosophical paper, reasoned out in form. I have signally failed; I have become far too excited. But let me, in conclusion, see what elements of rational statement I can fish out of so much turbulence. It will amount to little.

I have said that the Christian disciples of Aristotle were wrong in stating that God does not, and cannot, make his action so relative to his creatures as to render that relation constitutive of anything in his divine life. I have said on the other hand that God's so relating his action to his creatures has no tendency to show all his activity to be thus creature-related and none of it God-related, as (for example) the traditional doctrine of the Blessed Trinity declares it to be; and I have added that the religion lived by orthodox Christians implies that God's action realizes both levels of relation.

Moving on to philosophical ground, I have remarked that philosophers, if they find God at all, are likely to acknowledge him first in an action which somehow shapes the world as it runs. But I have gone on to say that they have no need, as philosophers, to stop there. The metaphysical passion, if they indulge it, can carry them on to acknowledge in God a prior actuality which is the whole cause why any world runs anyhow. And, I have said, it is the ultimate thrust of metaphysical inquiry which coincides most closely with the movement of religion. For religion is concerned with what God is in himself, and with his ultimate mastery over all existence.

I have warned you that your theologians of process are all too much inclined to cut God down to size and fit him upon a world which measures up to him extremely poorly; and I have called on Christians to rally round the Ark of the Covenant, and not to be fooled out of their faith.

Grace and the Human Will†

In this paper (if I ever write it) I shall make two distinct but not wholly disconnected endeavours. First, I shall classify in a rough and ready manner the several strands of St Augustine's thought about the insufficiency of the human will. Second, I shall make some jejune remarks on the merits of the case and in particular on the mutual relation which obtains between several of our conceptions of divine action exercised upon us.

John Lucas, in his paper,* concentrated on what is surely the most natural and immediately intelligible of the issues raised by the dispute between St Augustine and the Pelagians. We may ask the apparently straightforward question: 'What brought me into the way of salvation or led me to persevere in it? Was it I myself, or was it some other power or factor?' We may note, in passing, that while the first alternative (I myself) is, or at least appears to be, determinate, the second is not. It may have been Ambrose or a Bible-text or a little bird in the garden or a sore throat; perhaps even a gust of emotion, or a quickening of interest which fell on me quite apart from any choice, decision, act or virtue of mine. Here is a queer collection of things, but we put them all in one basket because, being no direct part or effect of my voluntary behaviour, they come to me as gratuitous, or unmerited. Speaking as a pious providentialist, I shall call them the Grace of God. Now, as Lucas said, Augustine and Pelagius must agree that no one strikes into the saving path, unless *both* factors are operative. No one becomes a Christian without antecedent conditions and present influences; no one becomes a Christian, but of his own will. It follows that, considered absolutely, the question, 'Was it I, or was

† A paper read to the Metaphysicals, *circa* 1964.
* 'Pelagius and St Augustine'; initially read to the Metaphysicals and now published in *Journal of Theological Studies*, Vol. 22 (April 1971), pp. 73–85 —Ed.

it the grace of God?' makes no sense. But, as Lucas said, the question will be interpreted by a limited conception of causality. Cause will mean the differential, or the manipulable, factor. Suppose an unvarying attitude on my part: then what caused my salvation was an alteration outside me, which brought my will, previously ineffective, into effective play. Suppose an unvarying background of (let us say) Christian society and institutions: then what caused my salvation was a fresh effort of decision or strenuity on my part.

Even so conceived, the question, 'Was it I, or was it the grace of God?' can be interpreted in two ways. It can be interpreted as a genuinely empirical question: we want to know in any given case which it was; and the asking of the question implies that some- times the one answer, sometimes the other, will be historically correct. 'Tom was converted by meeting a saint; Dick by pulling himself together and making a retreat.' These may be perfectly truthful, and also perfectly pious statements. It will sound less pious, of course, if we put the two statements in the generalized form: 'Dick achieved his own conversion; Tom was converted by the Grace of God.' And it may be that this linguistic indecency has something to do with Augustinian protests against Pelagian remarks. So long as we are talking about Tom, all is well—it is very evident he was not converted by his own efforts; it was the unmerited grace of God that he met Father Anastasias, or Sister Jemima. If, however, we go on to contrast the case of Dick, a man who laid hold of saving truth by his own endeavour, we shall still want to say that he (of course) like all Christians was *really* converted by the grace of God; but that here the intervenient character of the divine action was less striking because less external.

The moral is, that the form 'Was it I, or was it the grace of God?' is inappropriate for asking empirical questions. The empirical questions can be fairly asked; but not in these terms. The terms suggest a *philosophical* question: not about what happened in Tom's or Dick's conversion, but what happens in any and every conversion, or, indeed, adhesion to the faith. And, in spite of his special illustration of conversion from his own case, this is surely how Augustine understands the issue. The attitude of the human will is always in such a state, that the differential factor leading to

o

conversion must be sought in the unmerited action of influences ultimately deriving from God. Men's voluntary attitudes before conversion do, of course, differ in many ways; but not in ways which are significant for the achievement or non-achievement of conversion. Such appears to be the Augustinian answer. But a Pelagian answer is equally possible, and can even be made to sound equally pious, if we take this philosophical ground. For, it may be said, God's grace is not and cannot be the differential factor: it is changeless, impartial and superabundant, like the sunshine or the rain. But *recipitur secundum modum recipientis*: its effect is measured by the receptivity of our wills. It is difficult to believe that any real question is being discussed here, as between the Augustinian and Pelagian theses. An edifying sermon can be preached from either angle.

We observe, however, that on either side the sermon sounds good, so long as it leans on theological reasons; bad, if it takes its stand on anthropological or psychological grounds. The theological topic of the Pelagian is the universality of grace; the theological topic for the Augustinian is the divine initiative: and either affords a splendid text for sacred rhetoric. The anthropological topic of St Augustine is the universal impotence of the human will; that of Pelagius, the unalienable power or right of free choice. Now it is no use saying (with Pelagius) that every sane man who hears the gospel has the live option of embracing it; nor (with Augustine) that no one really exercises such an option at all, or anyhow not until the flank of choice has been virtually turned by the march of events.

We will here leave to speak of Pelagius, and consider St Augustine. His doctrine of the impotence of the will to achieve salvation is *either* a mere reverse statement of the divine initiative, *or* it is a psychological theory. If it is the former, its detailed application, or cash-interpretation, may be an open question. In what way does the divine initiative get in front of the human will? I might not know, or I might propose various answers. If, on the other hand, it is a psychological theory, it must be definite in form, and open to refutation.

St Augustine has, in fact, a psychological theory. One may say two things about it: that first, it is a bad theory; and second, it is an *ad hoc* theory. The general lines of his philosophical psychology appear to be neo-Platonist; and the neo-Platonist sages were libertarians. The special twist which St Augustine introduces does not seem to arise from that way of looking at the mind.

For us, perhaps, it may be simplest, and not seriously mis-leading, to draw out the Augustinian from the Aristotelian position. A man has the free choice of means, but always in view of a preconceived end, which simply does attract him, and so becomes the object of his βουλησις (*voluntas*).* This pre-conceived end, though it particularizes itself in individual objects or purposes, is conceived as general, like the object of every appetite *qua* appetite (hunger as such is for the nourishing).** Now according to Aristotle, and all the orthodox (i.e. optimistic) Greek philosophers, the human aspiration;[1] like every movement of nature, tends towards its proper goal. It may be biased by unhappy accident: a true education at the hands of others, or a consistent exercise of the rational faculties on our own part, will tend to liberate it. According to the neo-Platonists, the natural and best aspiration of everything is towards what is above it in the hierarchy: and so the human mind rises towards God, when it has the chance; and makes many particular choices or decisions in pursuit of its everlasting good. According to St Augustine, the fallen human mind simply lacks that care for its true object, which could motive an effective decision, or προαιρεσις, in pursuit of it. Fallen Adam may make many decisions, in implementation of his φαυλη φαντασια του αγαθου ['imperfect apprehension of what is good'; cf. *NE* 114a 32f.]; but none of them can raise him to the pursuit of a higher good.

The Augustinian psychology is doubly vicious. First, it dog-

* Although Farrer wrote βουλη—'deliberation', he most likely meant βουλησις —'desire' or 'inclination'; for these reasons: (1) it is the Greek equivalent of *voluntas* ('What the Stoics call βουλησις, we (*sc.* the Romans) call *voluntas*'— Cicero, *Tusculan Disputations*, IV, vi, 12); (2) βουλητα, which Farrer uses to develop the argument in the following paragraphs, is cognate with βουλησις, not βουλη; (3) 'deliberation' can only be accommodated to the philosophical argu-ment with difficulty, since προαιρεσις itself involves deliberation (see *Nicho-machean Ethics*, III, 2 and 3), and therefore cannot stand in opposition to it; (4) it is consistent with his criticism of the Augustinian doctrine as having the fixity of a fallen or depraved appetite (see p. 196 below). (5) he made the same slip of pen in the margin of his text of *Nicomachean Ethics*—Ed.

** *Republic*, IV, 437d; where Plato argues that appetite as such is the desire for the general means of satisfaction, rather than a particular satisfaction—Ed.

matizes *a priori* about empirical possibilities (i.e. what effective aspirations there are to be found among unevangelized mankind); and second, it hardens the line between βουλητα and προαιρετα.* It is allowable to interpret the Aristotelian distinction as innocently logical. In any choice we make between alternatives, there must be some good which (to our mind) stands above them, and of which they are to be conceived as the rival incarnations. But a good which transcends our choice on any given occasion may on another occasion become alternative to another object: the lover takes his love for granted when he is considering how to please his girl; he makes it the subject of choice, if he is driven to ask, 'my mistress or my country?' Nothing that can be seen as an alternative is barred from the field of choice; and so, though self-regarding satisfactions often serve as axioms of choosing, there is nothing to prevent their being weighed against the love of God—weighed, and found wanting too. Whereas for St Augustine the βουλητα of the natural man are fixed and determinate: his aspiration has not the universality of reason, even as a possibility; it has the fixity of an appetite.

St Augustine, then, rests his case for the supreme causality of grace on a psychological theory which has little to commend it. But, as we said, he can and does equally rest it on the sovereign initiative of God. Whatever the psychological facts may be, how can we, how dare we, deny that all good descends from above; that the best activity of the creature is one of obedience? Here again, a dubious mental philosophy comes to the aid of a theological axiom. The standard example of true thinking was the mathematical; and this was supposed to be a coincidence of our thought with a pattern of truth valid *per se*: a pattern of truth which, on the neo-Platonic view, was the substance of the divine mind. The true and free act of intelligence, then, turns out to be one of submission, or of obedience.

But when we have reached this point, it is time we observed that we have completely shifted our ground. The original question was: 'Who brought about my salvation? Did I? Or did grace, acting from without?' The question assumed that there are many things

---

* I.e. between 'desire' and 'deliberate choice'—*Nicomachean Ethics*, III. 2 1111b 26ff. Marginalia in Farrer's copy of *NE* indicate that he took this distinction as 'between moral and morally indifferent ends'—Ed.

which 'I' can do: for instance, I do perform the act of asking for baptism, of professing my faith, of doing this or that duty in obedience to its precepts. But (it asks), did I *come* to do these wholesome things by my own choice and effort, or because other influences occasioned me so to do?

The psychological theory, which we criticized just now, took a fresh distinction. There are many choices (it admitted) which I can and do make of myself; but there are others which may look open to me, but in reality they are not so. Whatever external influences play upon me, they will not evoke these closed choices. I must be mysteriously (one might almost say, miraculously) reborn, turned into another creature, before I can make them. Then, of course, I *shall* be free to do so. But now the highest metaphysical theory takes a different line. Even the healed and restored spirit, most freely acting, cannot act of itself—not, anyhow, in any truly positive direction: sin is ours, and yet sin is defective action, and only sinful in so far as it is imperfectly active. Now it must be obvious that, on this level, the thought-form has radically changed. We are no longer handling a simple distinction between what we can freely do, and what we cannot, either because it is done to us from without, or because it is not within our psychological repertoire to do it. We are now talking of that sort of act, which is most free and most truly our own (if any is) and we are saying that it is not simply free, or ours, it is an offprint of the divine will.

The form which is here being employed is obviously that of the transcendent scale. Our acts are free, in comparison of our *passiones*: and among our acts, some more truly free than others, namely, those which are, and deserve to be, sovereign in the hierarchy of our mind and will. But not even these are free in comparison of that freedom, which is and should be sovereign over all the world, and especially over us. Our best freedom is the highest freedom we know, and so it must stand to us as our type of what freedom is. Yet we are drawn to allege that there *is* a freedom, far more above this, than our most free acts are above our least.

According to the distinction with which we started, the way to experience grace is to find ourselves occasioned to do good by influences and forces outside ourselves: for then it will not be we

who act. According to the thought-form we are now using, the way
to experience grace will be to exercise our highest powers in the
freest and most truly personal way: for by so doing, we shall touch
the point of transition in the hierarchy of being, where the divine
action actively comes through into the creature.

The contradiction appears absolute: it may be broken down,
however. It is requisite only to recall that to label wholesome
external influences 'the grace of God' is not to specify or trace
the line of causality by which they descend to us from their divine
source. Some of these gracious influences are what profane lips
call accidents, and piety calls providences; and (by all admission)
the relation of such events to the divine will is wholly opaque to us.
But such events, on any showing, have no more than a secondary
and assisting role: they would be nothing by themselves. Children
might sing in the garden till they were hoarse,* without converting
the Saint; he might lecture himself hoarse, and be no more inclined to spend his enforced leisure in a salutary meditation. The
decisive influences were personal: God in Ambrose, God in
Monnica, God in Christ. And if Ambrose and Monnica, not to
name our Redeemer, were occasioned to holiness in turn by external influences merely, we should have an infinite regress, and
never come any nearer the Divine Cause. It remains that they
were holy, and transmitted the causality of God, by adherence to
him in the apex of their wills; and especially Christ by an inseparable adhesive and personal identity with godhead.

Nothing could be further from the pretence of philosophical
exactitude than this ramble round the field of Augustinian conceptions, in the course of which we have made one or two critical
remarks, but for the most part have accepted old-world ideas
which cry aloud for revision or analysis. We even sincerely talk of
drawing conclusions from such unexamined premises; but perhaps we can speak of pointing a moral.

It is a common enough case, that the sort of occasion most apt
to start religious reflections is not the most illuminating about
divine mysteries. A man is struck by awe and gratitude to observe
that his conversion was occasioned by circumstances quite outside
the scope of his will. 'And so,' says he, 'it was not I, it was the
grace of God.' But if he goes so far as to consider the operation of

* *Confessions*, Bk. 8, sec. 12—Ed.

God's grace, it is not in such externalities that it is even remotely intelligible: it is in the act by which he himself comes to adhere to the prior will of God for him, and in some manner to experience a continuity of the creaturely with the creative purpose.

There is, of course, something to be said on the other side. Just as self-love is an absurdity and humanity is only made amiable to us by being objectified in another face, so the expression (though not perhaps the influx) of grace is scarcely perceptible in ourselves —even where we do not distort and hinder it beyond recognition —but may be visible in others. That is to suppose that they and we are on a level. But it may not be so: we may be elementary Christians, they may be saints; not to mention Christ, who is Grace Incarnate. Moreover, even where there is no great disparity between Christians, others are uniquely the instruments of grace towards us by being Christians before us, and talking us into the speech of faith, as those who reared us talked us into our mother tongue.

But, metaphysically considered, the mystery of grace is not seen in the mutual or one-sided influences passing between those who receive it. It is seen in the influx of the divine will into the human. And if this is where the true mystery lies, then it cannot be that the recognition of grace can undermine an appreciation of man's free will. For free and sovereign actions on our part, anyhow actions of thought and of decision, are the chief occasions and, as it were, organs for the reception of actual grace. If we are told that our destiny is determined not by our free acts, but by conditions or influences outside our control, the effect is to enslave us. But if we are told that our most free acts are those most purely and pellucidly expressive of a will sovereign over all, the paradox cannot dismay us; it cannot deny the effect of a freedom which it supposes and upon which it offers a theological comment. Still less shall we be dismayed to be reminded that the grace active in the human will so operates as to make us dependent upon one another, as well for the supernatural gifts of God, as for natural charities and blessings.

Causes†

As the day of reckoning approaches, and I have to produce the paper I promised, I wonder again (as I have wondered on similar occasions in the past) what on earth induced me to undertake such an effort. I am an elderly administrator and I have utterly failed to keep up with the pace of contemporary discussion. I venture, it is true, to take a few pupils in ancient philosophy, but the charm of that discipline is, that it is virtually static. I have just read Mr Crombie's excellent volume on Plato, and reassured my intellectual sloth—his brisk and ingenious discussion leaves the landscape looking much as it always did. But you do not want to hear me stamping over classic ground; I must attempt some contemporaneous reflections. What made me say I would? I should like to say, 'Good nature'; I'm afraid I must say, 'Vanity'.

Well now—your Voltaire—Voltaire, I take it, was a deist. He regarded the claims of revealed religion as both silly and oppressive. But he would not see how to square the arithmetic of cosmology without a First Cause. My pupils cannot believe that the deists were in earnest. If a man was not a pious man, if he did not mean to have anything much to do with the Supreme Being, then, they say, he did not believe what he professed. But my pupils are wrong. You could be a sincere philosophical deist, and practise no religion at all. So strong, in the eyes of previous generations, was the causal argument.

Now in my own muddle-headed way I believe in a Supreme Being, and not, I dare say, principally on the strength of causal argument. Nevertheless one of the things I am moved to assert is that the Supreme Being is the First Cause: and so I cannot disinterest myself from the question how we should think or talk about causality; and whether our common thinking does or does

† A paper read to the Voltaire Society, 1963.

not employ causal concepts of such a sort as to make sense of the world's dependence on Transcendent Cause.

What I am saying is that a theologian must inevitably have an interest in a high, or realistic, or naïve, doctrine of causality; so I make a clean breast of the ground of my concern. But please do not think that I am going to offer a constructive causal argument for theistic belief. I am just going to ruminate in a very elementary way on causes as such. And I hope you will not think that I must be counted out from the start as a prejudiced witness. A man who has had certain experiences of human personality will resist a philosophical analysis which seems to depersonalize the human being: and why? because he does not find it adequate to his experience; and a man who attempts to live his life in the form of dependence on the Supreme Cause will similarly resist an account of causal relation which makes such a dependence nonsensical. For, says he (rightly or wrongly), we in a manner experience it. The only man who will escape all prejudices of this kind, and in every field, will be the man who has experienced nothing at all.

Enough of this. Let us talk about Causes. I will begin by suggesting a question, in the hope that it may give some sort of direction to the remarks which will follow. My question is, which of two statements, if either, we should be willing to accept. The first statement is this: Causality reduces to natural uniformity. A general belief in causality is the belief that some rule or rules expressing a uniformity of natural order will be found applicable to the occurrence of any event in the context in which it occurs. The second statement is this: A general belief in causality is the belief that actualities already actual when any development takes place have it in them to produce, and do produce, that development.

Of these two statements the first is (I hope) clear; the second, I know, is not. The first is clear, for there is no great mystery about the way in which an occurrence may conform to, or come under, a rule expressing a uniformity of pattern or of sequence in nature's working. But if we talk about actualities already actual producing, and having it in them to produce, the development which follows, everything is obscure. We do not know what the 'actualities' in question are, for an actuality is merely something that is actual, and all sort of things can be said to be actual: phenomena, states of affairs, processes, agents, substances. Again, we do not know what is meant either by 'producing' or 'having it in them to produce'. So, then, the second suggested statement is about as obscure, or ill-defined, as it could well be. Why, then, do we bother with it? Because it expresses that common-sense belief in the power, efficacy, or constrainingness of causes which Hume's thought was too honest to deny altogether, and too limited to explain adequately.

The first of our two statements, which reduces causality to natural uniformities, is only disputable if it is held to be exclusive. We may dispute, that is, the assertion that we have no meaningful idea of causality but uniformity of sequence. We cannot dispute the fact that uniformity of sequence is all that, in many fields, we can practically study. We must admit (for example) that uniformities of pattern or of sequence are the only sorts of causality which play any part in several of the more exact sciences. But it is still open to us to maintain that such sciences are abstractive. They study the uniformity-aspect of natural process, not the power or efficacy which displays itself in the events whose uniformity-aspect they study. But (we can say if we like) the fact that these sciences abstract from real causal power does not have any tendency to show that such power is an illusion. There are plenty of comforting analogies we can quote if we wish to take this view. The statistical method can be applied to human behaviour, and we can talk about population-trends and economic laws in abstraction from the living acts and voluntary choices of individual men. Yet we do not suppose that the applicability of such methods has any tendency to show that our belief in personal action or choice is illusory. Mrs Jones buys a cabbage because she decides to bake it with chestnuts in its hair* and set it before Mrs Smith, whom she has asked to supper because, poor dear, she has been having such an awful time with her burst pipes. This is a voluntary action if any action is, but the purchase of the cabbage goes to swell the economic statistics just the same. And so it may be that a real power or agency (though certainly not of a personal or voluntary kind) underlies the uniformities studied in the physical sciences.

We could say, if we wished, that these sciences study *pattern*,

---

* An odd metaphor, but it appears to be what Farrer wrote. Quite possibly a pun on bits of chestnut 'in its hair'—i.e. the leaves of the head of cabbage—Ed.

not *cause*, but that there are causes for the patterns all the same. But to deny that the sciences study causes at all, seems an odd way to talk; and the history as well of science as of language makes it more natural to speak of abstractions taken within causality itself, rather than of abstractions which disattend from causality and attend to something else.

Talking of the history of the causal idea, we may recall that ingenious if wrong-headed philosopher Robin Collingwood, who, in the most perverse of all his works, the *Essay on Metaphysics*, offers a treatise on the history of causal thinking. This treatise is intended to illustrate and support the general thesis of the book, which is that at any given time serious thinkers such as scientists are at the mercy of absolute presuppositions, or categories which they cannot question. These absolute presuppositions change from time to time and, looking back after the event, the historian of ideas can observe the fact; but that's all he can do, it seems, according to Collingwood. For instance, he says to us, you may suppose that serious thinkers have always been concerned with *causes*. But let me point out to you that serious enquiry, in different ages and in several fields, has been activated by very different conceptions of what a *cause* is.

The tendency of Collingwood's argument seems to be in the direction of a sort of idealism. The picture we form of the world at any given time is to be the product of crude experience on the one hand; and on the other, of principles of order or interpretation which the mind itself supplies and brings to its engagement with the crude data. One can easily see what in general such a doctrine means by taking the example of admittedly sophisticated and arbitrary approaches to the world of our experience. I shall not observe such facts as 'an acute example of an unsolved Oedipus complex' by the light of nature. I shall only observe such facts if I go round the place primed with the Freudian mythology and ready to plant on my human environment the questions it suggests. But now, Collingwood is saying, we all know where the Freudian models come from, how they were constructed and why. The great Sigmund put it all together as a practical method of classifying hysterical and other psychically regrettable phenomena—whereas the basic models and the basic questions in the mind of any age or culture are not put together *ad hoc* in this way. They are just there, haunting the period and conditioning its thinking, *malgré lvi*. Take, for example, says Collingwood, the idea most fundamental to all serious enquiry—the idea that there is a cause to be found. No genius invents the idea, as Freud invented Oedipus complexes and so forth. It underlies the invention of all ideas that are invented, and if it were not presupposed no such inventions could be made.

But neither can you say (pursues Collingwood) that there are just causes operating all around and anyone can see them, as easily as he can see cats and dogs. For if that were so, the causal concept could not have changed so radically as I show you it has, from one age to another. And the same historical demonstration will stop you from saying what Hume and Kant said in their different ways —that causal thinking is just the only way in which a mind like ours can do anything with its world. For in that case, why has causal thinking been done so differently at different times? Say if you like that it is the only way in which the mind of *the time* can make anything of its world; but admit that the mind of one time is not the mind of another, and that the mind of a given time is the fate of the men of that time.

Why should I ask you to lend your ears to an oration over Collingwood's remains? I can assure you that I mean neither to bury Robin, nor to praise him—I would gladly learn something from him though; for whatever he was or was not, he was a stimulating writer. And what strikes me about the history of causal thinking which he offers, is that it suggests a more interesting conclusion than that which he wants it to support. For what his historical account shows is by no means that the question about causes has been a varying but ultimate riddle propounded to the universe from age to age by a racial mentality which combines the changeableness of the chameleon with the inscrutability of the sphinx. Nothing of the sort; his story shows the progressive attempt to interpret environment through the model of one's own interaction with it. The first sort of cause to be talked about was the environmental factor occasioning a man to alter his conduct in a significant way: e.g. the *cause* of his quarrelling with his uncle was. . . . Next, we observed that, by ourselves behaving in a certain way, we could occasion others to act as we wished: we thought of *causing* them to change their minds. Then we saw that an analogous treatment could usefully be extended to physical bodies or natural forces. We had been used to make do with simple active verbs—we had pushed, we had displaced the stone. Now, finding that we could not, by pushing, displace it, we adopted an indirect method: by digging away the earth on the lower side of it, we caused it to roll. So we came to call the removal of the earth the *cause* of its rolling. Next we observed that natural forces might sometimes do the job for us: rainwater might wash the earth away and cause the stone to roll; so the action of one force or thing became the cause of the action of another force or thing, without our taking a hand in the matter. Nevertheless, since our interest remained practical and manipulative, we were inclined to limit the use of 'cause' to agents or acts occasioning effects which we desired either to produce or to prevent. If we wished to produce the effect we could assist its natural cause; if we wished to prevent the effect we could inhibit or remove or counteract the cause. And so, Collingwood remarks, in practical sciences like medicine we still talk of the causes of sickness or of recovery, and mean the conditioning factors by manipulation of which we may hope to prevent the one, or forward the other.

Such a limitation of view was a matter of convenience, rather than of principle. Once we had seen natural agents as causing one another to act, there was nothing to stop us from taking ourselves out of the picture, and contemplating a scene in which natural agents occasioned the action of natural agents, and so *ad infinitum*. So the grandiose scheme of perfect science, or of total explanation came into view. Could we but see what sorts of natural agents there were, and what they were apt to do, and how the action of one *caused* another to modify its action, we should understand the universe. Such an enterprise seemed to begin, as I was saying, with our taking ourselves out of the picture—but it was a *reculer pour mieux sauter*: by taking ourselves out of it, and studying the lines of it objectively, we put ourselves in the position to re-enter it with better effect. Since we could predict, we should know when and where to intervene; and understanding the structure of process, we might see how to manipulate it for our advantage.

There is only one more paragraph we need add to this perfunctory sketch of causal history. We divided the factors of total explanation into two: what natural agents are apt to do, and how they condition one another's doings. These two factors have a very different look. 'What agents are apt to do' suggests, if it does not actually require, teleological explanation: will not agents be apt to do what fulfils their tendencies? By contrast, 'The manner in which agents condition one another' excludes teleology and prescribes a treatment in terms of inflexible rule. Only consider: What can be meant by saying that an action on the part of one agent sets a condition for the action of another? Both agents, if you like, may act freely or purposively. But to say that one sets a condition for the action of the other can only mean that he imposes a necessity. Unless the condition set by the action of *a* for the action of *b* follows by an invariable uniformity from the nature of the event constituted by *a*'s action, then I cannot conceive what is meant by saying that *a*'s action conditions *b*'s. Well then: attention to agents, and what they are apt to do, gave scope to teleology; attention to the mutual conditioning of agents prescribed inflexible rule, and invited mathematical treatment.

Hence the glorious scientific revolution of the late Renaissance —to make physics exact, and bring it all under mathematical discipline, it was found convenient to ignore what natural agents are apt to do, and concentrate on how they mutually condition one another's doings. And, since we couldn't get rid of the agents altogether, we found it convenient to postulate that they were all very small, perfectly uniform, and apt to act in an absolutely one-track sort of way. The model from which everything started, the model of the living agent interacting with his environment, was still in play; but we made a distinction. Sometimes when I act upon a neighbouring being, it reacts—for instance, if I pull the cat's tail it scratches my face. Sometimes the neighbouring being does not react, it is simply misshapen or displaced: I push my thumb into the clay; I push the stone out of my path. Well then, let it be supposed that natural agents do not react, they are simply displaced. Their action is, in fact, a mere passivity. Hence the universe of Descartes and Newton. It was jolly for science; what was awkward was, you couldn't fit in agents who really do act or react, and not merely suffer displacements, e.g. you and me and the cat. And that, of course, was Descartes's headache.

Since those days, as is very well known, we have been driven by the facts to recognize that natural agencies do act, and react, like anything. But (anyhow at the physical level) we can still regard their action, however forcible, as simple or uniform; or anyhow such as to endure the invariable applicability of mathematical laws. Still, we are in a world of active beings once more, however elementary—which is kind of comforting for self-consciously active beings like you and me. We are not poor only children, like Descartes: we have got a world of physical brothers and sisters to play ball with us.

So much for my historical sketch of causal thinking, which is by no means so Collingwoodian as it set out to be—but there! I can't be bothered to follow him when I think he has got it wrong and the moral is unaffected in any case. What is the history of causal thinking? It is the history of the interpretation of our environment by the model of our own interaction with it. Not only has the application of the model been progressively extended: the fit of the model to the facts has also been progressively modified, and especially in modern times. And no wonder, for the clue is our own interaction with our environment; and we are conscious, voluntary agents, whereas the agencies of nature are not. So the fit of the clue to the facts is inevitably a misfit, and it is very natural we should have tried it this way and that way, to reduce the misfit as far as we could.

A most telling and informative example of causal thinking is Aristotle's. What is Aristotle's causal theory? The elements of it are derived from nothing more nor less than an analysis of the factors involved in an act of human craftsmanship. What we want to understand is how nature makes things, but since we have no immediate penetration or insight into her operations, we take the perspicuous example. When *we* make things we know how it goes, for we have the recipe. There is required some stuff (ὕλη or *deal*, says Aristotle,[1] for he is thinking of a carpenter) a form into which it is fashioned, a maker with the art so to fashion it, and a purpose to impel him. Here are Aristotle's four productive factors, or causes (so-called). Having got them, what does he do with them? Does he apply the model to nature, neat? Does he make the world out to be the handiwork of a supernatural craftsman? He does not. He breaks the four-factor pattern down to fit the natural facts. Everywhere he finds a pattern *analogous* to the craftsman-example, but it is never the same—except, of course, in other examples of human craft. Everywhere he labours to pick out his four factors: but the parts they play vary from case to case, and their mutual relation to one another varies equally. To take his own examples, it is one thing when a statuary makes a statue, another thing when a man begets a man.

Aristotle's causal doctrine may be highly individual and perhaps it was a nuisance that it held sway over the scientific mind for such a length of time. But in the sense that concerns us it is also highly typical of causal thinking in general. The human model is taken, being the most immediate or perspicuous: it is broken down to fit natural causalities because, after all, they are not the same.

Having come so far, I propose now to turn back and reconsider a comparison I casually made. By way of expounding Collingwood, I contrasted the causal idea in general with artificial and voluntarily adopted models such as those employed in the Freudian mythology. (The example was mine, by the way, not Collingwood's.) But now, is the contrast really so strong? Freud is concerned with a wide range of facts, namely, the attitudes of adolescent youths to their fathers and mothers. He picks out one history (which happens to be mythical) exhibiting an actual example of the relationship of a young male to father and mother, namely that of Oedipus. The merit of the instance is that it is clear—attitudes more or less disguised and always thwarted in civilized life are exhibited as actually fulfilled through a trick of fate. So Oedipus, the young male, becomes a clue to young males in general. But, of course, the model cannot be applied neat. It has to be more or less broken down to fit the instances. I did not kill my father or marry my mother. I did not even want to, in any ordinary sense of the word 'want'; I didn't fear, either, in the ordinary sense of the word 'fear', that I should be landed in doing it. But I suppose that, reared as I was in a traditional and somewhat patriarchal family, I had a handsome Oedipus complex, and solved it, though not quite in the Oedipodean manner.

Now to take the other side of the comparison. Here we are concerned with an even wider range of facts than adolescent maladjustments and adjustments—we are concerned with the whole field of agents conditioned in their action by the action of other agents. But here too we take for our model the luminous instance of the very thing we went to understand—the instance of the agent which is ourself, conditioned by, and conditioning, other agents. Here, too, the instance must be broken down, or modified, to cover the range; for just as I am not an Oedipus, so a cabbage, or a rag, or a particle is not a me.

So far the parallel holds. But we must be fair; we must concede Collingwood the differences. Whereas on the one side Freud did the thinking out, on the other side it was done by the convenient fictional character, man. Freud did it in one brainwave and a decade or two of clinical practice; man did it in all the history there has been. Freud's thinking about complexes was a serviceable addition to the battery of human skill; man's thinking about causes was the very nerve of human skill itself. Freud's mental invention was consciously made with a definite aim in mind; man's mental invention was as it were embodied and wrapped up in his expanding exploration and developing use of the world, and evolved *pari passu* with it. Collingwood is, I think, inclined to suggest that the practice of causal interpretation came first, and the reflection which brings the categories to light, is subsequent. And this may be the usual order. I do not see that it need be accepted as invariable. Kant may have merely codified the causal categories of Newtonian physics; but was not Aristotle creating an instrument for use?

I did not set out either to estimate the work of Collingwood or to describe the history of causal thinking. I set out to ruminate on causes and to see whether our causal beliefs are such as to support metaphysical inferences. I say, our causal *beliefs*, because when one comes to metaphysics, it is a question of what (after all due critical reflection) we *cannot but believe*. And so Collingwood thought; only what we *cannot but believe* was the phase of categorical form or of absolute presupposition, in force in our own time as applicable to the sciences. It was indeed odd that Collingwood should have been inclined himself to assert a metaphysical theology; for it seems strange to assert the real existence of a timeless ground for all historical change on the basis of a form of thought admitted to be itself a phase of historical change, the category of a passing hour. Surely the most you could say would be, that the world-picture of the time looks better with a deity in the top right-hand corner; that the world-picture proves its validity by its ability to organize the terrestrial phenomena; that sub-

P

sequent generations will doubtless alter the picture a good deal, so as to organize the phenomena in some ways more skilfully; and that we cannot possibly guarantee that in their picture the little baroque heaven at the top right-hand corner will retain its position.

Well now, I said I would not attempt anything so enormous as an argument for deistic belief; no, not even before the Voltaire Society, which is doubtless committed to a pious and tender regard for the convictions of its eponymous hero. All I want to do is to see what sort of beliefs about cause would conceivably support metaphysical inferences and what beliefs would not. And, reflecting on Collingwood's history of causes, I ask myself this question: Can I see in the whole human enterprise of causal explanation, from first to last, any features which are inseparable from it and whose future elimination from the ground is incredible? And if I can, then will these features of causal thinking support metaphysical inferences, or will they not? Of these two questions, the former is very much the easier to answer, so let us turn to it.

Yes, surely I can discern such features. Causal explanation is and can only be an interpretation of natural interactions by the clue, or the model, of our own interferences with our environment, and its interferences with us. To understand the world never was, nor conceivably could be, to construe it as patterns of *phenomena*. It must be construed as an interaction of real existences carrying on business as it were out there in space under their own names. But now, apart from any personal identity with my own body and any active identity with my bodily performances; and apart from my experience of impinging upon, and being impinged upon by, other things or forces, I have no conceivable clue to physical existence, or physical force, or physical interaction. So whatever is inseparable from the use of the human model, however sophisticated, will be intrinsic to causal thinking, and indeed to rational human experience altogether.

But before we ask what features of causal thinking are (for the reason given) inalienable; still more, before we think of asking whether they can be made to support Voltaire's deism or mine, we may as well reckon with scientific pragmatism. The scientific pragmatist is going to speak to the following effect: 'Your historical observations,' he will say to us, 'are no doubt of interest to historians; they are of no philosophical importance, and how could they be? You show us that causal thinking has been the progressive adaptation of a model derived from human action. But, as you have shown, the model has been progressively broken down, refined and whittled away; and the more we have got rid of the original human analogy the less it has got in our light and the more we have learnt about the workings of nature. Men began with the naïve *a priori* assumption that the model would cast light on nature and that nature's workings would be somehow manlike. I agree with you that, initially, we had no other clue, and no power of thinking otherwise. Nothing, indeed, could teach us any better, but experimenting with the facts. The model has been smashed against facts of physical experience; and we have learnt the real physicality of the physical by its refusal of the model, not by its conformity to it.

'I was edified (this orator continues) by the analogy you drew from the Freudian mythology; but I was disappointed that you stopped where you did. You should have pressed the comparison to the bitter end. You should have pointed out that the invoking of the Oedipus legend is only an initial move and that the scientific value of the doctrine is in direct proportion to its ability to liberate itself from the model. The psychologist who keeps treating each new patient as simply a young Oedipus-with-a-difference will be the merest horse-doctor of the soul. The competent practitioner does not measure the new case against Oedipus, he measures it against a mass of organized experience of adolescents in love-hate relationships with their parents. To force the model on the psychologist, to re-Oedipodize his de-Oedipodizing practice, would be utterly retrograde and anti-scientific. We cannot do without models, but we examine the models and recall the crudity of their provenance; not with the object of casting direct light on the field in which we apply them, but with the negative purpose of escaping the misleading suggestions they offer. In sum: everything that is objectively valuable in causal thinking is contributed by the evidence of the experimental data. Models are makeshift devices for formulating questions. Experiment not only supplies the matter of the answer, it corrects the form of the question, too. *Dixi.*'

Well, what a broadside! My timbers are shivered and my guns

out of action. How am I to sustain the engagement? All I can offer is a few little sneaking distinctions. It is in this matter of 'models'. First, there is the model which we may call arbitrary, extraneous, or frankly metaphysical: as, for example, when we use botanical or physical images in history; when we see institutions growing like trees, or forces of political sentiment in collision, combination, or equipoise. Second, and at the far opposite remove, is the model which many call typical. It is no metaphor or diagram of the realities to which it is applied, but an actual instance of the sort, it may be a specially clear, pure, complete, or exaggerated instance, but nevertheless an instance: and Oedipus is a case of the kind. It is plain that these two sorts of models do not work in at all the same sort of way. A metaphysical model may be indispensable, in the sense that, if we wish to handle great masses of fact, say in history, we shall be obliged to diagrammatize and very likely we cannot diagrammatize without models. A typical model will scarcely be indispensable, for we are likely to have access to other instances, as easily as we have access to the type-instance: no need to keep referring to Oedipus, since we can refer to the young males of our acquaintance and work out the common factors in their attitudes to their parents. But though these two sorts of models differ so widely in their manner of functioning, they have this negative characteristic in common, that they are neither of them informative in themselves. I mean that nothing is judged to be true of young males in general, on the strength of the Oedipus story; we only know it to be illuminating in so far as we see resemblances to it in the general observed pattern of young male life. And still less is anything judged to be true of historical process on the strength of arboreal growth, or in that of the balance of physical forces.

But now there is a third sort of model, which is neither simply typical, nor absolutely metaphorical, but somewhere between the two—the *graded* model: and when I say 'graded', I mean 'up-graded' or 'down-graded'. If the simplicities of animal behaviour are used as a clue to the interpretation of human conduct, the model is a down-graded model; if the explicit and word-using consciousness of man is used as a clue to the quality of animal consciousness, the model is an up-graded model. How then do such models work? They need be no more informative than the other two sorts: for instance, nothing can be judged to be true of human conduct from the model of animal instinct, except in so far as it is found to be true; the value of the model lies in its observable applicability and in nothing else.

But there is a special case of the graded model, and this we will call the privileged graded model. This is the case where we have an access to the model which is denied us in respect of the grade to which the model is applied. And such is the case, when we use our human consciousness as some sort of clue to the quality of animal consciousness. For we have an access to human conscious-ness, through personal awareness and mutual communication, which is denied us in respect of the beasts. And it seems indubit-able that in such a case—the privileged case—the model is in-formative. Though I am not such an ass as to suppose that being conscious is the same thing for the cat as it is for me, yet but for the informativeness of the human model, I should be able to give no content to my (very ill-defined) sense of the cat's subjectivity. To put it less artificially—I appreciate cats, as I appreciate men, by sympathy; but the sympathy is down-graded and pays an in-definable discount[2] in virtue of the fact.

Well now, to come to the point at last—what we have to say is that the model of our own interaction with environment, which we men have used from the beginning as the model for plotting the interaction of natural causes, is a privileged graded model, and therefore in some degree informative. It is a graded model evidently, and neither absolutely metaphorical nor simply typical. Not metaphorical, for I am an actual case of a physical agent in physical relation with a physical environment. But not simply typical either, for the rational animal is not typical of irrational and inanimate agencies. It is a graded model, then; but it is also a privileged model. For it is only in the case of our own action that we have the recipe for the direct exercise and enjoyment of causal efficacy; only in the case of the conditionedness of our own per-formance that we know what it is to suffer causal constraint.

So, then, the model is informative: but what information does it give? 'Not much, and nothing to the purpose', will (I imagine) be the answer of our scientific pragmatist—let us give him the floor once more, and hear what he says. 'If I thought', he declares, 'that your new distinctions about models implied a laying down of

the law for scientific thinking *a priori* and in advance of experi-
mentally ascertained facts, I'd fight you tooth and nail; for I'm
convinced that there are no such *a priori* rules for the construction
of scientific hypotheses. And why am I convinced? Because I've
done some physics, I know what the job is; and I've followed the
history of physical enquiry in the hands of our predecessors. So
I'd be convinced that any *a priori* law-making for physics must be
bogus. Fortunately, however, your remarks do not carry any such
sinister implications. Your model, you say, is informative. But
informative about what? About what I will venture to call the
substance of causation, not about the pattern of causality. 'About
the substance of causation'—about the very idea of acting, and
being acted upon; of exerting or of undergoing causal constraint.
It is this that we derive from our own active and passive bodily
experience. But all this is taken for granted in scientific enquiry,
before we start. We assume that there are real agencies out there in
physical space, doing what we do—to the extent, that is, of acting
and being acted upon. If there were no such interactive multi-
plicity of energies, there would be nothing for physics to study.
But physics does not proceed by developing the model, and cashing
the concept of mutual interaction; those who, like Descartes,
attempted such a course, reached conclusions which were experi-
mentally refuted. No: we simply aim at exact generalizations of the
patterns which (on the evidence available to us) the interactions
exhibit.

'Let me clarify the matter,' this orator continues, 'by referring
again to the hackeneyed example you cited some while ago. David
Hume confessed his embarrassment when he tried to account for
the notion of causal necessitation, efficacy or constraint; and the
explanation he did offer for it was both too extraneous to justify it
and too sophisticated to convince us. But Hume felt able to push
the whole puzzle aside, while he discussed the question of causal
sequence; of which he gave a fundamentally correct, if over-
simplified account, in terms of observed or expected uniformities.
Well now, you say that your model is informative; and I say that
so it is—it is informative precisely about that puzzle which
embarrassed Hume: it tells us how we come by the idea of causal
necessitation, or constraint; why we should believe it, and in what
sense, when we find ourselves applying it to the field of physical

nature. It is agreeable, indeed, to be able to solve the necessitation-puzzle, but the principles for construing sequential uniformities remain unaffected; we have simply to study them upon the object, and generalize them as best we can.

'Finally,' says our orator, 'I will turn to a topic for which I have little taste—your metaphysical theology. I will limit myself to raising one simple question. If you are asking whether the complex causal sequences which make up the world need to be traced back to a transcendent First Cause, in what direction do you look for an answer? To the mere idea of causativeness, of necessitating efficacy, or to the chains and patterns of causal uniformity which we find in the world? Do not you propose to fumble back along the chain from consequent to antecedent and so to reach a First Cause of all? And if that is your proposal, must not your argument wholly depend upon the sort of enchainments of causal sequence which the world-process actually exhibits? The issue for you cannot be what causation is, but what paths it follows; for it is only by plotting the paths that you can run them back to any supposed origin.

'Well then (my pragmatic orator proceeds—I thought I'd finished with him, but once mounted he's like the old man of the sea, I can't get him off my shoulders)—well then', says he, 'let us establish a conclusion, and a corollary to it. The conclusion is, that your causal model is a red herring, so far as the question of first cause is concerned. And the corollary is, that the question is exactly where it was before you brought your model in. And where was that? Had not it become clear to all unprejudiced enquirers, that the causal chains which science can establish are simply the workings of such uniformities of order as the world-process exhibits, and that the idea of tracing them back behind the world and out into the not-world is nonsensical?'

Whew! I believe the man has finished at last. He hasn't left me much time; never mind, I will at least have the last word—though of course it won't be the last word: my audience will see to that. What I will do is to take up the man's question. 'If,' he said, 'you are asking whether the complex causal sequences which make up the world need tracing back to a transcendent First Cause, or not, in what direction do you look for an answer? To the mere idea of causativeness, as the model prescribes it, or to the chains and patterns of causal uniformity we find in the world? That was the question, and I shall, of course, refuse to answer it, if it presented us a choice between mutually exclusive alternatives. For I am bound to say that the metaphysical theist must look in both directions at once.

It is a long time, surely, since any serious philosopher was so naive as to think of the First Cause as a first item in a homogeneous series of which the remaining items were natural agencies or natural events. We could not hope to reach the First Cause by fumbling back along the chain of observed causal sequence and extrapolating a bit at the back end. The First Cause was postulated because the finite causes known or supposed by us were seen as insufficient or defective: they were all very well in their way but they didn't do the job. What job? The job of causing.

The argument supposed two things: (a) that there is a standard of sufficient causation; (b) that natural causes, as known or imaginable, do not by themselves come up to the standard. Now the traditional philosophy had no doubt what the standard was: causation ought to be assimilable to implication. Otherwise put, if the world were to be self-explanatory, there ought to be some simple definable essence at the bottom of it from which all the seeming accidents of its history would follow by logical necessity. Since the causal series known to us or imaginable by us do not articulate the development of any such logical necessity, the world does not contain sufficient cause; and such cause must be sought outside or above it.

The empiricist movement, as everyone knows, destroyed this argument. It was shown to everyone's satisfaction that causal necessity had nothing in common with logical necessity, i.e. with valid implication. Since the idea of construing causal sequence in terms of logical consequence was merely grotesque, it became absurd to complain that natural causes failed to do the job because they could not be turned into a watertight implicational system. The standard tightness for causal systems on any level could only be derived from the best worked-out of such systems themselves; and every motive was removed for postulating a cause behind all causes, which should make them adequate to determine their effects.

Such appeared to be the position. What difference, if any, does my informative model make? It provides an alternative source for the idea of a standard causativeness which natural causes may fail to attain. For the model of causal efficacy is that causal efficacy for which we have the recipe in ourselves, when we produce an intended result.

Now this is the point at which my paper ought to begin, but this is the point at which it will have to end. As I said, it would be too great a work to attempt a constructive argument to a First Cause. Let's compromise. I would call on atheists and theists alike to agree with me that theism operates *de facto* with my model, and not with the classic model of logical implication as a standard for causal explanation. For when the theist feels in his bones the inadequacy of natural causes to do the job of causing, with what does he underpin them? With a self-implicatory essence? Certainly not: that is a sophism of the schools, not the form of religious belief.[3] No; the theist sees behind all causes the personal agent, the Creator, the supreme archetype of his own efficacity, the Intelligent Will, or voluntary intelligence, in whose likeness he has himself been made. Whether such a belief is the height of wisdom or the height of folly, that is how it goes; and even as a folly, an illusion, it becomes more natural to the mind of man when we see how man has thought, does think, and must think about natural causes.

Study Notes

Abbreviations used in the notes

FI   *Finite and Infinite*
GV   *The Glass of Vision*
FW   *The Freedom of the Will*
LAIU   *Love Almighty and Ills Unlimited*
SB   *Saving Belief*
SG   *A Science of God?*
FS   *Faith and Speculation*
CF   *A Celebration of Faith*

THE RATIONAL GROUNDS FOR BELIEF IN GOD

1 For the practical and philosophical implications of a 'provisional definition', see *FS*, 122; and *SB*, ch. 1.

2 See *FI*, ix (revised preface, 2nd edn.) where apprehension is defined *not* in terms of the perceptual analogy, but as expressing 'the idiom of action'—i.e. a cognitive or veridical response determined by the realities with which one interacts. (Cf. with the earlier treatment, *FI*, 7–10, 287ff.; for amplification, see *FW*, 135ff., 141 and 145f., 150ff., 184f., 188; and text, p. 21.

3 Cf. *FI*, 3ff., *SG*, ch. 5.

4 See text, pp. 149ff.; and *FW*, 151ff., esp. 155–6; *FS*, 42, 49–50, 126–7.

5. A reference to Berkeley, see *FS*, 127, 169; also, for the doctrine of God as 'Mind of the World', see 146ff., esp. 154, 159ff.; *SG*, 77ff.; and text, p. 186.

6 Cf. *FS*, 122–3, where the 'matrix of theistic reflection' is taken to be our implicit awareness of Sovereign *Will*. (See also pp. 133ff., and 145 where the 'practice' and 'logic of theistic belief' coincide 'in seeing the Primary Determinant as personal will'.)

7 In a letter to Edward Henderson (8 September 1966), Farrer wrote: 'You raised the question about my doctrine of space. I am a sort of Leibnitian Einsteinist. Space as a uniform continuum belongs to the form of visual representation. Real space is the field of conditioning

forces relatively to which any one real activity acts. So the universe is drawn together into a real space wherever there is an activity of which it constitutes the field and in so far as it is effective in such a field by really conditioning ("affecting") that activity. The world space of physicists or astronomers is a mental construction, a diagram which can never in fact be drawn in any fulness, diagrammatizing the mutual relations of all real spaces as though in one spatial field viewed from nowhere. Since God knows the truth, he does not see the world in a mental diagram of Newtonian Space but from the foci of all real spaces, that is, through the existences of all real creatures.—I am not, of course, a thorough-paced Leibnitian because other creatures really and not simply by representations enter into the "monadic" world of a given creature.' Cf. *FS*, 147ff., esp. 150; and *FI*, 239, where Farrer says that Leibniz's 'fundamental error [was] to make consciousness rather than activity his primary notion'.

8 For the concept of action in nature (the 'being of nature-in-itself' —*FW*, 185; cf. 171, 306) as *in pari materia* ('of the same logical order') with personal action, see *FW*, 183ff.; *FS*, 134. See also n. 2, 'The Physical Theology of Leibniz'.

9 See *FW*, 145ff., 152f., 155–6; *FS*, 49f., 126f.

POETIC TRUTH

1 For the 'voluntarist definition' of God—'all that he wills to be, and wills to be all that he is'—see *FS*, 118; *CF*, 56.

DOES GOD EXIST?

1 In later writings, Farrer disavows the formalist for the voluntarist explanation. See esp. *FS*, 116ff. and *FW*, ch. IX. (For his criticism of the Aristotelian notion of substantial form, see *FI*, 63f., 247ff.; and for his treatment of 'a doctrine of divine volitions', see *FW*, 303–12. For the cosmological implications of the notion of causality, see *FS*, ch. IX on 'First Cause'. Cf. n. 3, 'The Physical Theology of Leibniz'.)

2 For the changing role of the doctrine of Providence, cf. *FI*, 299 with the revised preface, p. viii. By the time of his final philosophical essay, Farrer had completely reversed the theological significance of the doctrines of creation and providence—see *FS*, 81.

3 The importance of the action-pattern as the divine *modus operandi* is developed in *FW*, chs. I–V, and ch. IX (esp. 178ff.), and applied to the 'prior action' of the Creator, 312ff. The doctrine of a divinely inspired 'super-pattern', implied in *FI*, 175ff. and spelled out in *LAIU*, 94–5, is involved in Farrer's account or creation (*SG*, 58f., ch. 5,

esp. 81, 87, 90), and the theodicy sketched in *LAIU* (*passim*, esp. 91–100; *CF*, 73; *FS*, 70–1, 78, 132–3). It is further refined on the model of mind-body in *FS*, chs. X–XI (see n. 2, 'The Prior Actuality of God').

4 See *FW*, 303ff.

5 In *FS*, Farrer settles on the 'definition' of God as 'Unconditioned Will', p. 118 (cf. 57); which raises the problem discussed in ch. VIII of giving content to a 'term standing for a personal action' (p. 124).

6 A reference to the Cartesian starting-point, described in *FI* as 'crypto-theism' (pp. 7, 10). Cf. *FI*, 7–10 and the revised preface—*FI*, ix—with *SG*, ch. 6 on 'Experimental Proof', esp. 107; and *FS*, chs. IV–VII in which the theistic 'clue' is located less in mental apperception than in volitional activity.

FAITH AND REASON

1 See text, p. 119, 'A Moral Argument for the Existence of God'.

2 See 'Revelation', *Faith and Logic* (Allen & Unwin, 1957); esp. p. 101.

3 Cf. *FI*, 8–9.

THEOLOGY AND ANALOGY, I

1 See *FI*, 2–3 for a vigorous critique of the 'revelationists'.

2 Farrer's bibliography: 'For a select list of the Catholic literature see T. L. Penido, *La Rôle de l'Analogie en Théologie Dogmatique* (1931), 12, and the index on pp. 451ff. for the principal texts in St Thomas and his scholastic commentators. For modern Protestant rejection of the doctrine see Karl Barth, *The Doctrine of the Word of God* (Eng. trans., 1936), esp. 43–4, 192, 274, 279, 383–99. Recent English philosophical discussions in E. L. Mascall, *Existence and Analogy* (1949), and D. M. Emmet, *The Nature of Metaphysical Thinking* (1945).'

METAPHYSICS AND ANALOGY

1 For the teleological implications of this suggestion, see *SG*, ch. 3, esp. 49ff.; and *FW*, ch. IV, esp. 58, 60, 76.

2 See n. 1, 'Commemorative Address on Berkeley'; and p. 210 text.

THE PHYSICAL THEOLOGY OF LEIBNIZ

1 'To be is to be perceived'; for Farrer's criticism of this and the substitution of his own 'esse est operari', see *FI*, 21, 31, 44. In *FS* (p. 114) he challenged the accuracy of this formula, while maintaining that 'a theology of being' might be based on energy or activity concepts.

For his treatment of the 'energy-concept' as physical ultimate, see *FS*, 82–5; and for the theological implications of the philosophy of action, see *FS*, 111–18.

2 For the content of physical reals, Farrer suggests a doctrine of 'associative imputation' borrowed from the 'idiom of activity' ('. . . a washed-out analogy of action to interpret the physical world', *FW*, 189), and balanced by an 'indefinable (or 'incalculable') discount' allowing for the anthropomorphism of activity-concepts. See *FS*, 178–91, esp. 184ff.; *FS*, 134. The expression, *in pari materia* (see n. 8 'The Rational Grounds for Belief in God') appears in all three major philosophical essays: *FI*, 230, 235; *FW*, 183, 185; *FS*, 134.

3 The idea that consciousness does 'real work'—i.e. cannot be reduced to physical or phenomenological occurrences—is of considerable importance.

In *FI*, Farrer reworks the Aristotelian notion of substantial form, emphasizing the vital conceptual and epistemological connections between consciousness and activity (*passim*; esp. 169–70, and chs. XIX–XXI where the metaphysical unity of the self—its explanatory capability—is taken as clue to the nature of reality).

In *FW*, Farrer sets out the logical priority of conscious intentions— indicated by the fact that physical actions respond to meaningful choice, pp. 78–80, also 40–6—as a solution to the mind-body problem. (Consciousness throws up a *tertium quid*, a third term involving large-scale action-patterns, operative between conscious intentions and physical execution—see ch. IV, pp. 99–100, 174. This 'bewitching' by higher mental states of minute physical components, leading them into combinations they would not otherwise attain, is connected with Farrer's doctrine of physical providence, the divine 'overruling' of physical nature—*FW*, 52, 58, 60, 85—which he later modified for a more natural and yet more mysterious 'causal joint'. See *SG*, 88, also 49, 76; *FS*, 62, 65, 66, 69, 72, 78, 80, 85, 142, 149.)

Finally, in *FS* (pp. 154, 161, 167), Farrer uses the causal efficacy of conscious intentions to provide an analogy of how God enters the subjectivity of the world's constituents: namely, a 'half-theology' of prior causality.

4 For another critique of Cartesian dualism, see *FW* 13ff. where Farrer concedes to Ryle that 'embodied consciousness' is our primary or basic conception of the self, but must be enlarged to account for two recalcitrant facts: 'mental activities or states which ignore their own bodily performance; and events in the nervous system not directly represented in consciousness' (*FW*, 18).

5 See *FW*, ch. II, 'The Seat of Consciousness', esp. p. 24.

6 See *FS*, 70–85 for Farrer's (ontological) treatment of a 'theology of nature'.

7 For the relation of God and world on the analogy of mind–body, see the 'theistic semi-naturalism' developed by Farrer in *FS*, chs. X–XI; esp. 146–8, 153–5, 157–9, 166, 169.

8 See also 'The Prior Actuality of God', pp. 178ff. text.

9 Agnosticism of the 'causal joint'; see *FS*, 65, 66, 110, 142, 146, 149; and n. 3 above.

A MORAL ARGUMENT FOR THE EXISTENCE OF GOD

1 In a letter to Diogenes Allen (2 April 1964), Farrer wrote: 'I think that a long and very subtle discussion would be needed to settle the "read in or read off?" issue. St Thomas would begin by pointing out that the very nature of things finite must surely be related in fact to their dependence on God (a believer must believe): why then is it denied that it can be "read off"? Only on the Calvinistic dogma of man's "depravity". But if it can be "read off" why do not all philosophers achieve the "reading"?—Why not compromise, and say that those who *do* "read off" are making an incipient move towards religious belief, and that the believer really does and can "read off", just as he really does and can interpret his own standing in relation to God?'

GOD AND VERIFICATION, 1

1 In *FS*, ch. VIII, Farrer suggests a pragmatic (i.e. operable or intentional, as opposed to formal) solution to the theological problem of analogy.

2 For the relation between Creative Act and creaturely activity, see *FS*, chs. IV–VI.

3 The 'smothered perception' is a reference to crypto- (or implicit) theism (*FI*, 10, 267f., 292; see also n. 6, 'Does God Exist?'). In later writings, Farrer reduced the cosmological 'demand' (see *FI*, 262) to a 'recognition' (*FW*, 312), or a 'requirement' (*FS*, 13, 130; *SG*, 33ff.); and modified the perceptual analogy to one based on intentional activity (see *FI*, ix, x).

4 The realm of human freedom—the reference is to Marcel's Gifford Lectures, *The Mystery of Being*. See text, 'Freedom and Theology'. For Farrer's development of this theme, see *FW*, ch. XV.

GOD AND VERIFICATION, 2

1 Cf. *GV*, 3; *FS*, 8of.

2 Farrer deals with the supernaturality of faith in 'Faith and Reason',

text, esp. pp. 61ff. In using the word 'apprehension' in connection with theistic apprehension, Farrer wrote (in a letter to Diogenes Allen, sometime in November 1963): 'The apprehension of God (or of our relation to him) is the act, or activity, of faith. (Apprehension is a bad word: all I mean is, that faith here plays the sort of part played by sensation and immediate supposition, in physical experience.)'

SIGNIFICATION

1 See *FW*, ch. VIII for Farrer's development of this position, esp. pp. 145–6; and for its theological implications, *FS*, 42, 49–50, 65–6.

COMMEMORATIVE ADDRESS ON BERKELEY

1 Cf. *FW*, 306. For the theological implications of this, see *FW*, 171, 311, 13 and 'The Physical Theology of Leibniz', esp. p. 94.

FREEDOM AND THEOLOGY

1 Farrer's rejection of Existentialism is equally strong. See *FW*, 300.
2 For that argument, see *FW*, 297–304; and 'A Moral Argument for the Existence of God'.

TRANSCENDENCE AND 'RADICAL THEOLOGY'

1 See *FS*, 70–1; 132–3; *LAIU*, 146–7.
2 In full-dress context, Farrer described the random collocations of physical activity characterizing the universe, even more vividly: 'If God creates energies he creates energies-in-act, and if energies-in-act then energies in mutual engagement, and if energies in mutual engagement then energies in perpetual change. We cannot conceive God as instituting anything physical, unless he institutes a piece of cosmic hurly-burly in full career, and with all its kaleidoscopic detail'. (*FS*, 83; cf. 150; also *FW*, 177; *CF*, 56, 61, 65; text, pp. 187–90.)
For the relation of God and universe on the analogy of mind–body, see *SG*, 76–91, esp. 80–1; and *FS*, 153–4. For Farrer's treatment of the 'energy-concept' as physical ultimate, see *FS*, 82–6; also *SG*, 69; *SB*, 50f.
3 See Farrer's reply to the review discussion of *SG* in *Theoria to Theory*, Vol. 1, 1966. For the space-time relation, see *SB*, 66–7; and for criticism of Newtonian physics, see *FS*, 150–1 and *SB*, 145.
4 Farrer's review, *Journal of Theological Studies*, New Series, 19 (1968), pp. 422–3.
5 An aphorism adapted from Mother Carey in *The Water Babies*

(ch. VII, by Charles Kingsley, 1863) and crucial to Farrer's doctrine of the divine and human complementarity. See *SG*, 90; *SB*, 51, 72, 5, 6, 7, 8, 82, 124; *CF*, 73,147; also *FW*, 312ff,; *FS*, 155; *LAIU*, 98ff.

THE PRIOR ACTUALITY OF GOD

1 Cf. *FS*, 162-3.
2 Cf. *FS*, 147ff., 153ff., 157ff., 163, 166.

GRACE AND THE HUMAN WILL

1 For Farrer's use of 'aspiration', see *FI*, 262; *FW*, 303ff.; *FS*, 26, 116.

CAUSES

1 See *FS*, 134ff. Aristotle (*Physics* II. 1) 194b (ΰλη 193a, 28).
2 See n. 2, 'The Physical Theology of Leibniz'.
3 Farrer's reply to Emmet (et. al., *Theoria to Theory*, Vol. 1 (1966), p. 75) is of importance here. By the definition of God as Unconditioned Will, 'science is not made ancillary to a preconceived theology; for what is preconceived is the bare concept of a first-causal actuality, which is only preconceived by being self-defined. The postulate of a First Cause which has any relevant firstness, or any relevant self-identity, is the postulate of transcendent will'. See also, *FS*. 123: 'Deity is as-it-were personal will, of so exalted a form as to be simply undetermined *a priori* in any respect.'

Chronological List of Published Writings: 1933-1973

1933
'A Return to New Testament Christological Categories', *Theology*, Vol. 26, pp. 304–18.

1936
Review of *The Doctrine of the Word of God*, and *God in Action* by Karl Barth in *Theology*, Vols. 32–3, pp. 370–3. (the former is Vol. 1, part 1 of the 2nd edn. of *Prolegomena to Church Dogmatics*).

1937
'Eucharist and Church in the New Testament', *The Parish Communion*, ed. A. G. Hebert, S.P.C.K, pp. 75–94.
Review of *Der christliche Glaube und die altheidnische Welt* (2 Vols.) by K. Prümm in *Journal of Theological Studies*, Vol. 38, pp. 95–7.
Review of *Religion and Reality: An Essay in the Christian Co-ordination of Contraries* by Melville Chaning-Pearce in *Church Quarterly Review*, Vols. 123–4, pp. 328–30.

1938
'The Christian Doctrine of Man', *The Christian Understanding of Man*, ed. T. E. Jessop, Vol. II, Oxford Conf. Series, Allen & Unwin, pp. 181–213.
Review of *Die Kirche und die Schöpfung* by Eugen Gerstenmaier in *Church Quarterly Review*, Vols. 125–6, pp. 345–6.

1939
' "The Blood is the Life" and the Blood of Christ in the New Testament', *Oxford Society of Historical Theology*, Vol. 1933–42/43, pp. 60–7 (abstract of a paper read 23 February 1939 on Eucharistic theology).
'The Theology of Morals', *Theology*, Vol. 38, pp. 332–41.
Review of *Philosophie de la Religion* by Paul Ortegat in *Journal of Theological Studies*, Vol. 40, pp. 100–1.

1940

Review of *The Problem of the Future Life* by C. J. Shebbeare in *Journal of Theological Studies*, Vol. 41, pp. 343-4.

1941

Review of *The Nature of the World, An Essay in Phenomenalist Metaphysics* by W. T. Stace in *Journal of Theological Studies*, Vol. 42, pp. 108-10.

Review of *The Realm of Spirit* by George Santayana in *Theology*, Vol. 42, pp. 123-5.

1942

Review of *The Philosophy of David Hume* by Norman Kemp Smith in *Journal of Theological Studies*, Vol. 43, pp. 229-32.

Review of *The Revelation of St John* by M. Kiddle (assisted by M. K. Ross) in *Journal of Theological Studies*, Vol. 43, pp. 227-29.

1943

Finite and Infinite, Dacre Press (2nd edn., 1959 with revised Preface; also published by Macmillan and Humanities, 1966).

'How was Jesus Divine?', *Socratic Digest*, No. 1, pp. 24-5.

1944

'Can we know that God Exists?' (editor's summary of a discussion by the Revd A. M. Farrer and Mr MacNabb), *Socratic Digest*, No. 2, pp. 12, 13.

1945

'Can Myth be Fact?', *Socratic Digest*, No. 3, pp. 36-44.

1946

'The Ministry in the New Testament', *The Apostolic Ministry*, ed. K. E. Kirk (repb. 1951 with 'New Foreword' by Farrer), Hodder & Stoughton, pp. 113-82.

Epigrams', *Theology*, Vol. 49, p. 238 (two poems).

Review of *Christ in the Gospels* by A. E. J. Rawlinson in *Journal of Theological Studies*, Vol. 47, pp. 77-8.

1947

Catholicity: A study in the conflict of Christian traditions in the West, Dacre Press (a report presented to the Archbishop of Canterbury by a committee of Anglicans of which Farrer was a member).

'The Extension of St Thomas's Doctrine of Analogy to Modern Philosophical Problems', *Downside Review*, Vol. 65, pp. 21–32 (reprinted as 'Knowledge by Analogy', supra pp. 69–81.
'On Credulity', *Illuminatio*, Vol. I, No. 3, pp. 3–9.
'Thought as the Basis of History', *The Listener*, Vol. 37 (20 March), pp. 424–5 (a broadcast talk on R. G. Collingwood).
'Does God Exist?', *Socratic Digest*, No. 4, pp. 27–34.

1948

The class of Vision, Dacre Press (Bampton Lectures).

1949

A Rebirth of Images: the Making of St John's Apocalypse, Dacre Press (also by Beacon Press, 1963 with a new Preface by Kenneth Burke; rebound in hard cover by Smith, 1964).

1950

Review of *Abelard's Christian Theology* by J. Ramsay McCallum in *Journal of Theological Studies*, New Series, Vol. 1, p. 221.

1951

'A Midwinter Dream', *University: A Journal of Enquiry*, Vol. I, pp. 86–90 (reprinted as 'A Theologian's Point of View', *The Socratic*, No. 5, 1952, pp. 35–8); abridged version reprinted as 'Theology and Philosophy', supra pp. 1–4).
A Study in St Mark, Dacre Press.
'Editor's Introduction', *Theodicy: Essays on the Goodness of God, the Freedom of Man, and the Origin of Evil* by G. W. Leibniz, ed. A. M. Farrer, tr. E. M. Huggard, Routledge and Kegan Paul, pp. 7–47 (excerpt reprinted as 'The Physical Theology of Leibniz', supra pp. 91–113).
'Messianic Prophecy', *Theology*, Vol. 54, pp. 335–42 (a sermon preached at Oxford, Hilary Term, 1951).

1952

The Crown of the Year (weekly Paragraphs for the Holy Sacrament), Dacre Press (also Morehouse-Barlow, 1953).
'A Liturgical Theory about St Mark's Gospel' (a review of *The Primitive Christian Calendar*, Vol. I, Introduction and text by Philip Carrington, Archbishop of Quebec), *Church Quarterly Review*, Vol. 153, pp. 501–8.

Review of *Holy Communion and Holy Spirit* by J. E. L. Oulton in *Theology*, Vol. 55, pp. 107-8.
Review of *The Originality of St Matthew* by B. C. Butler in *Journal of Theological Studies*, New Series, Vol. 3, pp. 102-6.

1953

'An English Appreciation', *Kerygma and Myth: A Theological Debate*, ed. H. W. Bartsch; tr. R. H. Fuller, S.P.C.K., pp. 212-23 (paperback, 1972).
'Loaves and Thousands', *Journal of Theological Studies*, New Series, Vol. 4, pp. 1-14.
'The Trinity in Whom We Live', *Theology*, Vol. 56, pp. 322-27 (originally a broadcast talk, 'Meditation for Trinity Sunday', 8 June 1952; reprinted in *Lord I Believe* as Chapter 2).

1954

St Matthew and St Mark (Edward Cadbury Lectures, 1953-4) Dacre Press (2nd edn., 1966; also by Macmillan).

1955

'Absolute', *Twentieth Century Encyclopedia of Religious Knowledge*, ed. Lefferts A. Loetscher, Vol. 1, Baker Book House, Grand Rapids, p. 3.
'Analogy', ibid., pp. 38-40 (reprinted as 'The Concept of Analogy', supra pp. 64-8).
'Being', ibid., pp. 120-1.
'On Dispensing with Q', *Studies in the Gospels*, ed. D. E. Nineham, Blackwell, pp. 55-88.
'The Queen of Sciences', *Twentieth Century*, Vol. 157, pp. 489-94.

1956

'An Examination of Mark 13. 10', a reply to G. D. Kilpatrick, *Journal of Theological Studies*, New Series, Vol. 7, pp. 75-9.
'The Dies Irae'. A New Translation, *Theology*, Vol. 59, pp. 155-7 (published separately in card-form by S.P.C.K., No. 3218, 1957).
'How do we know we have found Him?', *Christ and the Christian*, Mowbrays, pp. 21-7 (a sermon in a course of sermons on 'Evangelism in the Church', preached in the chapel of Pusey House, Oxford; reprinted in *Said or Sung* as 'Assurance', pp. 83-8).
'Important Hypotheses Reconsidered. VIII. Typology', *Expository Times*, Vol. 67, pp. 228-31.
A Short Bible, ed. with general introduction, Fontana, pp. 5-15 (published in the U.S. as *Core of the Bible*, Harper, 1957).

1957

'The Everyday Use of the Bible', *The Bible and the Christian*, Mowbrays, pp. 55–60 (a sermon in a course of sermons preached in the chapel of Pusey House; reprinted in *Said or Sung* as 'The Doctor of Divinity', pp. 147–52).

(new) 'Foreword', *The Apostolic Ministry* (repb. from 1946), pp. v–xviii.

The New Testament, ed. with a general introduction and note to each book, Collins, pp. 7–19.

'Revelation', *Faith and Logic*, ed. B. G. Mitchell, Allen & Unwin, pp. 84–107.

'A Starting Point for the Philosophical Examination of Theological Belief', *Faith and Logic*, ed. B. G. Mitchell, Allen & Unwin, pp. 9–30 (reprinted as 'A Moral Argument for the Existence of God', supra pp. 114–33).

1958

The Freedom of the Will (Gifford Lectures for 1957), Adam and Charles Black (2nd edn.—Scribners, N.Y., 1960; London, 1963—includes a 'Summary of the Argument', pp. 316–20; also published by Macmillan and Humanities).

Lord I believe; Suggestions for turning the Creed into Prayer, Faith Press (2nd edn., revised and enlarged, reissued by S.P.C.K. in paperback, 1962; also Seabury, 1962; Morehouse-Barlow, 1959).

1959

Introduction to *The Easter Enigma: An Essay on the Resurrection with Special Reference to the Data of Psychical Research* by Michael C. Perry, Faber & Faber, pp. 11–16.

'On Looking Below the Surface', *Oxford Society of Historical Theology*, Vol. 1959–60, pp. 3–18 (a Presidential Address, 22 October 1959, replying to Miss Helen Gardner's Riddel Lectures in *The Business of Criticism*, O.U.P., 1959).

'Predestination', *Christianity According to St Paul*, Mowbrays, pp. 37–44 (a sermon in a course of sermons preached in the chapel of Pusey House, Oxford).

1960

'In the Conscience of Man', *God and the Universe*, Mowbrays, pp. 30–7 (a sermon in a course of sermons on 'Signs of God' preached in the chapel of Pusey House, Oxford).

Said or Sung (an arrangement of homily and verse), Faith Press (published in the U.S. as *A Faith of Our Own*, with Preface by C. S. Lewis, World Publishing Company, 1960).

1961

'The Gate of Heaven' (a pamphlet-sermon preached at the patronal festival of St Edward's House, Westminster).

Love Almighty and Ills Unlimited (containing the Nathaniel Taylor Lectures for 1961), Doubleday (published in England by Collins, 1962; Fontana, 1966).

'Messianic Prophecy and Preparation for Christ', *The Communication of the Gospel in New Testament Times*, Theological Collections, 2, S.P.C.K., pp. 1–9 (originally a sermon at Oxford, 1958), pp. 1–9.

1962

'Continence', *Lenten Counsellors*: A Catena of Lent Sermons, Mowbrays, pp. 83–90 (published in the U.S. by Morehouse-Barlow as *These Forty Days*: Lenten Counsels by Twenty-one Anglicans).

'The Descent into Hell and the Ascent into Life', *The Gospel of the Resurrection*, Mowbrays, pp. 13–18 (a sermon in a course of sermons preached in the chapel of Pusey House, Oxford; reprinted as 'Gates to the City' in *A Celebration of Faith*, Hodder & Stoughton, pp. 95–9).

1963

Bible Sermons by C. F. Evans and A. M. Farrer, Mowbrays, pp. 32–57 (a course of sermons preached in the chapel of Pusey House, Oxford, to which each contributed four sermons).

'Inspiration: Poetical and Divine', *Promise and Fulfilment*, ed. F. F. Bruce, T. and T. Clark, pp. 91–105.

'Mary, Scripture, and Tradition', *The Blessed Virgin Mary: Essays by Anglican Writers*, eds. E. L. Mascall and H. S. Box, Darton, Longman & Todd, pp. 27–52.

'Objections to Christianity', *Theology*, Vol. 66, pp. 317–18 (a poem).

An untitled sermon on Psalm 26.11–12 at St Margaret's, East Grinstead, on St Margaret's Day, 1962, *St Margaret's Half-Yearly Chronicle*, Vol. XVI, pp. 2–6.

1964

'The Datum in Divine Revelation', *Oxford Society of Historical Theology*, Vol. 1964–6, pp. 10–11 (abstract of a paper read on 19 November 1964; related to Chapter 6, *Faith and Speculation*).

Matriculation Sermon in the Chapel of the Good Shepherd (Friday,

30 October at Evensong), *The Bulletin* (of the General Theological
Seminary, New York), pp. 15–17.
The Revelation of St John the Divine: Commentary on the English Text,
O.U.P.
Review of *Models and Mystery* by Ian T. Ramsey in *Journal of Theological
Studies*, New Series, Vol. 15, pp. 489–90.
Saving Belief, Hodder & Stoughton (paperback, 1967; also by More-
house-Barlow, 1965).

1965

The Triple Victory (Christ's temptations according to St Matthew),
Faith Press (paperback; also by Morehouse-Barlow).

1966

'The Christian Apologist', *Light on C. S. Lewis*, ed. J. Gibb, Harcourt
Brace and World, N.Y., pp. 23–43.
Reply to 'Review Discussion of "A Science of God?"' by Dorothy
Emmet, Ted Bastin, Margaret Masterman, *Theoria to Theory*, Vol. 1,
pp. 55–75.
Review of *Philosophie du fait chrétien* by Henk Van Luijk in *Journal of
Theological Studies*, New Series, Vol. 17, p. 553.
Review of *St Anselm's Proslogion* by M. J. Charlesworth in *Journal of
Theological Studies*, New Series, Vol. 17, p. 502.
A Science of God?, Bles, London (published in the U.S. as *God is not
Dead*, Morehouse-Barlow, 1966).

1967

Faith and Speculation (containing the Deems Lectures for 1964),
Adam and Charles Black (paperback.).

1968

'The Eucharist in I Corinthians', *Eucharistic Theology Then and Now*,
Theological Collections, 9, S.P.C.K., pp. 15–33.
'Infallibility and Historical Revelation', *Infallibility in the Church:
An Anglican-Catholic Dialogue*, Darton, Longman & Todd, pp. 9–23.
Review of *The Bounds of Sense: An Essay on Kant's Critique of Pure
Reason* by P. F. Strawson in *Journal of Theological Studies*, New
Series, Vol. 19, pp. 420–1.

1969

Review of *The Cambridge History of Latin, Greek and Early Mediaeval
Philosophy*, ed. A. H. Armstrong in *Religious Studies*, Vols. 3–4, pp.
287–8.

1970

A Celebration of Faith, ed. L. Houlden, Hodder & Stoughton (paperback, 1972).

1973

'Free Will in Theology', *Dictionary of the History of Ideas*, Scribner's, N.Y.